W9-AXJ-825

**AWARD-WINNING CHEF MARC VETRI WANTED TO WRITE HIS FIRST BOOK ABOUT PASTA.** Instead, he wrote two other acclaimed cookbooks and continued researching pasta for ten more years. Now, the respected master of Italian cuisine finally shares his vast knowledge of pasta, gnocchi, and risotto in this inspiring, informative primer featuring expert tips and techniques, and more than 100 recipes.

Vetri's personal stories of travel and culinary discovery in Italy appear alongside his easy-to-follow, detailed explanations of how to make and enjoy fresh handmade pasta. Whether you're a home cook or a professional, you'll learn how to make more than thirty different types of pasta dough, from versatile egg yolk dough, to extruded semolina dough, to a variety of flavored pastas—and form them into shapes both familiar and unique. In dishes ranging from classic to innovative, Vetri shares his coveted recipes for stuffed pastas, baked pastas, and pasta sauces. He also shows you how to make light-as-air gnocchi and the perfect dish of risotto.

Loaded with useful information, including the best way to cook and sauce pasta, suggestions for substituting pasta shapes, and advance preparation and storage notes, *Mastering Pasta* offers you all of the wisdom of a pro. For cooks who want to take their knowledge to the next level, Vetri delves deep into the science of various types of flour to explain pasta's uniquely satisfying texture and how to craft the very best pasta by hand or with a machine. *Mastering Pasta* is the definitive work on the subject and the only book you will ever need to serve outstanding pasta dishes in your own kitchen.

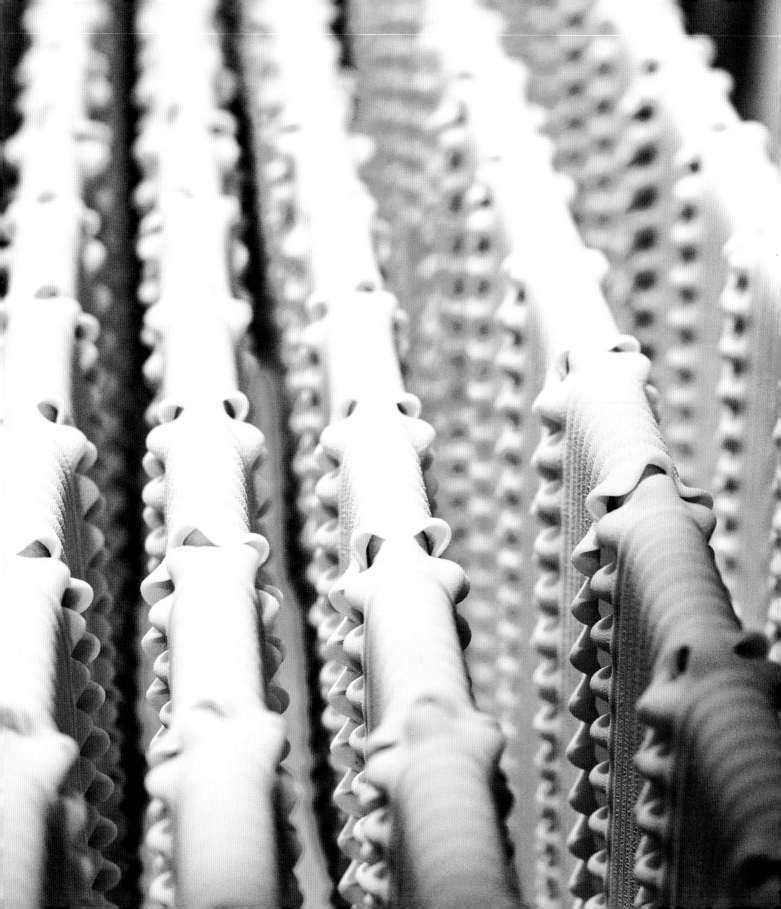

THE ART AND PRACTICE OF
HANDMADE PASTA,
GNOCCHI, AND RISOTTO

# MASTERING PASTA

## MARC VETRI
with David Joachim

Photography by Ed Anderson

TEN SPEED PRESS
Berkeley

TO MOM AND DAD FOR THEIR UNCONDITIONAL LOVE,
GUIDANCE, AND SUPPORT.

# CONTENTS

# RECIPE LIST

# PASTA SENSIBILITY

*Life is a combination of magic and pasta.*
—FEDERICO FELLINI

**SOMETIMES I FEEL LIKE MY LIFE IS ONE LONG SHEET OF PASTA.** Every day takes on a different shape or filling. Some days are remarkable, and some days I want to forget. But in the end, the sheet keeps rolling on. For me, a life without pasta would be a life without music, a life without love. No dish in history has as many variations, colors, motifs, tastes, textures, and subtleties as a dish of pasta. It's like a symphony that sounds a little different each time it is played. When you enjoy a truly inspirational dish of pasta, you ooh and ahh, like when hearing a blues riff from B. B. King for the very first time. It's a simple magic that makes you smile.

I see it in my restaurants every day. Guests laugh and tell stories around the table while sipping a beautiful Barbera or Chianti and filling their bellies with all manner of delicious food. But things kick into high gear when the pasta course comes out. They look bewildered and amazed. "Look at this one!" "Check mine out!" Each thinks his or hers is the best until they pass the dishes around. They end up loving every pasta in a different way. People just adore pasta. It's a simple fact. There's something about the shape, the feel of it in your mouth, and the combinations of flavors that make you giddy.

Pasta turns you into a teenager again. It breaks my heart when I see people boiling pasta to death, throwing it on a plate, and dumping any old sauce on top. That is not a proper dish of pasta. That is more like Cheez Whiz on French fries.

To this day, pasta is misunderstood. First, many chefs and home cooks think about it as two separate things: pasta and sauce. But pasta is a singular thing. A good pasta dish is like a good marriage. In it, two things become one. It is no longer Bill Smith and Jane Smith, or pasta and sauce. It becomes The Smiths, or a dish of pasta.

Second, and I fault myself for this as well, wheat is misunderstood. Whenever anyone used to ask me, "What kind of flour do you use?" I would reply, "Get a bag of double-zero flour. Here's a good brand." Not anymore. Flour is as vital to pasta as the marriage of noodle and sauce—maybe even more vital. It is at the very heart of every noodle with great texture—and great flavor. Yes, I said flavor. Flour has flavor! And after reading this book, you will understand why.

In *Mastering Pasta*, I teach you not only how to create and enjoy truly inspirational pasta but also how to use different flours without relying on just one brand. This book explains why classic pastas work and how to create your *own* classics. Great dishes like *spaghetti al pomodoro* and *fettuccine alla bolognese* withstand the test of time because they perfectly balance texture and flavor. *Mastering Pasta* shows you what makes any dish of pasta tick, how to craft dozens of shapes, how to marry pasta and sauce, and how to bring together flavors and textures without complicating the plate. I share with you some of my favorite doughs, fillings, and flavor combinations. And I discuss other *primi* on the Italian menu, including gnocchi, risotto, and *rotolo*.

Pasta has always been one of the most difficult things to teach young cooks. But it shouldn't be. Pasta is as simple as getting dressed in the morning. You've stocked your closet with this and that, and then just let yourself get inspired by what's happening that day.

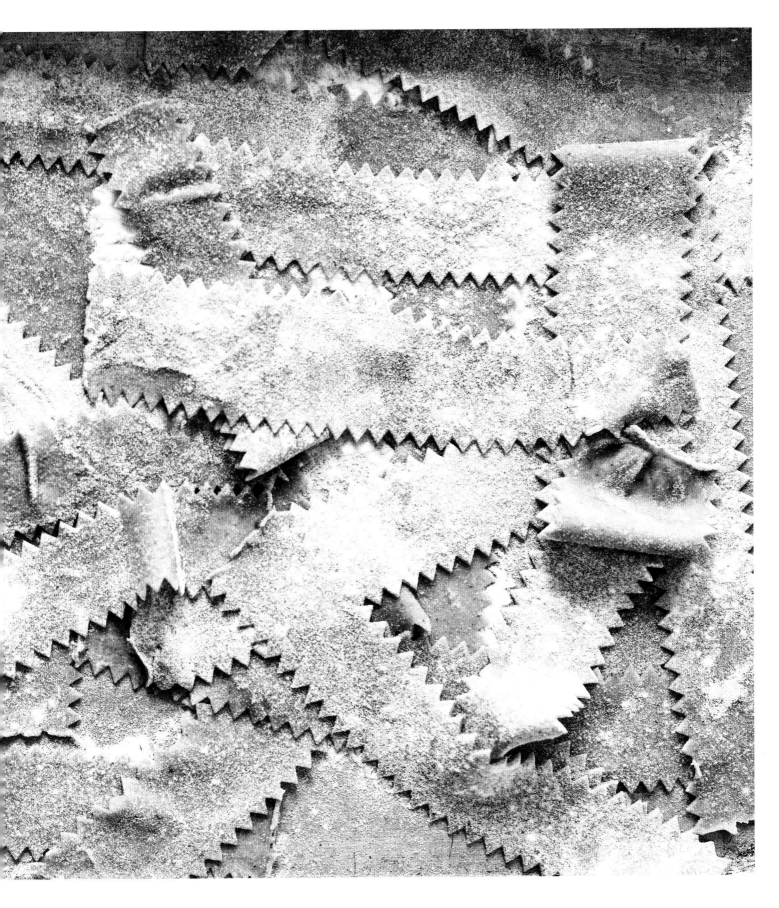

# 1

—

# TRADITION AND INNOVATION

**IT SEEMS ANACHRONISTIC TO WRITE A BOOK ON PASTA IN A WORLD OF INCREASING ACCELERATION.** Why roll out pasta by hand when you can buy it from a refrigerated case? Why search out Italian artisanal dried pasta made in the same style for hundreds of years when the corner store has pasta that looks pretty much the same? And forget about making risotto! Boiled rice in a microwave is quick, cheap, and gets the job done.

But does it really? I believe it does not. I also believe that pasta is not as time-consuming as many people make it out to be. Just the thought of making homemade pasta is so daunting to some cooks that they won't even try. That is precisely why I have written this book—to dispel the myth that pasta is complicated to make. Of course, understanding everything about pasta could take a lifetime, but you'll get incredible results just by knowing the ingredients better and how they come together.

In these pages, you'll find pasta history and science, but this book is really intended to inspire you to make pasta at home. Put it out of your mind that pasta requires a master's degree. It consists of two simple ingredients: flour and liquid. That's it. The liquid can be water, eggs, or almost any other flavored liquid or combination of flavored liquids. It's not the act of making pasta that makes it intimidating. It's the centuries of history behind it. The fear of doing something wrong. The age-old battle between tradition and innovation.

Well, I'm here to tell you that the Italian pasta tradition is one of innovation! The union of flour and water has taken on hundreds of forms out of necessity, creativity, and, in some cases, pure whimsy. To this day, the history of Italian pasta making has been a never-ending quest to fully realize what can be achieved in a plate of pasta. And this quest has consumed nearly my entire life. In that time, I have come to understand a very crucial thing about Italian cuisine: I know nothing about it.

Although I was born into a Sicilian American family that got together every weekend for big Sunday suppers, have lived in Italy, have worked in restaurants for thirty years, and have been going back and forth between Italy and the

## Recipes Need Cooks

It may not be all that apparent, but the difference between a recipe and a gorgeous plate of food is you. Think of it this way: cooking from a recipe is sort of like driving from a GPS. Follow the directions and you get to your destination. But you still have to drive the car. You still have to cook the dish. And cooking means responding to your environment, tasting the ingredients to see how much seasoning they need, observing the texture of pasta dough to see if it needs more flour or water, and feeling the thickness of the noodles to decide whether it's right for the dish you are making.

A recipe doesn't just work or not work. The cook makes a recipe work. That isn't to say that the recipes in this book haven't been tested. They have been tested multiple times in multiple kitchens by multiple cooks of various skill levels. But the exact composition of the ingredients you use, the heat level of your stove, the humidity in your kitchen, and numerous other factors will influence your success. Food has so many changing variables that absolute consistency is impossible. Let's say you make pasta in the winter. Pasta dough absorbs some moisture from the air, so you might need to add more water to the recipe because the air is less humid at that time of year.

I have been as meticulous as possible in explaining all of the variables that can affect the recipes, such as the freshness of your flour, the volume and weight measurements of your ingredients, and the humidity of your environment. But it's up to you to be aware of these factors when you cook.

The idea is to be engaged. Engage yourself in the act of cooking. Look at the recipes as a guide, not as gospel. Read the accompanying text to learn more, combine that information with your experience, however vast or limited, and roll it all together to create a dish that you want to taste. The recipes here are written so that you can make pastas and sauces ahead of time and then mix and match them the way you like. They offer that flexibility. Just keep in mind that no one can master pasta to the extent that he or she is done learning about it. Even the moisture and warmth of your hands makes a difference in the exact amount of flour or water you need to add to pasta dough. The only true path to the quest of mastering pasta is to continue making it. And I hope this book inspires you to do just that.

United States for the last twenty years, I can say now more than ever that I have not yet even scratched the surface of Italian food. For me, this is a beautiful statement—a statement both humble and confident. After all, you would think that someone who has spent so much of his life studying one subject would come to understand it fully. Yes, I know a fair amount about Italian cookery, but how can any one person ever understand all the subtleties of Italian cuisine? There are so many regions and so many centuries of history and culture, all changing and evolving into what Italians cook today.

That's why it's difficult for Italians to change particular dishes. The dishes were born of a specific context. To change the dish would be to erase the context and, to some extent, erase its soul. Someone wants to put cream in *bucatini all'amatriciana*? Of course Italians will get upset! That's just not how it's made. Respecting tradition is an important part of this cuisine.

On the other hand, Italians encourage innovation. They love that special something, that little twist or personal touch when they sit down to eat. With pasta, it's all about respecting traditions but being open to taking a dish somewhere new.

How do you know when you've gone too far? I walk that line every day in my restaurants. I have deep respect and admiration for Italian cuisine and its traditions. But I have curiosity and creativity, too. What if I used this ingredient instead of that? What if I presented the flavors this way instead of that way?

Not long ago, I was in Rome enjoying an amazing meal with Oretta Zanini De Vita at Piatto Romano. Oretta has written dozens of award-winning books on Italian food, history, and culture, including the incredible *Encyclopedia of Pasta*. As we bit into perfectly chewy *maltagliati* with a simple sauce of tomatoes and chiles, the chef, Francesca, came to the table.

"I will be serving rigatoni with intestines." Oretta responded to her, "Yes, definitely rigatoni." "Oh?" I asked, Why not spaghetti?" They both looked at me like I was crazy and said, "Non si fa!" (You just don't do that!) Of course I asked why. Francesca explained, "It just doesn't go." She went on to say that sometimes you can substitute capellini in this

dish but not spaghetti. Confused, I looked at Oretta. "No," she said. "Never spaghetti."

That exchange reinforced my belief that Italian food traditions are anchored in familiarity. A certain region has made a certain dish a certain way for so many years that changing it is unheard of.

Oretta elaborated on the matter. "When you make *bucatini all'amatriciana*, you have tomatoes, some *guanciale*, and pecorino. That's it. Very simple. It's because of the landscape and what grew there years ago. Italian food is about culture. Tomatoes grew there, sheep and pigs grew there, and they had dry pasta because of the air between the volcanic mountains and the sea. Dishes came about because of that. So to take years of tradition and change it would almost be sacrilege. However, nowadays, sometimes you don't have *guanciale*. Maybe you have pancetta. So maybe you think, 'I will substitute that.' Or maybe you have only Parmigiano, or a different type of pasta. No *bucatini*, but you have rigatoni. All of these things are logical substitutions that can be made without changing the dish. But adding cream? Or spinach? That wouldn't make sense."

And that's where you draw the line. You cannot drastically change the sauce and still call it by the same name. Many different sauces can go with many different shapes. But pastas and sauces should be substituted only within reason. And the reason is not always a scientific or gustatory one. On the contrary, it may simply be because "this goes with the dish and that doesn't." This is the kind of understanding that gives us respect for tradition in cuisine. But it also leaves the door open to innovation.

# 2

## WHEAT FLOUR

**TO UNDERSTAND PASTA, YOU HAVE TO GET A HANDLE ON WHEAT.**
This beautiful, amber grain is the main ingredient in pasta, accounting
for 50 to 75 percent of the weight of most pasta doughs, both fresh and
dried. Even so, when making fresh pasta, most chefs just grab a bag of
tipo 00 flour from Italy. At one time, I did the same thing. Double-zero flour
is traditional. It works. Why risk anything else? But then I got to thinking:
I love to experiment with different wheat flours from local farmers for my
breads. Why not experiment with different wheat flours for my pasta?
To learn more about wheat, I attended "Seeds: Cultivating the Future of
Flavor," a conference organized by chef Dan Barber that was held at the
Stone Barns Center for Food and Agriculture in upstate New York. Plant
breeders, farmers, and chefs from all over the world came together in a
single room to discuss one thing: how to grow more delicious food—

particularly grains. Ferran Adrià, Michel Bras, David Bouley, and many other chefs were there, but the guy who captured my attention most was Dr. Stephen Jones, a wheat breeder from Washington State University. Dr. Jones talked about delicious breeds of wheat that couldn't be sold on the commodity market because although they had great flavor when milled for whole wheat flour, they didn't work for bread making on an industrial scale. In other words, they were too nutritious for our commodity wheat market. We tasted a few simple breads made with these flours, and their flavors just blew me away. It was like I'd never tasted wheat before.

I thought, maybe these wheat varieties would make great pasta, too? I've always sought out the best ingredients for my kitchens. Over the years, I've developed relationships with farmers and growers to provide my guests with the best-tasting varieties of vegetables and fruits and the highest-quality breeds of animal meats. Maybe it was time to work with my local farmers to develop the best flours for pasta. Dr. Jones inspired me to dive into the subject of wheat.

## ANCIENT AND MODERN WHEATS

Wheat breeding is nothing new. This cereal grass was one of the first plants cultivated by humans and is the third most widely grown grain in the world, after rice and corn. Chalk it up to wheat's mild flavor and unique proteins. When wheat is ground into flour and mixed with water, its proteins can be formed into a huge range of different breads, noodles, and dumplings. That helps to explain why wheat is now the number one source of plant-based protein around the world and the most widely planted human food crop in the United States.

Two of the earliest cultivated types of wheat were durum and emmer (*farro*). These ancient wheats are still vital to Italian food culture today. The wheat plant evolved on its own for millennia, and as a result of mating and cross-breeding with other grasses, a new wheat species, *Triticum aestivum*, appeared about eight thousand years ago. We started cultivating this new species because it made a more elastic dough than the ancient wheats, making it possible to create a greater variety of food. Although centuries old, this "modern" bread wheat now accounts for 90 percent of

## Wheat Anatomy

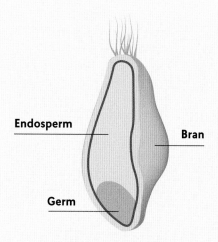

Like other grains, a wheat berry consists of three basic components: bran, germ, and endosperm. The bran is the hard, fibrous outer layer. Buried inside is the germ, which is high in vitamins, minerals, and essential fatty acids. Give the germ some soil, water, and light and it grows into a new, live wheat plant. The rest of the wheat berry, about 80 percent of its total volume, is called the endosperm. This is the white, puffy interior that gets ground into white flour. It's mostly starch and about 9 to 17 percent protein, depending on the wheat variety.

the wheat grown in the world, with the remainder consisting mostly of durum used to make dried pasta.

For cooks, the main variables in types of wheat before it is milled are the growing season and protein content of the grain itself. Wheat grown in the spring tends to contain more protein than wheat grown in the winter. Hard wheat is developed to have a high protein content; soft wheat has less. The smaller amount of protein means that soft wheat creates tender doughs and batters for soft fresh pasta, cakes, and cookies. Higher protein hard wheat produces more sturdy doughs and the structure needed for bread and dried pasta.

## MILLING AND FRESHNESS

The variety of wheat you use isn't the only thing that determines how the flour behaves in the kitchen. How it's milled and stored makes a big difference. Since Neolithic times, stones have been used to grind grains down to smaller pieces. They didn't call it the Stone Age for nothing! Today, modern millstones consist of two disk-shaped stones that grind wheat berries into flour. When stone-ground, all three basic parts of a whole grain are ground together. The soft, white endosperm ends up in very fine pieces, and the tougher, dark bran and tan germ end up in large pieces. To refine stone-ground wheat flour, millers pass it through a series of sieves to achieve various grades of so-called dirty white flour that retains some of the bran and germ.

In the mid-1800s, steel roller mills were developed in the United States and Europe. They promised to take us out of the Stone Age, but I'm not so sure they improved our health. Roller mills do away with the bran and germ right off the bat, and then they grind just the soft, white endosperm. They're not designed to make whole-grain flour. In fact, most of today's "whole wheat" flour is not made of intact wheat berries ground into flour. It's actually refined roller-milled white flour with some bran and germ added back in. In contrast, true whole-grain stone-ground flour is made by grinding intact wheat berries into flour between stones and then sifting to various grades of fineness. Be careful, however. The US Food and Drug Administration (FDA) does not currently regulate the term *stone-ground*, so look for stone-ground flour from reputable millers.

The biggest problem with roller-milling wheat is that it removes the most flavorful and nutritious parts of the grain, the bran and germ. That's done in part because refined white flour can be stored longer. The germ has a high oil content, which can make flour go rancid relatively quickly, so removing it extends the shelf life of the flour. But that convenience comes at a price. Most flour on the market tastes old and stale. As Dr. Jones likes to say, "When you

gain functionality, you need to watch it because you can lose flavor, too."

This point was driven home when I spent a day visiting Dr. Jones at his Bread Lab in Mount Vernon, Washington. The lab, a key part of Washington State University's plant-breeding program, brings together farmers, millers, bakers, and food scientists to study and bake with different wheat varieties. It's basically a room with professional bread ovens on one side and high-tech flour and dough-testing machines on the other. The day I visited, we turned the Bread Lab into the Pasta Lab and studied pasta dough. Dr. Jones and the resident baker, Jonathan McDowell, ground a bunch of flours for me to work with and we made pasta.

Like most chefs, I'm keenly aware of how important freshness is to the best flavor of most ingredients. But in the past, I didn't think much about how old flour was. Most chefs don't. They just order bread flour or pizza flour or all-purpose flour without thinking about freshness and flavor. Until that day in the lab, I never realized how important freshness is for flour. Yes, freshly ground wheat actually has flavor! And different varieties have different flavors. We made pasta with freshly ground varietals like Soissons, Tevelde, McGuire, and Dayn. We used whole eggs, no eggs, egg yolks, water only, and olive oil. We also made the same pastas with big-name brands of commodity flour and then tasted the two versions side by side. The results were staggering. The commodity flours made the familiar mild-tasting earthy pasta that most people are used to. But the freshly ground flours brought forward other flavor profiles. You could taste tobacco and nuts. You could smell flowers, fruit, and freshly cut grass. I'm talking about pasta cooked and served with absolutely nothing on it. This plain boiled pasta tasted incredible!

One variety in particular, Red Russian, smelled complex in the bag but failed in the bakery. It was high in protein, 14.1 percent, but the protein wasn't strong enough to make bread. So I asked them to grind the Red Russian wheat berries very finely, like tipo 00 flour, the grind I normally use for fresh pasta. Pasta flour is usually ground fine so that the dough passes easily through the rollers. With this freshly ground whole wheat flour, we made a basic egg dough, rolled it by hand, and cut it into *pappardelle*. Just boiled and put on a plate, it was like no pasta I had ever tasted.

The texture was soft but chewy and the flavor was pronounced: earthy, nutty, and fruity all at once. It was light-years ahead of any other whole wheat flour I've ever used to make pasta. And none of these flavors was detectable in the pastas made with commodity flours. The textures were similar, but texture is something you can manipulate by mixing flours together to change the protein content. Flavor, on the other hand, cannot be replicated.

This is an extremely important point. As soon as you crack a wheat berry, its flavor and aroma begin to dissipate. Within two days of grinding wheat berries into flour, nearly half of the flavorful oils—as well as many of the healthful nutrients—will oxidize. Within three days, 90 percent of the volatile flavor compounds in the flour will have been simply lost to the air. Think of wheat berries like coffee beans. For the best taste, you need to grind them fresh and use them right away. Otherwise, all the flavor and aroma just fade away.

The temperature of the grain matters, too. For the best taste, it's a good idea to freeze grains before you mill them. Traditionally, the first-milled grains of the season were milled cold, right after the winter. These cold-milled grains produced the most sought after, highest-quality flour because more of the volatile flavors and aromas remained in the grain. According to Glenn Roberts, who founded Anson Mills and produces some of the best-tasting grains a chef could ever hope to cook with, "Milling temperature determines how flavor develops in flours. If viable grain is milled cold, the resultant flour retains fresh milled flavors and is considered 'live' flour because the bio structure of viable grain is retained in cold milling. This class of flour is a different food form than flour milled at ambient temperature, especially if the flour is aspirated with ambient air during or after milling. Ambient-temperature milled flours are oxidized and become an element in the canon of the preservation kitchen, whereas live flours are perishable and, from antiquity to modern times, they should be used immediately in cookery and/or baking or stored cold to preserve their fresh milled flavors. Live flour performance is radically

## Italian Flour Terms

American grain mills usually label flour by their intended usage, such as bread flour, cake flour, and so on. Most Italian flours, on the other hand, are labeled with numbers to indicate the fineness of the grind. Tipo 00 (type 00) is ground superfine, like talcum powder. Tipo 0 is ground slightly coarser, and types 1 and 2 have the coarsest textures. Double-zero flour is often—but not always—ground from low-protein varieties of soft wheat (grano tenero in Italian), meaning that the flour is best suited for cakes, pastries, and soft fresh pasta. Tipo 0 is usually—but not always—ground from slightly higher protein wheat, making it a good all-purpose flour for fresh pasta and delicate breads. Tipo 1 and tipo 2, which tend to be ground from high-protein wheat, are good for sturdy breads.

But don't go by the numbers alone. Strictly speaking, these numbers refer only to the fineness of the grind. It's possible to buy a finely ground tipo 00 flour that's milled from high-protein wheat, and that flour may be best suited to sturdier doughs such as pizza dough. When in doubt, check the protein content of the flour and match it to the texture you're trying to achieve. In general, use lower protein flours for softer textures and higher protein flours for sturdier textures. That's why factory-dried pasta is made from hard, high-protein durum wheat (grano duro). It helps the dough hold its shape as a dried noodle. Semolina is the coarsely ground yellow endosperm of durum wheat and is used to make extruded and dried pastas. But keep in mind that durum wheat can also be ground finer and sold as durum flour.

different in pasta and bread making when compared to oxidized or ambient milled flours."

Am I suggesting that you grind your own flour to make pasta? It's not out of the question. Chefs go above and beyond for vegetables, meat, fish, and even cheeses, so why not wheat? Whole wheat berries stay fresh for years. The hard outer layer protects all of the vital nutrients and flavors inside. You could buy wheat berries from a local farmer, store them at room temperature or freeze them in a paper bag, and grind them cold into flour whenever you need it. KitchenAid makes an inexpensive burr grinder attachment that quickly grinds one pound (454 g) of wheat berries into flour. If you want to grind larger volumes of flour, reasonably priced tabletop mills are available. Or, you can buy fresh flour from a local miller. More and more millers are showing up at farmers' markets to sell different varieties of locally grown wheat. So if you really want the best-tasting fresh pasta, you need to make the effort to get your hands on freshly milled flour.

Fresh flour behaves a little differently from aged flour, however. Over time, flour reacts with oxygen and moisture, causing its proteins to combine with one another and create longer chains of protein. As a result, doughs made with aged flour are more stable and elastic, producing higher-rising breads. But they're not as flavorful. Again, "when you gain functionality, you lose flavor." Fortunately, that kind of sturdy functionality is not as essential when you're making fresh pasta. The flavor of the flour is more important.

## GLUTEN QUANTITY AND QUALITY

Wheat is complicated stuff. As already mentioned, the amount of protein in wheat is an important factor that partly determines its functionality. But the *quality* of that protein matters just as much as the quantity. By quality, I'm referring to how the protein is constructed on a molecular level. The quality matters because when you mix wheat flour with water or other liquids, the protein in the grain forms a web, or network, called gluten, which is what holds the mixture together as dough. The more you mix, the stronger the network becomes. And if the flour is high in protein and the protein has a strong quality, the gluten network is also

strengthened. Chewy breads call for strong protein and long kneading times to develop a sturdy gluten network. Light, fluffy cakes call for weak proteins and just a little mixing to minimize gluten development. Fresh pasta is somewhere in between. A moderate amount of protein in the flour and some gentle kneading allows you to form elastic dough that can be rolled out into long sheets that hold their shape.

In pasta dough (and in bread and pizza doughs, for that matter), the gluten network is considered both elastic and plastic. That means the dough stretches and bounces back (elastic), and it can be molded into shapes that stay put (plastic). In general, the dough used to make fresh ravioli has more elasticity, while the dough used to make dried penne has more plasticity. The relative elasticity and plasticity of any wheat flour dough is determined by the gluten *quality* or how the protein is constructed, specifically the ratio of the two primary components of gluten: glutenin and gliadin. Stick with me here. We're gonna dig into this a little bit!

Elasticity is largely governed by the glutenin component and plasticity by the gliadin component. Glutenin is of particular interest in bread flours. A glutenin molecule consists of subunits that align themselves in different ways that ultimately make the gluten network in the dough stronger or weaker. Glutenin subunits that align themselves in a

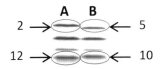

*Here are samples of two different wheat varieties. Sample A (low gluten strength) has gluten subunits 2+12, and sample B (high gluten strength) has subunits 5+10. The other bands represent various subunits that have less of an effect on the strength of the dough.*

2+12 pattern create a weaker gluten network. Those aligned in a 5+10 pattern create a stronger gluten network. See the image on page 13 for more detail. Basically, this means that wheat flours with 2+12 glutenin subunits are considered low-strength cake and pastry flours. Those with more 5+10 subunits are considered high-strength bread flours. All-purpose flour is generally a mix of both types of flour for a moderate protein content and moderate amount of elasticity and plasticity. According to Dr. Jones, "Most commodity bread flours that you have access to in the United States are 5+10 wheats."

I know this is pretty technical. But it really helped me understand the difference between, say, Italian dried penne pasta and Chinese hand-pulled noodles. The penne is made with high-protein semolina wheat with a high degree of plasticity, so the pasta can hold its shape. Chinese hand-pulled noodles, in contrast, are made with a lower protein flour with a high degree of elasticity, so they can be easily stretched by hand. The cool thing was that Dr. Jones showed me all of these wheat properties with high-tech food-science gizmos at the Bread Lab. Various machines with names like farinograph, alveograph, and consistograph are used to measure the strength, elasticity, plasticity, extensibility, viscosity, and shear tolerance of wheat doughs. It's crazy, fascinating stuff.

## CHOOSING FLOUR

So where does this leave the aspiring pasta chef? With lots of exciting possibilities!

Sure, you can just grab a bag of tipo 00 off the shelf to make fresh pasta. It's traditional, and it works. You can even use all-purpose flour. But you can achieve extraordinary results by experimenting with different varieties of flour—especially freshly milled flour.

For instance, for fresh pasta, I usually make my basic Egg Yolk Dough (page 26) with 75 percent tipo 00 flour for pasta and 25 percent durum flour. The durum flour raises the overall protein content and gives the pasta a slightly chewier texture and better durability for shaping. The net protein content of these two flours is about 11.5 percent, close to the protein content of bread flour. So I experimented with using 100 percent bread flour instead. It worked great. The grind is a little coarser, which creates a more rustic, less silky pasta, but that works perfectly if you're pairing the pasta with a more rustic, chunky sauce. Of course, a finely ground bread flour would make silkier pasta.

After playing around with pasta dough for years, I've developed all kinds of recipes. I call for several different types of flour in the recipes in this book. Most of them are wheat flours you can buy off the shelf, like tipo 00, durum, semolina, whole wheat, and stone-ground. Some are nonwheat flours like oat, buckwheat, chestnut, almond, pistachio, and corn—and even cocoa. I suggest making the recipes as they are written the first time around. But remember this: *there is no single perfect flour for pasta making.* Once you make a recipe and get a feel for how the dough rolls out, cooks up, and tastes, experiment with different flours. Buy some freshly milled stone-ground flour from a local farmer and turn it into fettuccine. Or grind some *farro* into flour with a home grain mill and cut the dough into *pappardelle*. It all depends on the kind of pasta you want to make. Thick or thin. Tender or chewy. Fresh or dried. Mild or bursting with flavor. The world of pasta is an endless sheet of possibilities.

# Gluten Allergies

This is a highly controversial subject, but here's my two cents: wheat is not bad for most people. A recent review of research on wheat and health published in the *Journal of Cereal Science* concluded that wheat is actually good for most people. Only 1 percent of the US population is gluten intolerant and about 6 percent are gluten sensitive. The other 93 percent of Americans can enjoy a wide variety of healthful wheat foods. It's true that eating fewer refined wheat products and more whole-grain wheat products can have a beneficial effect on your overall health. But wheat is not addictive, and the starch in it is not drastically different from other starches.

Modern wheat, *Triticum aestivum*, is the same wheat species that has been used to make bread for at least eight thousand years. What changed in the 1960s is that new varieties of *T. aestivum* were developed (using traditional plant-breeding techniques) that could withstand higher levels of chemical fertilizers and modern harvesting methods. Those semidwarf wheats helped increase production. But what may be more important is how these wheats led to a drastic reduction in the time it takes to turn dry flour into packaged baked goods. Wheats for making commodity flours have been specifically bred to withstand the high-speed mixing required for making bread products quickly on an industrial scale. This is good for production and profits but maybe not so good for our health. First of all, we're adding excessive amounts of vital wheat gluten to bread products. Vital wheat gluten is basically refined white flour hydrated into dough and then washed of its starch, so you're left with a mass of almost 80 percent wheat protein. It's like pure gluten, which adds structure and elasticity to bread doughs and helps them rise faster—

especially whole wheat bread doughs. Ironically, the added gluten may be making these "healthy" whole-grain breads less tolerable to our digestive systems.

During the natural fermentation and rising of traditional yeast breads, the enzymes in wheat dough (called proteases) break down gluten proteins, and when the gluten is broken down, it is easier for our bodies to digest. But in modern industrial baking, natural fermentation does not occur. Dry flour becomes plastic-bagged bread in an average of just three hours. That means the gluten proteins remain largely intact in these breads, so they are more difficult for us to digest. Personally, I prefer to eat naturally fermented yeast breads.

Fortunately, pasta is not fermented or baked, so it remains largely unaffected by these changes in modern industrial bread baking. Plus, dried pasta is made from a completely different species of wheat, *T. durum*, so it remains unaffected by the controversy over modern bread wheat, *T. aestivum*. But if you are a fan of gluten-free products in general, bear this in mind: annual sales of these products are expected to exceed $15 billion by 2016. Food companies are more than happy to capitalize on food trends and supply the public with what it demands. To ensure truth in labeling, the FDA recently defined the term *gluten-free* as "containing no more than 20 parts of gluten per million." But is an industrially produced bread product labeled "gluten-free" your most healthful choice? Back when fat was the nutritional villain of the moment, fat-free food products flooded the marketplace. But they turned out to be less healthy for us than foods made with natural, healthy fats. Could the gluten-free craze be headed in the same unhealthy direction?

# Wheat Flour Characteristics

Specific qualities of wheat flours vary widely by breed and brand. In general, here is the protein content and functionality you can expect from various types of flour. Some brands of flour also list the protein content on the package or on the brand's website. In this book, I call mostly for wheat flours like durum, semolina (the coarsely ground endosperm of durum), tipo 00, all-purpose, whole wheat, bread, and stone-ground. I also call for some nonwheat flours in chapter 7, Playing with Flavor (see page 137). Wouldn't it be great if there was a whole category of pasta wheats to play with, just as there is a category of bread wheats?

| WHEAT FLOUR PROTEIN, STRENGTH, AND ELASTICITY | | | |
| --- | --- | --- | --- |
| **WHEAT FLOUR** | **PROTEIN % BY WEIGHT** | **GLUTEN STRENGTH** | **ELASTICITY** |
| Vital gluten | 65–80 | Strong | High |
| Farro (emmer) | 16–17 | Moderate | Low |
| Durum | 14–15 | Strong | Low |
| Whole wheat | 12–14 | Strong | Moderate |
| Stone-ground | 12–14 | Strong | Moderate |
| Semolina | 12–13 | Moderate | Low |
| Tipo 00 for pizza | 12–13 | Strong | Moderate |
| Bread | 11.5–14 | Strong | High |
| Unbleached all-purpose, northern US | 11–12 | Strong | Moderate |
| Unbleached all-purpose, national US | 10–12 | Strong | Moderate |
| Bleached all-purpose, national US | 10–12 | Moderate | Moderate |
| Bleached all-purpose, southern US | 8–10 | Moderate | Moderate |
| Tipo 00 for pasta | 8–10 | Moderate | Moderate |
| Pastry | 8–9 | Weak | Low |
| Cake | 6–8 | Weak | Low |

Sources: theartisan.net; thefreshloaf.com; *On Food and Cooking* by Harold McGee; caputoflour.com; USDA National Nutrient Database for Standard Reference

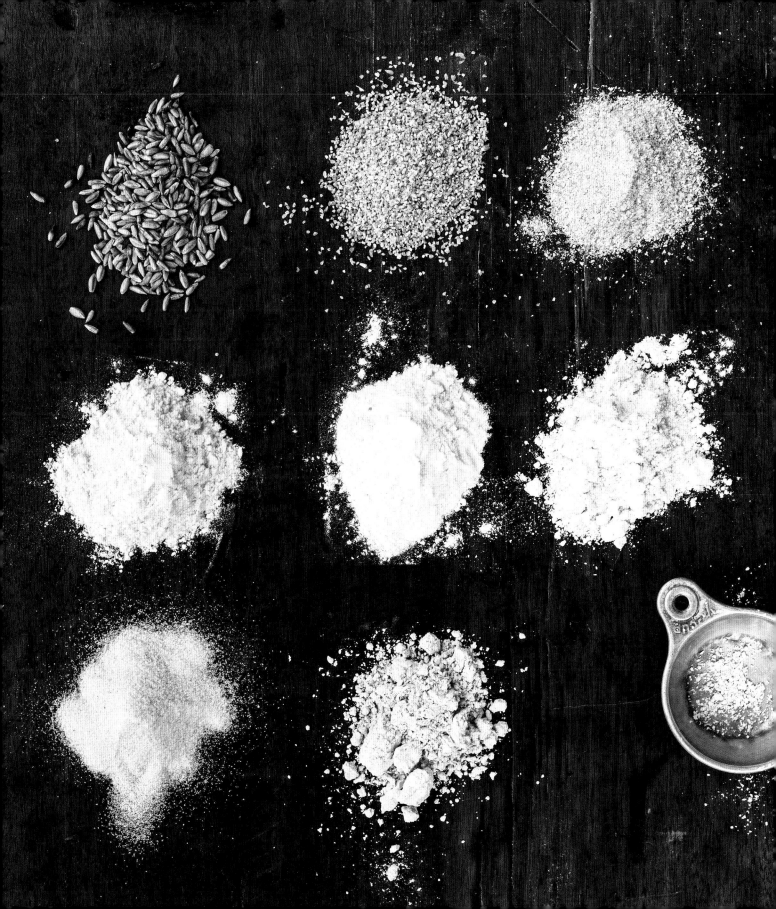

# 3

## FRESH PASTA

**WHEN I EAT A GREAT PLATE OF PASTA, I LET OUT A LITTLE SHOUT.**
Ask anyone who has worked with me. They'll tell you that when I eat a new dish, I smell it first, close my eyes to sharpen my senses, and then taste. If I like it, my body does a quick shake and out comes this little "ha!" Everyone starts to laugh. I don't do it for effect or to get a response. It's something uncontrollable. Something takes over my body. But it's more than just a release. It's a pure expression. It's saying that a beautiful balance has just happened. Everything came together and presented a unique sensation. That's when I know it's perfect. A fettuccine with just a slight bite wraps around a beautiful *ragù*. *Garganelli* with their sauce sucked up inside the tubes squirt all over your mouth when you bite into them. These sensations don't just happen out of the blue. I've always believed that a great plate of food results from two things: beautiful products and careful technique.

One without the other will only ever achieve a certain level of cuisine. To reach the "ha!" level, you must have both.

In my quest to learn ever more about a great dish of fresh pasta, I took some friends to a restaurant in the middle of Tuscany where I worked twenty years ago. La Chiusa sits on a hillside in the village of Montefollonico, just outside Montepulciano. Overlooking the vineyards, we enjoyed three different pasta dishes for lunch: fresh tomatoes and chiles with *pici*, tagliatelle with white truffle, and ricotta-filled ravioli (page 81). We all helped make the pastas that morning. Near the end of the meal, the owner, Umberto Luccherini, drove up and got out of his car, standing tall just as I remembered him, cigar in hand. "Hai vista paradiso?" Umberto asked. (Are you seeing paradise?) Indeed. La Chiusa is one of those gorgeous Tuscan places that you dream about. As if frozen in time, it's the same as it ever was. Even the head chef, Dania, was still radiant and vivacious. She had run out earlier that morning to get her hair done and had just returned, ready to cook. She used to walk the line in the kitchen wearing high heels and a cocktail dress, and then would put on an apron and start cooking the most beautiful dishes. As a young chef, I thought that was hot! But it was the pasta at La Chiusa that really got me going. "Pasta, pasta, pasta," said Dania with a smile. "Forty years of it! I've had it up to here with pasta," she gestured, half-joking, half-serious.

The pasta, like everything else at La Chiusa, is timeless. After all these years, there are still no pasta machines in the kitchen, and every day the dough is rolled out by hand on wooden boards with rolling pins. The pasta woman I worked with two decades earlier had just retired a few weeks before we arrived. But the new pasta woman, Rosa, made it the same way as before. We spent the entire morning mixing, kneading, rolling, shaping, and filling dough and talking about the craft I love.

I use lots of different recipes for fresh pasta. Some have eggs, some have oil, some have no eggs, some have no oil. But in all of them—and every Italian will tell you this—"La farina è la cosa più importante." (Flour is the most important thing.) More than any other ingredient, flour changes the texture of the dough and the way it stretches, the way the pasta feels in your mouth, and how it tastes. Read the Wheat Flour chapter (see page 9) to dig deep into the details. Keep in mind, too, that adding or omitting ingredients is not only about the results you get. This is crucial to understand. Some ingredients originally made their way into pasta dough or were left out for economic or cultural reasons. If you were wealthy, you could afford to drop a few eggs into the pasta dough. Or if it was a holiday, maybe you splurged with an egg or two. But if you were poor and it was just another day, you used flour and water. Maybe you added whatever was handy. Maybe some olive oil. In other words, many pasta dishes evolved out of necessity. Or whimsy. Or pure luck. So don't overthink it. There is no right or wrong way. There is just the way it's been done for centuries and the way it has evolved.

I am going to walk you through a basic fresh pasta recipe from La Chiusa. It's easy to do and helps explain how the ingredients you add alter the dough.

On the day we visited, Rosa put two tablespoons (30 ml) water and two tablespoons (30 ml) olive oil into a bowl. Then she cracked in six whole eggs and mixed. She poured in tipo zero flour—without measuring of course—and I asked, "Why not use double zero?" (I like to use double zero because it creates a fine dough that becomes a little more compact and easier to roll out.) She explained that she likes the pasta a little tighter and thus prefers the zero flour. So you can use zero or double zero, keeping in mind the texture will be a little coarser with zero. Maybe you want it coarser because of the sauce you're planning to make. The kind of flour you use also depends on what type of flour you can get your hands on—the fresher the better, of course, because freshness equals flavor—and what you are trying to achieve in the pasta.

After the zero flour, she added about half as much beautiful stone-ground whole wheat flour. Of course I asked why. Because when I use double-zero flour, I add some durum flour to the mix. Durum flour is milled from hard wheat while double-zero flour for pasta is usually milled from soft wheat; I add the durum because I like a little bite in the pasta. Rosa adds stone-ground flour for bite, too, but it has some of the wheat bran and germ still in it, so you see nice brown and tan specks throughout the dough, and those specks add beautiful flavor and nutrients like iron, magnesium, and potassium.

Rosa uses whole eggs, but I often use egg yolks because they add richness from the fat and a firmer texture from

the protein. That firmness and richness work better with the double-zero flour. With whole eggs, you're getting the whites too, and they are mostly water and protein. Whole eggs could water down a double-zero dough and make it too soft. The point here, however, is that you can *manipulate* the dough by varying flours and using whole eggs or egg yolks to lower or raise the protein in the whole mix. All of the proteins are giving the dough structure and chew.

Rosa mixes the dough by hand continuously for about six minutes. It's important to mix. How much you mix depends on the flours you use and whether you want the dough to be tender or chewy. Either way, everything not only has to come together but also be smoothly incorporated. She kneads and kneads, developing gluten in the dough,

which makes the dough firmer and helps the pasta hold its shape. Will the dough made with zero flour be harder to roll out than my double-zero dough? Of course it will. Zero flour is coarser than double zero, and Rosa added some even coarser stone-ground flour on top of that. But the egg whites thin out the dough, so it will still roll out pretty thinly, and it will cook up beautifully. With the flours she used, egg yolks alone might make this dough too hard to roll and cause it to rip. So her recipe is spot-on.

What are we learning here? Very simply that pasta dough can be changed and varied and played with however you want if you understand the properties that each ingredient brings to the dough. Once you have that knowledge, you can make *any* pasta you can imagine.

## FRESH PASTA TUTORIAL

Erase the image of a labor-intensive process and a messy kitchen with flour and egg all over the place. It's really not like that. Actually, it's quite the opposite. With a little flour and some liquid, your hands, and a rolling pin, you have the power to create the most beautiful plates of food. Fresh pasta is one of the easiest and simplest things to make. Let's take it step-by-step, from understanding the ingredients to the rolling, cutting, boiling, and saucing of the pasta.

### Flour

Wheat flour is the primary ingredient in pasta, accounting for 50 to 75 percent of the weight of most doughs. It's the gluten protein in flour that creates the structure of the dough, both its elasticity (the dough stretches and bounces back) and its plasticity (it can be molded into shape and holds that shape). The starch in wheat flour absorbs water, and when the pasta is cooked, that starch sets the structure of the noodle and gelatinizes, or forms a creamy paste. That gelatinized starch is what you taste when a beautifully cooked noodle just melts in your mouth as you chew it.

Depending on the flour you use and its protein content, the pasta will be softer or chewier. Semolina from high-protein durum flour (12 to 13 percent protein in the semolina) makes factory-dried pasta chewier. Low-protein tipo 00 flour (8 to 10 percent protein) makes fresh pasta silkier. Maybe you want to pick a higher-protein flour for a thick, chewy *pappardelle*. Or maybe you're making ravioli and want the dough superthin and silky, which means a lower-protein tipo 00 could be the way to go. (To check the protein content of different flours, see the chart on page 16.) How finely the flour is ground makes a difference, too. Tipo 00 flour is like baby powder and makes a more supple dough that's easier to roll. Tipo 2 flour and coarsely ground whole wheat flours give you a coarser, more rustic feel in the mouth. Different grinds measure differently, so you have to be careful. For example, 100 grams fine tipo 00 flour is about ⅔ cup in volume, but 100 grams all-purpose flour, which is ground a little coarser, is about ¾ cup. Weights are constant, so measure by weight if you can. But don't go too crazy with these details. You can pull almost any decent-quality flour off the shelf and make great pasta with it!

### Water

Without water, the gluten in wheat would never form into dough. When you add water, the wheat proteins suck up about 200 percent of their weight in moisture. Adding more water just thins out the dough. The water can add minerals, too, if you have hard water. Or it can add other flavors if you use flavored water. Squid ink is a popular flavored water for pasta, but you can use any flavored liquid. Vegetables and fruits are 70 to 95 percent water, so sometimes I puree them and use the puree for part of the water in pasta dough. Even egg yolks are 50 percent water.

There's also water in the air, especially if it's a humid day. This is extremely important to keep in mind. Because of humidity, every few months we have to change the grind setting on the coffee grinders at all of my restaurants to get the espresso machines to work properly. In the winter, when there is less humidity, we use a fine grind of coffee. In the summer, when the air is thick, we use a coarse grind. A fine grind in the summer just won't let any water through because the air is too moist. Some of the runners and busboys think they can simply change the dose of coffee grounds, but the dose should remain the same. The grind needs to be adjusted. That's also why the exact same pasta dough recipe with the exact same flour will work differently in the winter than it will in the summer. The grind of the flour—and even whether it is stone-ground or whole wheat flour—will change the amount of water the dough will absorb. After flour, water is the single most important ingredient in pasta, no matter where it comes from.

### Eggs and Oil

A typical pasta dough formula is 1 whole egg per 100 grams flour. And for every 3 whole eggs, 1 tablespoon olive oil, and 1 tablespoon water. So a basic recipe would be 300 grams of flour, 3 eggs, 1 tablespoon olive oil, and 1 tablespoon water. That will make great fresh pasta every time, regardless of the flour you use. The egg whites add protein and water; the egg yolks add protein and fat. The protein firms up the dough and the water thins it out so it can be rolled. The fat weakens the gluten network and makes the pasta more tender. Oil is fat, too, so the oil does the same thing as the egg yolk, but it adds the flavor of olive instead of egg. You could also use

pistachio oil or any other liquid fat. One other advantage of egg yolks is that they contain a natural emulsifier called lecithin, which stabilizes the starch in the dough. When the pasta cooks, the egg yolk proteins coagulate, firming up the pasta and giving it some chew. Plus, egg yolks are yellow and add awesome color to pasta. The *tajarin* of Piedmont are made with forty egg yolks per kilogram of flour, and those noodles glow as yellow as the sunrise.

## Salt

I don't usually add salt to my pasta doughs. Sometimes I will for flavor and to tighten up the dough. Salt makes the gluten network stronger, which is important if the dough will be heavily manipulated by hand. That's why many handmade Sardinian pastas like *culurgiones* (see page 107) include salt, which ensures the dough will hold up as you twist and fold it. For most pastas, though, I like a more delicate dough. If you do add salt, keep in mind that the pasta will absorb some salt from the salted boiling water, so don't go overboard.

## Mixing

Some people dump the flour on a board, make a well, pour the wet ingredients in the well, and then stir the wet ingredients into the flour. Rosa mixes her wet ingredients together in a bowl with a fork, then stirs in the flour with a fork. Wet to dry, dry to wet—it doesn't matter. Some people use a food processor. Others use a stand mixer. I've tried all mixing methods. For large volumes at the restaurant, I use a stand mixer. But for small volumes at home, I like to mix and knead the dough by hand. Touching and playing with the dough is half the fun! Stretch it like Play-Doh. Make Stretch Armstrong. Have a good time with it!

## Rolling

Sushi chefs spend years just cleaning fish to learn their craft. So it goes with a great pasta maker. It can take years of rolling out dough to master it. Before you roll, let the dough rest for twenty to thirty minutes. That relaxes the gluten network you just kneaded into existence, so the dough will roll out more easily. Then you can use a rolling pin, a rolling machine, pinch off pieces with your fingers—there are all sorts of ways to shape pasta. But most of the time, we roll.

For the fewest scraps and least waste, roll the dough into the shape of the pasta you're making. For round ravioli, use a pin to roll the dough into a circle. I like to use a rolling pin rather than a machine. It's like meditation. There's a methodical satisfaction to rolling out a perfectly thin circle of pasta dough with a simple long rolling pin. I use one about 3 feet (1 m) long and 1½ inches (4 cm) in diameter. If you can't find one at a local shop, look for one online (see Sources, page 249).

At the restaurant, we usually use electric rolling machines. It's just easier for that kind of volume. For home kitchens, KitchenAid makes a great attachment that's pretty inexpensive. Either way, do yourself a favor and skip the hand-crank models. If you are rolling sheets between metal rollers anyway, go electric! It's not *rustico* or any better to do it with a hand crank. And the cost of a hand crank that will do the job right is about the same as the cost of a roller attachment. We tested all the recipes in this book with an electric roller that turned out sheets about 6 inches (15 cm) wide. Arcobaleno (see Sources, page 249) also makes a pretty mac daddy pasta sheeter, if you want to go that route.

Just make sure you go slowly through the settings as you roll. An electric roller gradually thins out the dough, just like when you roll by hand. If you make it too thin too fast, the pasta rips and gets bunched up in the machine, and then you will have to reroll. If you reroll too much, more flour gets into the dough and it gets harder to work. It's best to start on the widest setting of your machine, roll the dough through that setting a couple of times, and then set the roller to the next narrowest setting. Roll it through each setting a couple of times until you get to the thickness you want. Once you get good at it, you can set the machine to a higher speed so the dough passes through a little faster, but don't skip thickness settings as you roll.

When the pasta becomes thin enough that you can start to see light through it, you have to handle it more gently. I mean, it's superthin at this point—as thin as 1/32 inch (0.8 mm). Try not to grab the dough from the center. I like to pick up the end of the sheet, feed it into the machine, and then drape the rest of the sheet over the backs of my hands. That way, my hands are like guides underneath the pasta, and the whole setup works like a conveyor belt. You just guide the sheet into the machine. Guiding it in is more important than guiding it out. If the pasta goes in crooked, it will bunch up and tear. Thick pastas are more forgiving, so if you're new to pasta making, start with thicker ones like fettuccine and lasagna. Ravioli dough is generally thinner. Try it when you get good at rolling dough.

Is there an ideal thickness for all pasta? I go by the theory that the more egg yolks you use, the thinner you have to roll the pasta. An all-yolk dough needs to be thin because otherwise it would be too hard and chewy from all the protein. But a dough made with whole eggs can be rolled a little thicker because the water in the whites dilutes the dough, so it's not as chewy. And if it's an eggless dough, you can roll it even thicker. You have to consider the shape, sauce, and filling, too. Let's say you're making lasagna, where you layer sheets of pasta between layers of filling. There's only one stratum of pasta between two layers of filling, so I make the sheet a bit thicker to ensure a good balance between pasta and filling. But for *rotolo*, where you roll the filling up in the pasta like a jelly roll, you have more pasta and less filling, so I roll *rotolo* pasta a little thinner to make sure there isn't too much pasta overall. Whenever there's a filling—in lasagna, *rotolo*, or ravioli—it's all about the pasta-to-filling ratio.

## Cutting

The simplest pastas are cut by hand. *Pappardelle*, *fazzoletti*, tagliatelle, *tagliolini*—they are all rectangles, squares, or strands cut with a knife. Roll out the dough and cut it with a knife or a machine. It's up to you. If you're making a lot of pasta, a machine is faster. But by hand is always more satisfying. And it's fun to use cutting wheels with different edges so the cuts aren't all straight lines.

## Boiling

Now, this is the step that differentiates pasta from bread. Yes, some bread doughs are boiled, but most breads are baked. For pasta, boiling is what makes it go from raw to cooked. What happens is that the boiling water causes proteins in the flour to firm up the noodle. Egg proteins also coagulate and firm up the pasta. At the same time, starch in the flour absorbs water and swells, forming a thick paste (in a process called gelatinization). The paste is what creates the soft, creamy texture of pasta as you eat it, and the protein creates the chew. That's how you get the al dente texture that's both creamy and chewy at the same time.

Use plenty of water. If you don't, when you drop in the pasta, it takes longer to get the water back up to a boil, and the pasta soaks rather than boils. About 5 quarts (4.7 L) of water per pound (454 g) of pasta is right. For that amount of water, I like to sprinkle in about 2½ tablespoons (23 g) of kosher salt. Use less if you must, but salt both flavors the pasta and tightens the proteins, so it's an important ingredient for firming up the dough. Drop in your pasta, give it a stir so it doesn't stick, and then get the water boiling again as fast as you can: crank the heat, cover the pot—whatever it takes. Boiling quickly is what gets the heat to the center of the noodle before the outside gets mushy. Test a piece by chewing it. It should taste pretty chewy but also like it won't be too chewy in a couple of minutes from now. If you're going to toss the pasta with sauce or even bake it with sauce—especially a liquidy sauce—take the pasta out of the water when it's slightly underdone. It will cook and soften up more in the sauce. To simplify draining, I like to lift the pasta straight from the water with a spider strainer or tongs.

## Saucing

You know those commercials where they show a plate of cooked pasta with a pile of sauce on top? That's bullshit. It leaves out one of the most important steps: marrying pasta and sauce. A plate of pasta should be one thing, not two. You have to mix the pasta and sauce together. The starch on the outside of the pasta is the glue. And there's starch in the pasta water, too. I usually add some pasta water to the sauce to thicken it and help the pasta and sauce come together. You want to use the starch to emulsify all the ingredients together. The real trick, though, is mixing. Just like when you make risotto, you have to stir. Or toss. Or shake the pan. That agitation rubs the pasta and sauce together until they become one thing. I usually do this over some heat, so the two become one more easily. Even if the sauce is just oil and water, it should be creamy. As with a vinaigrette, agitation causes the oil and water to come together and get creamy. And creamy is what I love about a dish of fresh pasta. Yes, oil and water do mix. If you're adding cheese, add it off the heat so the cheese does not curdle.

# EGG YOLK DOUGH

MAKES ABOUT
1 POUND (454 G)

Here's my basic fresh pasta dough. I do riffs on this recipe for most of the pasta dishes in this book. It uses a 3 to 1 ratio (by weight) of tipo 00 flour to durum flour. The durum flour gives the dough extra strength and chew. The egg yolks make it rich and tender. For the riffs, I change out the flours or eggs or add other ingredients to achieve different tastes and textures. This recipe makes enough for about 4 sheets of pasta that are 5 to 6 inches (13 to 15 cm) wide, each 4 to 5 feet (1.3 to 1.5 m) long if rolled to ⅟₃₂-inch (0.8 mm) thickness; 3 to 4 feet (1 to 1.3 m) long if rolled to ⅟₁₆-inch (1.5 mm) thickness; and 2 to 3 feet (61 cm to 1 m) long if rolled to ⅛-inch (3 mm) thickness. That's enough to make about 80 four-inch (10 cm) squares for cannelloni or lasagna, 95 two-inch (5 cm) squares for ravioli, or 150 one-inch (2.5 cm) squares for small ravioli.

| | | |
|---|---|---|
| 1 cup plus 2 tablespoons (170 g) tipo 00 flour, or 1¼ cups plus 2 tablespoons (170 g) all-purpose flour, plus some for dusting | 7 tablespoons (55 g) durum flour<br><br>9 egg yolks | 1 tablespoon (15 ml) extra-virgin olive oil<br><br>3 tablespoons (45 ml) water, plus more as needed |

Combine both flours in the bowl of a stand mixer fitted with the paddle attachment or mix together the flours on a work surface and make a well in the center. On medium speed, or with your fingers, add the egg yolks, oil, and water, adding them one ingredient at a time and mixing just until the dough comes together, 2 to 3 minutes. If necessary, add a little more water, 1 tablespoon (15 ml) at a time, for the dough to come together.

Turn the dough out onto a lightly floured work surface and knead it until it feels silky and smooth, about 5 minutes, kneading in a little tipo 00 flour if necessary to keep the dough from sticking. The dough is ready if when you stretch it with your hands, it gently pulls back into place.

Shape the dough into a ball then flatten the ball into a disk. Cover the dough and set it aside for at least 30 minutes or wrap it in plastic wrap and refrigerate it for up to 3 days. You can also freeze the dough for up to 3 months. (Thaw the dough overnight in the refrigerator before using it. Alternatively, thaw it quickly in a microwave oven on 50 percent power in 5-second increments, just until cool to the touch.)

To roll out the dough, cut it into 4 equal pieces. If you have a very long work surface, you can cut the dough into fewer pieces. Let the pieces sit, covered, at room temperature for 10 minutes if chilled. The dough should be cool but not cold. Shape each piece into an oval wide enough to fit the width of your pasta roller. Lightly flour your work surface and set the pasta roller to its widest setting. Lightly flour 1 piece of dough, pass it through the roller, and then lightly dust the rolled dough with flour, brushing off the excess with your hands. Pass the dusted dough through the widest setting again. Set the roller to the next narrowest setting and pass the dough through, dusting again with flour and brushing off the excess. Pass once again through the roller. Fold the dough in half lengthwise over itself and cut about ¼ inch (6 mm) off both corners at the fold. This folding and cutting helps to create an evenly wide sheet of dough. Continue passing the dough once or twice through each progressively narrower setting. For thicker pasta like *corzetti*, *chitarra*, *pappardelle*, fettuccine, and tagliatelle, you want to roll the dough about ⅛ inch (3 mm) thick—setting 2 or 3 on a KitchenAid attachment—or about as thick as a thick cotton bedsheet. For sheet pastas like lasagna and cannelloni, you want to roll it a little thinner, just under ⅛ inch (2 mm) thick, and for *rotolo* thinner still,

CONTINUED

about 1⁄16 inch (1.5 mm) thick—setting 4 or 5 on a KitchenAid attachment, or about as thick as a thin cotton bedsheet. For ravioli, you want to roll the pasta a little thinner, to about 1⁄32 inch (0.8 mm) thick or setting 6 or 7 on a KitchenAid; ravioli sheets should generally be thin enough to read a newspaper through. As you roll and each sheet gets longer and more delicate, drape the sheet over the backs of your hands to easily feed it through the roller. You should end up with a sheet 2 to 5 feet (61 cm to 1.5 m) long, 5 to 6 inches (13 to 15 cm) wide, and 1⁄8 to 1⁄32 inch (3 to 0.8 mm) thick, depending on your roller and the pasta you are making.

To cut the pasta sheet into the pasta shape for the dish you are making, lay it on a lightly floured work surface and use a cutting wheel or knife, or the cutter attachment on the pasta machine. If you want to hold the pasta after cutting it, dust it with flour, cover it, and refrigerate it for a few hours, or freeze it in a single layer, transfer the frozen pasta to a zipper-lock bag, and freeze it for up to 1 month. Take the pasta straight from the freezer to the boiling pasta water. That's what I usually do.

EGG YOLK AND BREAD FLOUR DOUGH If you don't have tipo 00 and durum flour, you can use all bread flour, which has a protein content similar to the mixture of the two flours and is just slightly coarser in texture. Use 1⅔ cups (228 g) bread flour (about 11.5 percent protein) in place of the tipo 00 and durum flours, and proceed as directed for Egg Yolk Dough. Makes about 1 pound (454 g).

RICH EGG YOLK DOUGH For a deep yellow, superrich-tasting dough, replace the water and oil with egg yolks. The extra yolks create a very silky, delicate dough. Use 3 cups (455 g) tipo 00 flour and 20 egg yolks, and proceed as directed for Egg Yolk Dough. Makes about 1½ pounds (680 g).

WHOLE EGG AND EGG YOLK DOUGH For some added richness along with the sturdiness of protein in whole eggs, I like a mixture of yolks and whole eggs. Use 1 teaspoon (5 ml) extra-virgin olive oil, 3 whole eggs, and 3 egg yolks. Proceed as directed for Egg Yolk Dough, adding water only if necessary for the dough to come together. The whole eggs already add quite a bit of water. Makes about 1¼ pounds (567 g).

WHOLE EGG, EGG YOLK, AND BREAD FLOUR DOUGH Here's a good dough for thin strand pastas like *tagliolini*. Use 3¼ cups (445 g) bread flour (about 11.5 percent protein), 7 egg yolks, 3 whole eggs, 1 teaspoon (5 ml) extra-virgin olive oil, and a pinch of kosher salt. Proceed as directed for Egg Yolk Dough. Makes about 1½ pounds (680 g).

WHOLE EGG, BREAD FLOUR, AND STONE-GROUND WHEAT DOUGH This dough has a nice bite from all the protein in the bread flour, stone-ground flour, and whole eggs. Try it whenever you want a little more chew. Use 1½ cups (205 g) bread flour (about 11.5 percent protein), ¾ cup (90 g) stone-ground wheat flour, ¼ teaspoon (0.75 g) kosher salt, 3 eggs, 1 tablespoon (15 ml) extra-virgin olive oil, and 1 tablespoon (15 ml) water. Proceed as directed for Egg Yolk Dough, adding more water if necessary for the dough to come together. Makes about 1 pound (454 g).

WHOLE EGG AND WHOLE WHEAT DOUGH Try this dough with Tripe Lasagna with Whole Wheat Pasta (page 68). The high protein and fiber content of the dough gives it a nice, chewy texture that perfectly contrasts with the creamy tripe filling. Use 4 cups plus 2 tablespoons (495 g) finely ground whole wheat flour, 4 eggs, 1 tablespoon (15 ml) extra-virgin olive oil, and 2 tablespoons (30 ml) water. Proceed as directed for Egg Yolk Dough. Makes about 1¾ pounds (794 g).

WHOLE EGG AND SEMOLINA DOUGH The perfect dough for *chitarra*, the square strands cut on guitar-like strings. Use 2½ cups (418 g) semolina, 4 eggs, 2 tablespoons (30 ml) extra-virgin olive oil, and a little water at a time. Proceed as directed for Egg Yolk Dough. Makes about 1 pound (454 g).

CORZETTI DOUGH A soft, velvety dough for Liguria's classic flat disks of dough. I make mine the Piedmontese way, with a little oil for richness. Use 2 cups (300 g) tipo 00 or 2 cups plus 6 tablespoons (300 g) all-purpose flour, 1 egg, 2 tablespoons (30 ml) extra-virgin olive oil, and ½ cup (118 ml) water. Proceed as directed for Egg Yolk Dough. You can knead this one for a little less time—just until the dough feels soft and smooth. Makes about 1 pound (454 g).

CULURGIONE DOUGH This is a semolina dough similar to that used for extruded pasta. But the semolina is hydrated with about 50 percent of its weight in water instead of the 25 to 30 percent used for extruded pasta. That allows it to be shaped fresh by hand into ravioli such as *culurgiones*. Skip all of the ingredients in the Egg Yolk Dough; instead, use 2 cups plus 2 tablespoons (355 g) semolina, ¾ cup (178 ml) water, and 1 teaspoon (3 g) kosher salt. Proceed as directed for Egg Yolk Dough, mixing everything on medium speed until the dough is kneaded and soft, about 7 minutes. The dough should hold a dimple when poked with your finger rather than spring back. It will also look somewhat white. Makes about 1 pound (454 g).

# PAPPARDELLE WITH RABBIT RAGÙ AND PEACHES

MAKES 4 SERVINGS

I've always been fascinated by the way fruits play so well in savory cooking. Porcini and peaches. Oxtail with Italian mustard fruits. Duck with grapes. When we started making this rabbit *ragù*, it needed a little pop, but adding vinegar or lemon juice wasn't enough. Fruit gave it so much more—acid, sugar, aroma, and something to bite into. *Pappardelle* are traditionally cooked with a *ragù* made from game meats, and in Tuscany, the game is often wild hare or rabbit.

PASTA SWAP For a *ragù* like this, I prefer a thicker noodle. That's why I went with *pappardelle*. But square *fazzoletti* make a great substitute. They will wrap around the meat and sauce nicely and give you a big bite of pasta.

1 rabbit (about 3 lb/1.4 kg)

Kosher salt and freshly ground black pepper

3 tablespoons (45 ml) grapeseed or canola oil

⅓ cup (41 g) peeled and chopped carrot

⅓ cup (34 g) chopped celery

⅓ cup (56 g) chopped red onion

⅓ cup (79 ml) dry white wine

¾ cup (135 g) cherry tomatoes, halved

8 ounces (227 g) Egg Yolk Dough (page 26), rolled into sheets about ⅛ inch (3 mm) thick

¼ cup (60 ml) extra-virgin olive oil

6 tablespoons (85 g) unsalted butter

¼ cup (25 g) grated Parmesan cheese, plus some for garnish

2 ripe peaches, halved, pitted, and thinly sliced

Heat the oven to 350°F (175°C).

Rinse the rabbit and remove the innards and excess fat deposits. Reserve the innards for another use. Remove the hind legs and forelegs by driving your knife straight through the hip and shoulder joints. Cut each leg in half through the center joint. Snip through the breastbone with kitchen shears, and then cut the rabbit crosswise into 6 to 8 pieces. Season the rabbit pieces all over with salt and pepper.

Heat the grapeseed oil in a Dutch oven over medium-high heat. When the oil is hot, add the rabbit pieces, in batches if necessary to prevent crowding, and sear them, turning them once, until they are golden brown on both sides, about 5 minutes per side. Transfer the pieces to a platter as they are done.

Add the carrot, celery, and onion to the same pan and cook over medium heat until the vegetables are lightly browned, about 4 minutes. Pour in the wine and simmer, scraping up any browned bits on the pan bottom, until the liquid

evaporates, 2 to 3 minutes. Return the rabbit to the pan along with the tomatoes. Pour in enough water to come three-fourths of the way up the sides of the ingredients. Cover the pan and braise the rabbit in the oven until it is tender and the meat pulls easily away from the bone, 1 to 1½ hours.

Let the rabbit cool slightly in the pan, then shred the meat and discard the skin and bones. Pass the vegetables and braising liquid through a food mill fitted with the medium die, or pulse them briefly in a food processor just until the vegetables are finely chopped but not pureed. Return the *ragù* to the pan. If it is thin and watery, boil it over medium heat until it has reduced to a thick consistency similar to that of tomato sauce.

Return the shredded meat to the *ragù*. Taste it, adding salt and pepper until it tastes good to you. You should have about 2 cups (473 ml) *ragù*. Use it immediately, or transfer

CONTINUED

it to an airtight container and refrigerate it for up to 3 days or freeze it for up to 2 months. Reheat the *ragù* before proceeding with the recipe.

Lay a pasta sheet on a lightly floured work surface and trim the edges square. Cut the sheet crosswise into strips a little less than 1 inch (2.5 cm) wide, preferably with a fluted cutter. Repeat with the second sheet. Dust the strips with flour, cover them, and use them within 1 hour or refrigerate them for up to 4 hours. You can also freeze them in a single layer, transfer them to a zipper-lock bag, and freeze them for up to 1 month. Take the pasta straight from the freezer to the boiling pasta water.

Bring a large pot of salted water to a boil. Drop in the *pappardelle* and cover the pot to quickly return the water to a boil. Cook the pasta until it is tender but still a little chewy when bitten, about 2 minutes. Using a spider strainer or tongs, drain the pasta by transferring it to the pan of *ragù*. Reserve the pasta water.

Add the oil and butter to the pan and cook over medium-high heat, tossing and stirring vigorously, until the sauce reduces slightly, becomes creamy, and coats the pasta, about 1 minute. Add a little pasta water if necessary to create a creamy sauce. Remove the pan from the heat and stir in the Parmesan. Keep the pasta moving until pasta and sauce become one thing in the pan. Taste it, adding salt and pepper until it tastes good to you. Stir in the peaches.

Dish out the pasta onto warmed plates and garnish each serving with some Parmesan.

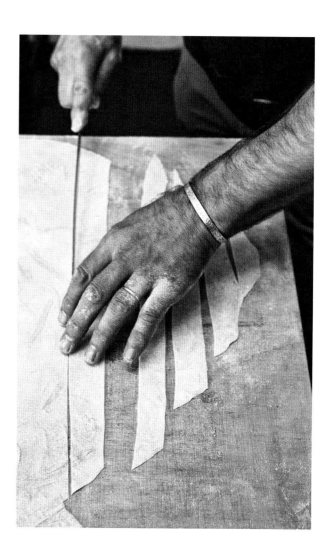

# CORZETTI WITH RED BELL PEPPER CREMA

MAKES 4 TO 6
SERVINGS

This pasta always starts a conversation. People look at a design stamped on pasta and ask where it came from and who made the stamp. Years ago, Italian royalty had the family crest carved into *corzetti* stamps made from olive or walnut wood. Nowadays, gourmet stores in Italy sell all kinds of inexpensive stamps, but occasionally you find some beautiful antique ones for sale (look in Chiavari, a little town in Liguria). The pasta medallions are essentially flat and typically served with a creamy sauce like Liguria's classic basil pesto.

PASTA SWAP A wide, flat noodle holds a creamy sauce like a towel. Other wide, flat noodles like *fazzoletti* and *maltagliati* would be great here.

5 red bell peppers

1 tablespoon (15 ml) sherry vinegar

6 tablespoons (90 ml) olive oil

Kosher salt and freshly ground black pepper

1 pound (454 g) Corzetti Dough (page 29), rolled into sheets about ⅛ inch (3 mm) thick

4 ounces (113 g) Italian fior di capra cheese (mold-ripened goat cheese)

Roast the peppers whole on a grill, under a broiler, or right over the gas flame on your stove top, turning them several times, until completely blackened on all sides, 4 to 5 minutes per side. Transfer them to a bowl, cover, and let steam for 10 to 15 minutes. Peel off and discard the skins, and then pull out and discard the cores and seeds.

Put the roasted peppers and vinegar in a blender and blend until completely smooth, 1 to 2 minutes. Slowly add 4 tablespoons (60 ml) of the oil until the *crema* thickens. Taste the *crema*, adding salt and pepper until it tastes good to you. Use the *crema* within a few hours or refrigerate in an airtight container for up to 2 days.

Lay a pasta sheet on a lightly floured work surface. Using the base of a *corzetti* stamp or a round cutter 2½ inches (6 cm) in diameter, cut out circles of dough; you should have a total of 50 to 60 circles. Stamp each circle with the *corzetti* stamp to imprint its design. If you don't have a stamp, leave the circles as they are. Or press the tines of a fork into them to imprint their shape. Repeat with the remaining pasta sheets. Dust the *corzetti* with flour, cover them, and use them within 1 hour or refrigerate them for up to 4 hours. You can also freeze them in a single layer, transfer them to a zipper-lock

bag, and freeze them for up to 1 month. Take the pasta right from the freezer to the boiling pasta water.

Bring a large pot of salted water to a boil. Drop in the *corzetti* and cover the pot to quickly return the water to a boil. Cook the pasta until it is tender but still a little chewy when bitten, about 3 minutes.

Meanwhile, pour the red pepper *crema* into a large, deep sauté pan with the remaining 2 tablespoons (30 ml) oil and a few grinds of black pepper. Add a few tablespoons (45 to 60 ml) of pasta water and cook over medium-high heat until the sauce is nice and creamy, 2 to 3 minutes.

Using a spider strainer or slotted spoon, drain the pasta by transferring it to the pan of sauce. Toss and stir vigorously until the sauce reduces slightly and coats the pasta, about 1 minute. Add a little more pasta water if necessary to create a creamy sauce. Keep the pasta moving until pasta and sauce become one thing in the pan. Taste it, adding salt and pepper until it tastes good to you.

Dish out the *corzetti* onto warmed plates, placing them in concentric circles. Shave the fior di capra over the top.

# MALTAGLIATI ALL'ARRABBIATA

**MAKES 4 SERVINGS**

There are only a couple of differences between this sauce and the tomato and basil sauce on page 124. Each starts with tomatoes and garlic sweated in olive oil, but the *arrabbiata* gets punched up with red pepper flakes and the herb is parsley—a fair amount of it. Otherwise, they're both simple, straightforward sautés of tomatoes and aromatics. The pasta here is scraps of freshly rolled egg pasta. Use leftovers from making another pasta, or use fresh sheets and cut them into irregular rectangles, diamonds, squares, triangles, or whatever. *Maltagliati* means "badly cut," so don't make them too perfect, or too big or too long. About 3 inches (7.5 cm) square is right. If you opt for dried pasta, use about 2 cups (150 g) of a short shape. And add as much red pepper flakes as you like. It's not *arrabbiata* without some kick.

PASTA SWAP So many pastas work in this dish. I use *maltagliati* to make it more luxurious. But you can easily used dried penne, ziti, or another short shape to make it more traditional.

---

¼ cup (60 ml) extra-virgin olive oil

1 clove garlic, smashed

1 cup (240 g) whole canned San Marzano tomatoes

8 ounces (227 g) Egg Yolk Dough (page 26), rolled into sheets about ⅛ inch (3 mm) thick

¼ teaspoon (0.5 g) red pepper flakes

3 tablespoons (11 g) chopped fresh flat-leaf parsley

Kosher salt and freshly ground black pepper

2 tablespoons (13 g) grated Parmesan cheese

---

Heat the oil and garlic in a large, deep sauté pan over medium heat. Keep the heat on medium so you don't burn the garlic. A little brown is okay. After about 2 minutes, add the tomatoes, crushing them with your hand as you add them to the pan. Lower the heat to medium-low and cook the tomatoes until they lose their raw tomato flavor, about 10 minutes.

Lay a pasta sheet on a lightly floured work surface. Cut the sheet into irregular shapes about 3 inches (7.5 cm) square. This pasta is traditionally made from pasta scraps, so the pieces should not be perfect. Just cut them any which way. Repeat with the second sheet. Dust the pieces with flour, cover them, and use them within 1 hour or refrigerate them for up to 4 hours. You can also freeze them in a single layer, transfer them to a zipper-lock bag, and freeze them for up to 1 month. Take the pasta right from the freezer to the boiling pasta water.

Bring a large pot of salted water to a boil. Drop in the *maltagliati* and cover the pot to quickly return the water to a boil. Cook the pasta until it is tender but still a little chewy when bitten, about 2 minutes. Using a spider strainer or slotted spoon, drain the pasta by transferring it to the pan of tomato sauce. Reserve the pasta water.

Add ½ cup (118 ml) of the pasta water, the pepper flakes, and the parsley to the pan and cook over medium-high heat, tossing and stirring vigorously, until the sauce reduces slightly, becomes creamy, and coats the pasta, about 1 minute. Keep the pasta moving until pasta and sauce become one thing in the pan. Taste it, adding salt and pepper until it tastes good to you.

Dish out the pasta onto warmed plates and garnish each serving with some of the Parmesan.

# GARGANELLI ALLA CARBONARA

MAKES 4 TO 6
SERVINGS

Compared with other pasta dishes, this one forms a slightly thicker robe of sauce around the pasta. The sauce is almost like a savory crème anglaise—super rich and creamy. Just cook it slowly so you don't curdle the eggs. Very slowly. That's the biggest problem with carbonara. This dish should not taste like scrambled eggs. Just be patient. The eggs will eventually thicken up and make the sauce ultracreamy. Trust me. The results are worth it.

PASTA SWAP *Garganelli* comes from the word *gargarnel*, which means "chicken's gullet" or esophagus. It's the perfect shape for sucking up sauce. You could also use fatter tubes like *paccheri* or longer, skinnier tubes like *bucatini*. As long as you choose a big, chewy pasta, it will go well with the creamy sauce.

1 pound (454 g) Egg Yolk Dough (page 26), rolled into sheets about ⅛ inch (3 mm) thick

8 ounces (227 g) pancetta, diced

1 cup (160 g) finely chopped white onion

4 eggs, well beaten

2½ cups (250 g) grated Parmesan cheese, plus some for garnish (optional)

Kosher salt and freshly ground black pepper

Lay a pasta sheet on a lightly floured work surface and trim the edges square. Cut the sheet into 2-inch (5 cm) squares. Place a *garganelli* comb or gnocchi board on your work surface with the lines running perpendicular to the edge of the surface, or securely tape a large, clean fine-toothed pocket comb to a clean part of the surface. Flour it lightly. To form each *garganello*, place a square of pasta on the comb or gnocchi board so one of the corners is pointing in the same direction as the teeth of the comb. Lightly flour a wooden dowel ¼ inch (6 mm) in diameter (or use a clean pencil) and lay it over the pasta perpendicular to the teeth of the comb. Fold the bottom corner of the pasta over the dowel, then roll the pasta loosely onto the dowel. Roll back and forth on the comb or board a couple of times, pressing gently into the ridges of the comb to seal the edges of the pasta and create a ridged quill shape similar to penne. Slide the pasta off the dowel and set it on a floured rimmed baking sheet. Repeat with the remaining sheets. Dust the tubes with flour, cover them, and use them within 1 hour or refrigerate them for up to 4 hours. You can also freeze them in a single layer, transfer them to a zipper-lock bag, and freeze them for up to 1 month. Take the pasta right from the freezer to the boiling pasta water.

Bring a large pot of salted water to a bowl. Drop in the *garganelli* and cover the pot to quickly return the water to

a boil. Cook the pasta until it is tender but still a little chewy when bitten, about 2 minutes.

Meanwhile, cook the pancetta in a large, deep sauté pan over medium heat until it renders its fat and starts to brown lightly, 3 to 4 minutes. Add the onion and cook it until it is tender, 3 to 4 minutes. When the pasta is ready, using a spider strainer or slotted spoon, drain the pasta by transferring it to the pan of pancetta and onion. Reserve the pasta water.

Add 2 cups (473 ml) of the pasta water to the pan and cook the mixture over medium-high heat, tossing and stirring vigorously, until the sauce reduces slightly, gets creamy, and coats the pasta, about 2 minutes. Add the eggs and cook gently over medium-low heat, tossing and stirring, until the eggs thicken and create a velvety sauce, 2 to 3 minutes. The eggs should not scramble and form curds; they should thicken and create a creamy sauce. When the sauce is creamy, remove the pan from the heat and stir in the Parmesan. Keep the pasta moving until the cheese melts and pasta and sauce become one thing in the pan. Taste it, adding salt and pepper until it tastes good to you.

Dish out the pasta onto warmed plates and garnish each serving with additional Parmesan, if you like.

# FETTUCCINE WITH CORN CREMA
# AND CHARRED GREEN ONIONS

MAKES 4 TO 6
SERVINGS

Every summer in July, this dish goes on the menu at Amis, and it stays on until we get the last of the sweet corn in the fall. Fresh corn with charred green onions is one of those combinations that should be up there with tomatoes and basil. The sweet freshness of the corn and slight bitterness of the green onions make an awesome contrast. The creamy corn puree and the delicate chew of the green onions are another delicious contrast. This dish has a great look, too, with bright green on bright yellow.

PASTA SWAP Any thick noodle works well here. Try *pappardelle* or *corzetti*.

1 pound (454 g) Egg Yolk Dough (page 26), rolled into sheets about ⅛ inch (3 mm) thick

2 tablespoons (30 ml) olive oil

2 tablespoons (21 g) finely chopped yellow onion

2 large ears corn, shucked and kernels cut from cobs

¼ cup (60 ml) water

Kosher salt and freshly ground black pepper

3 small green onions, trimmed

1 chunk ricotta salata cheese, for grating (optional)

Lay a pasta sheet on a lightly floured work surface and trim the edges square. Cut the sheet into 9-inch (23 cm) lengths. Fit your stand mixer or pasta machine with the fettuccine cutter and set it to medium speed. Feed 1 length of dough at a time through the cutter, dusting the dough lightly with flour as it is cut into strands. Coil the fettuccine into nests and set them on a floured rimmed baking sheet. Repeat with the remaining sheets. Use the fettuccine immediately or freeze in an airtight container for up to 1 month. Take the pasta right from the freezer to the boiling pasta water.

Heat 1 tablespoon (15 ml) of the oil in small saucepan over medium heat. Add the yellow onion and sweat it until it is soft but not browned, 2 to 3 minutes. Add all but ¼ cup (40 g) of the corn kernels and the water. Simmer the corn gently until it is heated through and almost tender, 3 to 4 minutes. Taste the mixture, adding salt and pepper until it tastes good to you. Transfer the mixture to a blender and puree until smooth.

Heat a cast-iron skillet over high heat until it is smoking hot. Add the green onions and cook, turning once, until charred on two sides, about 1 minute per side. Remove the skillet from the heat, transfer the onions to a cutting board, and

chop finely. Heat a large, deep skillet over medium heat and pour in the remaining 1 tablespoon (15 ml) oil. When the oil is hot, add the reserved ¼ cup (40 g) corn kernels and the chopped green onions and cook, stirring, for 1 minute, then stir in the corn *crema*. Keep warm over very low heat.

Bring a large pot of salted water to a boil. Drop in the fettuccine and cover the pot to quickly return the water to a boil. Cook the pasta until tender but still a little chewy, 4 to 5 minutes. Using a spider strainer or tongs, drain the pasta by transferring it to the pan of sauce. Reserve the pasta water.

Add about ½ cup (118 ml) of the pasta water and cook the mixture over medium-high heat, tossing and stirring vigorously until the sauce reduces slightly, becomes very creamy, and coats the pasta, about 2 minutes. Keep the pasta moving until pasta and sauce become one thing in the pan, adding a little more pasta water if necessary to create a creamy sauce. Taste it, adding salt and pepper until it tastes good to you.

Dish out the pasta onto warmed plates and grate the *ricotta salata* over the top.

# TAGLIATELLE WITH TRADITIONAL BOLOGNESE

MAKES 4 SERVINGS

How traditional is tagliatelle in Bologna? In the 1970s, the mayor of Bologna approved a law specifying that the noodles for authentic tagliatelle Bolognese must measure exactly 8 mm (5⁄16 inch) when cooked and served. There is even a gold *tagliatella* of regulation size in the Bologna Chamber of Commerce. The vegetables should be very finely cubed (called *brunoise*) for this dish. If you like, chop them in a food processor, using short pulses just until the vegetables are finely chopped. If you don't have a meat grinder, use preground beef and veal. Or, you can partially freeze the two meats as directed and then pulse them in a food processor until finely chopped but not pureed. If veal shoulder isn't available, use any fatty cut of veal from the shoulder, leg, or belly. And don't forget the milk. The meat soaks it up, creating a nice creamy texture and pretty red-orange color.

PASTA SWAP Bolognese sauce is thick enough to cling to anything. You can twirl it with spaghetti and it gets wound up among the noodles. Or you can toss it with rigatoni and it gets caught inside the tubes. Use whatever pasta you want here.

5¼ ounces (150 g) beef chuck, cubed

5¼ ounces (150 g) veal shoulder, cubed

6 tablespoons (85 g) unsalted butter

3 tablespoons (45 ml) extra-virgin olive oil

½ yellow onion, minced

1 small carrot, peeled and minced

2 celery stalks, minced

2¾ ounces (78 g) pancetta, finely chopped

½ cup (118 ml) dry red wine (such as Sangiovese, Barbera, or whatever you'll be drinking with the meal)

½ cup (120 g) whole canned San Marzano tomatoes

About 2 cups (473 ml) veal stock (page 242) or beef stock (page 242)

½ cup (118 ml) milk, heated to a boil

Kosher salt and freshly ground black pepper

12 ounces (340 g) Egg Yolk Dough (page 26), rolled into sheets about ⅛ inch (3 mm) thick

¾ cup (75 g) grated Parmesan cheese

Put a bowl and all of the parts of a meat grinder in the freezer for 20 minutes. Put the beef and veal cubes in a single layer on a rimmed baking sheet and freeze the meat until partially frozen, about 20 minutes.

Grind the cold meats on the medium die of the chilled meat grinder into the cold bowl and reserve.

Heat 3 tablespoons (43 g) of the butter and all of the olive oil in a large, deep sauté pan over medium-high heat. When the butter begins to foam, add the onion, carrot, celery, and pancetta and cook, stirring occasionally, until the vegetables and pancetta begin to brown, 4 to 5 minutes. A little color

adds a nice flavor here. Add the ground meats and continue cooking, breaking up the meats with a spoon, until they brown a little. Pour in the wine to deglaze the pan, scraping up any browned bits on the pan bottom and cooking until the liquid almost evaporates, 1 to 2 minutes. Add the tomatoes, crushing them with your hands as you add them to the pan. Cook for a few minutes, then add enough of the stock to barely cover the ingredients. Turn down the heat to medium-low and simmer, uncovered, until the tomatoes break down completely and the flavors are blended, about 45 minutes. If the stock completely evaporates, add a little more stock, a few spoonfuls at a time.

Add the milk and cook until the milk nearly evaporates and disappears into the meat, 5 to 7 minutes. Taste the sauce, adding salt and pepper until it tastes good to you. Cover and keep warm over low heat or refrigerate in an airtight container for up to 3 days. (If refrigerated, reheat the sauce before proceeding.)

Lay a pasta sheet on a lightly floured work surface and trim the edges square. Dust the sheet with flour, brushing off the excess, and then fold the sheet in half lengthwise to make the sheet narrower. Fold it in half again lengthwise to make it even narrower. Using a sharp knife, cut the dough cross-wise into slices about ¼ inch (6 mm) wide. Dust the pasta with flour, and then pick up the strands and drop them onto the work surface to dust them all over with the flour. Coil the strands into nests and place them on a floured rimmed baking sheet. Repeat with the remaining sheets. Cover the pasta and use it within 1 hour or refrigerate it for up to 4 hours. You can also freeze the pasta in an airtight container for up to 1 month. Take the pasta right from the freezer to the boiling pasta water.

Bring a large pot of salted water to a boil. Drop in the tagliatelle and cover the pot to quickly return the water to a boil. Cook the pasta until it is tender but still a little chewy when bitten, 2 to 3 minutes.

Meanwhile, add 1 cup (237 ml) of the pasta water and the remaining butter to the sauce and cook over medium-high heat until the liquid reduces slightly and starts to get creamy, 5 to 7 minutes. Using a spider strainer or tongs, drain the pasta by transferring it to the sauce in the pan. Toss and stir vigorously until the sauce becomes creamy and coats the pasta, 1 to 2 minutes. Remove the pan from the heat and stir in ½ cup (50 g) of the Parmesan. Keep the pasta moving until the cheese melts and pasta and sauce become one thing in the pan. Taste it, adding salt and pepper until it tastes good to you.

Dish out the pasta onto warmed plates and garnish with the remaining Parmesan.

# FARFALLE WITH CHORIZO AND FAVAS

MAKES 4 SERVINGS

For the record, the Italian word *farfalle* means "butterflies," not bow ties. And homemade farfalle are softer and more delicate than dried ones, so they need a lighter sauce. This one works great because the favas and bits of chorizo get caught up in the folds of the pasta. In this dish, I prefer the smooth texture of Pantaleo cheese, a hard, aged goat cheese from Sardinia. Look for Pantaleo at cheese shops or well-stocked supermarkets such as Whole Foods. Or substitute *fiore sardo* or another aged, firm goat's or sheep's milk cheese for grating.

PASTA SWAP Even though this sauce has bits of sausage and beans, the overall taste is light and fresh. *Fazzoletti* or fettuccine would work well here.

| | | |
|---|---|---|
| 1½ pounds (680 g) young fava beans in the pod | 12 ounces (340 g) soft Spanish chorizo | 1 cup (113 g) grated Pantaleo cheese |
| 8 ounces (227 g) Egg Yolk Dough (page 26), rolled into sheets about ⅛ inch (3 mm) thick | ¼ cup (60 ml) olive oil | Kosher salt and freshly ground black pepper |
| | ⅓ cup (56 g) finely chopped yellow onion | |

Have ready a large bowl of ice water. Bring a large pot of salted water to a boil. Shell the fava beans, discard the pods, and blanch the beans in the boiling water for 1 minute. Using a spider strainer or slotted spoon, transfer the beans to the ice water to stop the cooking. Pinch open the pale green skin on each bean and pop out the bright green fava. You should have about 1½ cups (170 g) peeled favas. Use them within 1 hour or cover and refrigerate for up to 8 hours.

Lay a pasta sheet on a lightly floured work surface and trim the edges square. Cut the sheet into 2 by 1-inch (5 by 2.5 cm) rectangles, preferably with a fluted cutter to create a ruffled edge on the two short sides of each rectangle (these will be the opposite ends of each "butterfly"). To form each *farfalla* (see photos, page 44), place your index finger in the center of a rectangle and place your thumb and middle finger on the straight edges of the rectangle on opposite sides of your index finger. Your fingers and thumb should be lined up in a row parallel with the ruffled edges of the rectangle. Pinch your thumb and middle finger toward your index finger in the center, keeping your index finger in place to help create the folds. As the pasta folds up, remove your index finger

and firmly pinch the folds of pasta together in the center to hold the shape. The ruffled edges should remain unpinched. Place the farfalla on a floured rimmed baking sheet and dust with a little flour. Repeat with the remaining pasta rectangles and then the remaining sheet. You should have 60 to 70 *farfalle*. Cover the pasta and use it within 1 hour or refrigerate it for up to 4 hours. You can also freeze them in a single layer, transfer them to a zipper-lock bag, and freeze them for up to 1 month. Take the pasta straight from the freezer to the boiling pasta water.

Cut each chorizo in half lengthwise, then cut crosswise into half-moons about ⅛ inch (3 mm) thick. Heat the oil in a large, deep sauté pan over medium heat. Add the onion and sweat until soft but not browned, 2 to 3 minutes. Add the chorizo and favas and cook, stirring occasionally, until heated through, 2 to 3 minutes.

Meanwhile, bring a large pot of salted water to a bowl. Drop in the *farfalle*, in batches if necessary to prevent crowding, and cover the pot to quickly return the water to a boil. Cook

CONTINUED

the pasta until it is tender but still a little chewy when bitten, about 2 minutes. Using a spider strainer or slotted spoon, drain the pasta by transferring it to the pan of sauce. Reserve the pasta water.

Add about 1 cup (240 ml) of the pasta water to the pan and cook the mixture over medium-high heat, tossing and stirring vigorously, until the sauce reduces slightly, becomes creamy, and coats the pasta, about 1 minute. Add a little more pasta water if necessary to create a creamy sauce. Remove the pan from the heat and stir in ¾ cup (85 g) of the cheese. Keep the pasta moving until pasta and sauce become one thing in the pan. Taste it, adding salt and pepper until it tastes good to you.

Dish out the pasta onto warmed plates and garnish with the remaining Pantaleo cheese and a grind of pepper.

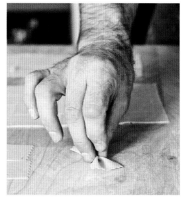

# FAZZOLETTI WITH CRAB AND BURRATA

**MAKES 4 SERVINGS**

While writing this book, I asked my chef de cuisine, Adam Leonti, how he came up with this dish. He told me, "It's your dish. Remember that pescatarian who came in one night?" Then it all came back to me. The guest didn't eat meat—only fish—but she wasn't impressed by the variety of fish on our menu at the time. I opened up the fridge and saw a Dungeness crab. I knew that we had just bought some fantastic *burrata*, so I made a pasta dish with the crab and the cheese. *Fazzoletti* means "handkerchiefs," and these little squares of pasta fold over themselves, the crab, and the *burrata* in a beautiful way. The old rule that says "no cheese with seafood" has always been a mystery to me. You can have cheese with seafood. A gentle *burrata* adds tremendous texture and flavor to the crab here. For a sharper punch of flavor, substitute sorrel for the parsley. By the way, the pescatarian left very happy!

PASTA SWAP This combination also works great in lasagna. Use the Heirloom Tomato and Burrata Lasagna (page 68) as a starting point, and then make layers with the crab, *burrata*, and pasta.

12 ounces (340 g) Egg Yolk Dough (page 26), rolled into sheets about 1⁄16 inch (1.5 mm) thick

¾ cup (180 ml) olive oil

⅓ cup (56 g) finely chopped yellow onion

12 ounces (340 g) jumbo lump crabmeat, picked over to remove any shells and cartilage

2 tablespoons (8 g) chopped fresh flat-leaf parsley, plus some for garnish

2 tablespoons (6 g) chopped fresh chives, plus some for garnish

1 tablespoon (15 ml) fresh lemon juice

6 ounces (170 g) burrata cheese

Kosher salt and freshly ground black pepper

Lay a pasta sheet on a lightly floured work surface and trim the ends square. Cut the sheet into 2½- to 3-inch (6 to 7.5 cm) squares and dust them lightly with flour. Repeat with the remaining sheets. You should have 60 to 70 *fazzoletti*. You can use the *fazzoletti* immediately, or you can freeze them in a single layer on a floured rimmed baking sheet, transfer them to a zipper-lock bag, and freeze them for up to 1 month. Take the pasta right from the freezer to the boiling pasta water.

Bring a large pot of salted water to a bowl. Drop in the *fazzoletti*, in batches if necessary to prevent crowding, and cover the pot to quickly return the water to a boil. Cook the pasta until it is tender but still a little chewy when bitten, about 2 minutes.

Meanwhile, heat the oil in a large, deep sauté pan over medium heat. Add the onion and sweat it until it is soft but not browned, 2 to 3 minutes. When the pasta is ready, using

a spider strainer or slotted spoon, drain the pasta by transferring it to the pan of onions. Reserve the pasta water. Add about 1 cup (240 ml) of the pasta water to the pan and stir vigorously over medium-high heat until the liquid reduces and thickens slightly, 1 to 2 minutes.

Add the crabmeat, parsley, chives, and lemon juice and cook over medium-low heat, tossing and stirring vigorously, until the sauce becomes creamy and coats the pasta, about 1 minute. Add a little more pasta water if necessary to create a creamy sauce. Remove the pan from the heat and stir in the *burrata*. Keep the pasta moving until pasta and sauce become one thing in the pan. The cheese should just start to get warm and melty. Taste the pasta, adding salt and pepper until it tastes good to you.

Dish out the pasta onto warmed plates and garnish with a grind of pepper and some parsley and chives.

# 4

—

# BAKED SHEET PASTA

**GIULIANO BUGIALLI HAS WRITTEN SOME OF THE GREATEST COOKBOOKS ON ITALIAN FOOD.** *Bugialli on Pasta* is a classic. When I heard that he lived in Philadelphia—just three blocks from Vetri—I was floored. I had to meet him. Cook for him. Show him the restaurant. Pick his brain. Anything!

In the spring of 2011, my chef de cuisine at Vetri, Adam Leonti, went to Bugialli's website to find his number. When we called, we figured we'd get an assistant or something. Nope. Giuliano Bugialli answered the phone. We talked with him for a while and asked him to come by the restaurant one morning just to hang out and chat. He reluctantly agreed. Bugialli is very soft spoken and doesn't like to be fussed over.

We were all very excited that morning. The entire kitchen crew arrived early, and we had a bunch of questions. A true legend was coming to talk with us. We waited and waited. The hours passed, and we started to think that maybe he had the wrong date, that he wasn't going to show up.

That afternoon, utterly disappointed, we accepted that it wasn't going to happen. So we started prepping for the day.

About a half hour later, I was looking at the reservations for the night. The receptionist working the phones had been with us for about four months at that point. He overheard us talking about Bugialli and how disappointed we were. Then, with a strange look on his face, he mentioned that an older gentleman had stopped by earlier that morning. But he told the gentleman to leave.

"Leave?!" I screamed. "Why would you do that?!" He said, "Well, I had never seen all of you here so early in the morning. I assumed you were in a meeting, and I told him to come back later." I looked at Adam, and Adam looked at me. We were dumbfounded. You *never* tell someone to leave. You ask. You come to the kitchen and ask.

So we called him back. We called and called. No response. Finally, Bugialli answered the phone. He said he wasn't mad. But we could tell that he was. We asked him very nicely to come back. Adam even baked some biscotti, but Bugialli didn't want them. We dropped off the biscotti with his doorman anyway. We asked Bugialli to reschedule. He said he would think about it.

About six months later, on a Saturday, I saw him at a farmers' market in Rittenhouse Square. I introduced myself, as we had never officially met, and I told him that we would love the opportunity to correct the mistake that had been made. A couple of weeks later, Adam called him again and he agreed to come in.

We decided to make something new to surprise him. We knew that he loved artichokes and mint. He mentioned them all the time in his books. How about a new pasta dish? At the time, we were completely obsessed with cannelloni. So we braised some artichokes with onion, chopped them fine, and mixed in a little ricotta to make a filling. The mint we julienned into a fresh salad dressed with olive oil and lemon juice. We piped some béchamel onto the cannelloni, blasted them in the oven to crisp up the pasta, and spooned the mint salad over each one.

The Artichoke Cannelloni with Mint Salad (page 61) was one of Bugialli's favorite dishes that evening. After dinner, he came back to the kitchen and told us stories about his father's wine collection, his love of well-farmed vegetables, and his

cooking school in Florence. It was the night we'd all been waiting for. After attempting to cook for Giuliano Bugialli for well over a year, it was well worth the wait.

Our persistence paid off, but the cannelloni were the key to that evening. And they started with a simple sheet of pasta. Fettuccine, *pappardelle*, tagliatelle, *tagliolini*, lasagna, ravioli—almost all fresh pasta starts with a simple sheet. Sure, we'll get to all the different shapes and crazy interesting things you can make, but one of the simplest and most underrated forms of pasta is sheet pasta.

Sheets can be layered into lasagna, rolled up like pinwheels, or stuffed and folded like crepes. It's a great foundation to build on. When I teach pasta classes, I always start with rolling out the pasta and talking about dishes you can make with a sheet.

The sheet pastas in this chapter—cannelloni, lasagna, *rotolo*, and *fazzoletti*—are all baked in a hot oven. Baking is part of their DNA. For most other pastas, you toss the pasta with sauce until you develop a *crema* in the pan, that is, until the pasta and sauce stick together. It's different with baked pasta. You just create layers of flavor and pop the dish in the oven. For beginners, it's a great place to start, and for the advanced, it's ideal for experimenting.

Lasagna is the simplest because you literally build layers of pasta and filling. For cannelloni, you cut squares, then wrap the pasta around the filling. For *fazzoletti*, you also cut squares, but you spread the filling on the pasta, then fold it into triangles like you would a crepe. To make *rotolo*, you lay out a whole sheet of cooked pasta, roll up the filling inside like a pinwheel, and then slice and bake each pinwheel. When you make these sheet pastas, give yourself plenty of room to work. You'll be blanching the sheets in boiling water—sometimes whole sheets—so it helps to have a long countertop, a large wooden board, or a kitchen table roomy enough to lay out the cooked noodles.

Whenever you're filling pasta, whether lasagna or ravioli, it's important to match the stuffing to the pasta. Let's say you like the filling from Asparagus and Egg Yolk Rotolo (page 53) and want to use it in a different baked pasta dish. That smooth, creamy filling works best with several thin sheets of lasagna rather than a couple of thick sheets. Think about how the stuffing and the pasta will feel in the

mouth when the whole dish is done. Pioppini Cannelloni with Romanesco Salad (page 66) is another good example. We wrap up whole mushrooms and béchamel in cannelloni. We leave the mushrooms whole to show off their beautiful texture. The little brown caps poke out the ends of the pasta tubes. Think about the visual and textural appeal of the dish as you're building it.

But these are the nitty-gritty details. Sheet pasta is not hard to make. Try this: Cut a sheet of pasta into squares, blanch the squares, pat them dry, and put them on a greased rimmed baking sheet. Put some butter and cheese on the squares and put the baking sheet in a 400°F (200°C) oven. I just want you to see what you're capable of making with little or no effort. Leave the oven light on so you can watch what happens. The pasta will start to shrivel. Slowly it will brown. Butter melts all around and into the pasta, and the cheese bubbles up. Just before it gets too brown, take it out. It will be the greatest pasta cracker you've ever eaten. Now, do the same procedure again, but sprinkle some fresh herbs on it. So simple. Start there and you'll understand how easy it is to make something delicious with little more than a sheet of pasta. Of course, you can always make it more complex if you want. But the trick is to keep it simple and delicious! That cannelloni we made for Giuliano Bugialli was a classic Roman artichoke preparation stuffed into cannelloni. Presenting it with a creamy filling and crunchy-edged pasta is what made it special.

And I have to say, that's actually my favorite part of all the baked pastas in this chapter—that contrast of creamy and crunchy. No matter which baked pasta you make, it's important to leave some of the pasta exposed or hanging over the edges of the pan. In Italy, we used to fight over those crispy edges!

# ASPARAGUS AND EGG YOLK ROTOLO

MAKES 4 SERVINGS

"Everything tastes good fried," is the old saying in the kitchen. Bread it and fry it and it will taste good. Well, I'm going to take us down another road. Everything tastes good with an egg on it. Especially asparagus and pasta. Taste it for yourself!

3 tablespoons (45 ml) olive oil, plus some for drizzling

2 pounds (907 g) asparagus, trimmed of woody ends, then cut crosswise into 1-inch (2.5 cm) pieces, tips reserved

1 small clove garlic, smashed

Kosher salt and freshly ground black pepper

4 ounces (114 g) Egg Yolk Dough (page 26), rolled into a sheet about ⅟₁₆ inch (1.5 mm) thick

2 cups (473 ml) taleggio béchamel (page 245), refrigerated until firm

4 tablespoons (57 g) unsalted butter

¼ cup (25 g) grated Parmesan cheese, plus some for garnish

4 egg yolks

Heat 2 tablespoons (30 ml) of the oil in a large sauté pan over medium heat. Set the asparagus tips aside. Add the remaining asparagus and the garlic to the pan and cook, tossing now and then, until the asparagus is tender but not browned, 4 to 5 minutes. Remove and discard the garlic.

Transfer the asparagus to a food processor and puree until smooth. If the asparagus is watery, drain the mixture in a fine-mesh sieve for 20 to 30 minutes. The consistency should be somewhat like pancake batter. Taste the puree, adding salt and pepper until it tastes good to you.

Bring a large pot of salted water to a boil. Drop in the entire pasta sheet and blanch it for 30 seconds, stirring and separating it with tongs to keep the sheet from sticking to itself. Carefully remove the pasta sheet and lay it out on kitchen towels or paper towels. Trim the edges square.

Spread the béchamel evenly over the entire sheet of pasta, all the way to the edges. Then spread the asparagus mixture evenly over the béchamel. Starting from a short side, tightly roll up the sheet. The *rotolo* should look like a jelly roll. Wrap the roll tightly in plastic wrap and refrigerate until firm, at least 1 hour or up to 4 hours.

CONTINUED

Heat the oven to 500°F (260°C). Generously butter a shallow 2-quart (2 L) baking dish, or, for individual servings, butter four 2-cup (473 ml) baking dishes. Using a sharp plain-edged or serrated knife, trim the ends of the *rotolo*, then cut it crosswise into four slices, each about 1 inch (2.5 cm) thick. Lay the slices flat in the baking dish(es) and top each slice with 1 tablespoon butter and 1 tablespoon Parmesan.

Bake the *rotolo* until heated through and lightly browned on top, 10 to 15 minutes. Remove from the oven and top each slice with 1 egg yolk. Return the slices to the oven and bake until the yolks begin to set but are still runny in the middle, 1 to 2 minutes.

Meanwhile, heat the remaining 1 tablespoon (15 ml) oil in a sauté pan over medium heat. Add the asparagus tips and cook, tossing occasionally, until tender, 1 to 2 minutes. Taste the asparagus, adding salt and pepper until it tastes good to you.

Transfer the *rotolo* slices to warmed plates if baked in a single dish, or leave in the individual baking dishes. Top each slice with some Parmesan, a drizzle of oil, and a grind of pepper. Serve the asparagus tips alongside.

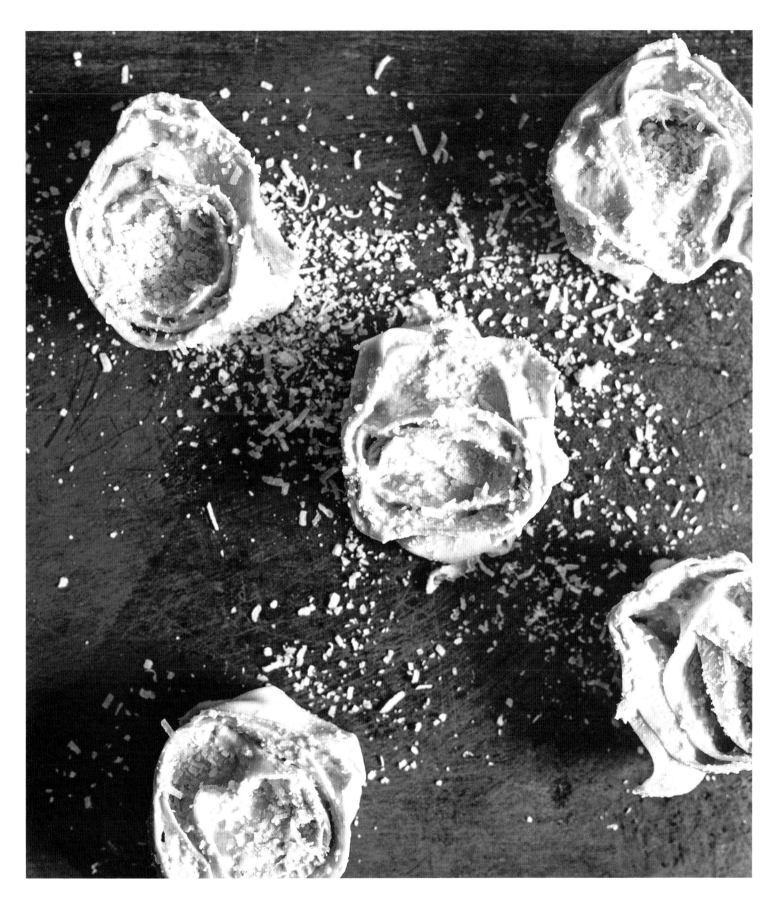

# SUMMER SQUASH FAZZOLETTI
# WITH GARLIC CHIVE OIL

MAKES 6 SERVINGS

Baked *fazzoletti* are almost like ravioli. You cut big squares of fresh pasta—about 5 inches (12 cm) square—spread some filling on each square, fold it over into a triangle, fill it again, and fold it one more time into a smaller triangle. Then you brown the triangles in the oven and end up with crispy pasta edges with a creamy center. I just love that contrast. If you can't find *stracciatella* cheese for this dish, puree 12 ounces (340 g) *burrata* in a blender or food processor. Or just use the center cream in *burrata*; it's basically the same thing as *stracciatella*. In some ways, the garlic chive oil is the star here. The dish is okay without it, but that final touch makes a huge difference. You will not need all of the oil for this dish. Use the remainder as a dip for bread or drizzle it on eggs, fish, or vegetables.

### GARLIC CHIVE OIL

½ bunch garlic chives, about ½ cup packed (24 g)

½ bunch chives, about ½ cup packed (24 g)

1 cup (237 ml) extra-virgin olive oil

### SQUASH FAZZOLETTI

1½ cups (12 oz/340 g) ricotta impastata cheese (see page 241)

12 ounces (340 g) stracciatella cheese

Kosher salt and freshly ground black pepper

2 tablespoons (30 ml) extra-virgin olive oil

2 yellow summer squashes (about 6 oz/170 g each), trimmed and julienned

2 zucchini (about 6 oz /170 g each), trimmed and julienned

2 cloves garlic, smashed

3 sprigs thyme

12 ounces (340 g) Egg Yolk Dough (page 26), rolled into sheets about 1⁄16 inch (1.5 mm) thick

1½ cups (150 g) grated Parmesan cheese, plus some for garnish

1½ cups (355 ml) béchamel (page 245), warmed

To make the garlic chive oil, combine all of the ingredients in a blender and blend until the mixture is as smooth as possible, 2 to 3 minutes (there will still be flecks of chives). Use it immediately or refrigerate in an airtight container for up to 3 days.

To make the *fazzoletti*, stir together the ricotta and *stracciatella* in a bowl. Taste the mixture, adding salt and pepper until it tastes good to you.

Heat the oil in a sauté pan over medium heat. Add the squashes, zucchini, garlic, and thyme and sweat the squashes until they are soft and pliable but not browned, 5 to 7 minutes. Remove the pan from the heat and taste the mixture, adding salt and pepper until it tastes good to you. Let the mixture cool in the pan.

Lay a pasta sheet on a lightly floured work surface and trim the edges square. Cut the pasta into 5-inch (12 cm) squares. Repeat with the remaining sheets. You should get 6 squares from each sheet or 18 total. Use them immediately, or freeze them in a single layer, transfer them to a zipper-lock bag, and freeze them for up to 1 month. Take the pasta straight from the freezer to the boiling pasta water.

Heat the oven to 475°F (245°C). Turn on the convection, if possible. Generously butter 2 rimmed baking sheets or six 2-cup (473 ml) individual baking dishes.

Have ready a large bowl of ice water. Bring a large pot of salted water to a boil. Working in batches to prevent crowding, drop in the pasta squares and cover the pot to quickly return the water to a boil. Blanch the pasta for

15 to 20 seconds, stirring gently to prevent sticking. Using a spider strainer or tongs, immediately transfer the pasta squares to the ice water to stop the cooking. Lay the squares flat on clean kitchen towels or paper towels and pat them dry.

Place equal amounts of the squash and ricotta mixtures in the middle of a square (about 3 tablespoons/43 g total), leaving the garlic and thyme in the pan. Top with 1 teaspoon (2 g) Parmesan. Fold the square in half over the filling to form a triangle, gently spreading out the filling to make the pasta as flat as possible. Repeat the step with more squash and cheeses, placing them in the center of the triangle, and fold the triangle in half again to form a smaller triangle; leave the pasta a little lumpier in the center like ravioli. Repeat with the remaining pasta squares and filling. Place the *fazzoletti* on the prepared baking sheets or in the prepared baking dishes, allowing 3 *fazzoletti* per serving and leaving a little room between them. Spread a scant tablespoon (15 ml) of béchamel over the entire surface of each *fazzoletto*, and then sprinkle with the remaining Parmesan.

Bake the *fazzoletti* until bubbly and lightly browned on top, 6 to 8 minutes.

Divide the *fazzoletti* among warmed plates if baked on baking sheets, allowing 3 *fazzoletti* per serving, or leave in the individual baking dishes. Top each serving with a drizzle of the garlic chive oil and garnish with Parmesan.

# ARTICHOKE CANNELLONI WITH MINT SALAD

MAKES 6 SERVINGS

Giuliano Bugialli used to live just around the corner from Vetri in Philadelphia. If you don't know who Bugialli is, he ranks up there with Marcella Hazan as one of the all-time great champions of classic Italian cooking. When he finally came in for a meal at the restaurant, a story that I recount on page 49, this was his favorite dish. In Rome, the traditional way to serve artichokes is braised with mint (the dish is called *carciofi alla romana*). It's the same combination here, but we stuff the artichokes into cannelloni and serve them with a fresh mint salad. The recipe makes modest portions, so it's perfect as a first course.

3 quarts (3 L) water

2 tablespoons (30 ml) fresh lemon juice

14 baby artichokes

6 tablespoons (90 ml) olive oil

¼ cup (42 g) finely chopped red onion

2 tablespoons (28 g) ricotta impastata cheese (see page 241)

Kosher salt and freshly ground black pepper

8 ounces (227 g) Egg Yolk Dough (page 26), rolled into sheets a little less than ⅛ inch (3 mm) thick

2 cups (473 ml) béchamel (page 245), refrigerated

12 fresh mint leaves

Combine the water and 1 tablespoon (15 ml) of the lemon juice in a bowl. Working with 1 artichoke at a time, snap off and discard the tough, dark green leaves until you are left with only yellow and light green leaves. Cut off the tough top of the artichoke (about ½ inch/12 mm). Trim the dark green parts from the bottom of the artichoke until only white and light green are visible. It will seem like barely any artichoke is left, but you will have reduced it down to the best part for eating. Cut the artichoke in half lengthwise. As each artichoke is trimmed and halved, drop it into the lemon water to keep it from browning.

Heat 4 tablespoons (60 ml) of the oil in a large, deep sauté pan or Dutch oven over medium-high heat. Remove the artichokes from the water. When the oil is hot, add the artichokes, cut side down, and cook until they are golden brown, 4 to 5 minutes. Add the onion and cook, shaking the pan now and then, until the onion is lightly browned, 4 to 5 minutes. Add enough water to cover the pan bottom (about ¼ cup/60 ml) and bring the liquid to a simmer. Turn down the heat to low, cover the pan, and braise the artichokes until they are tender and the pan bottom is nearly dry, about 20 minutes, adding as little water as necessary to keep the artichokes from scorching.

Transfer the artichokes and onion to a cutting board, let them cool until they can be handled, and then finely chop them. Save a few small spoonfuls of artichokes for garnish, if you like. Transfer the rest of the artichokes and onion to a bowl and stir in the ricotta. Taste the filling, adding salt and pepper until it tastes good to you. Spoon the filling into a zipper-lock bag, seal closed, and refrigerate for at least 1 hour or up to 1 day.

Lay a pasta sheet on a lightly floured work surface and cut it into 4-inch (10 cm) squares. Repeat with the remaining sheets. You should get 8 to 10 squares from each sheet, or 16 to 20 total. As you work, lightly mist the pasta with water to keep it from drying out.

Bring a large pot of salted water to a boil. Working in batches to prevent crowding, drop in the pasta and cover the pot to quickly return the water to a boil. Blanch the pasta for 15 to 20 seconds, stirring gently to prevent sticking. Using a spider strainer or slotted spoon, transfer the pasta squares to kitchen towels or paper towels, laying them flat and patting them dry. The pieces will be delicate and some may stick, but you should have plenty.

CONTINUED

# PIOPPINI CANNELLONI WITH ROMANESCO SALAD

MAKES 6 SERVINGS

Pioppini mushrooms have long, cream-colored stems and caps that range from light to dark brown. They look similar to mushrooms labeled beech, *nameko*, and *shimeji* (and you can substitute those), but pioppini have darker caps and a deep forest aroma. Their texture is soft like asparagus, so they don't need much heat. Stuffed inside pasta squares, all the mushrooms need is a little white sauce. The pickled onions and olives in the salad give the whole thing some acidity and spark.

8 ounces (227 g) Egg Yolk Dough (page 26), rolled into sheets a little less than ⅛ inch (3 mm) thick

3 cups (710 ml) béchamel (page 245), refrigerated

8 ounces (227 g) fresh velvet pioppini mushrooms

1 cup (100 g) grated Parmesan cheese

Red pepper flakes, plus some for sprinkling

1 cup (71 g) tiny romanesco or cauliflower florets

¾ cup (120 g) pickled red onions (page 246), julienned

12 Gaeta olives, pitted and halved

¼ cup (20 g) packed small fresh flat-leaf parsley leaves (a little mint is nice in there, too)

2 tablespoons (30 ml) extra-virgin olive oil

1 tablespoon (15 ml) white wine vinegar or champagne vinegar

Kosher salt and freshly ground black pepper

Lay a pasta sheet on a lightly floured work surface and cut it into 4-inch (10 cm) squares. Repeat with the remaining sheets. You should get 8 to 10 squares from each sheet, or 16 to 20 total. As you work, lightly mist the pasta with water to keep it from drying out.

Bring a large pot of salted water to a boil. Working in batches to prevent crowding, drop in the pasta and cover the pot to quickly return the water to a boil. Blanch the pasta for 15 to 20 seconds, stirring gently to prevent sticking. Transfer the pasta squares to kitchen towels or paper towels, laying them flat and patting them dry. They will be delicate and some may stick, but you should have plenty.

Heat the oven to 500°F (260°C). Turn on the convection, if possible. Spoon the refrigerated béchamel into a zipper-lock bag and seal closed, then snip a corner from the bag and pipe some of the béchamel into a 2½- to 3-quart (2.5 to 3 L) baking dish or 6 individual baking dishes, spreading it to create a thin layer.

Pipe a line of the béchamel ¾ inch (2 cm) thick along one edge of each pasta square. Break the mushrooms from the cluster into individual mushrooms and place a line of mushrooms (about 8) over the béchamel on each pasta square. Starting at the filled side, use the edge of the towel to lift and tightly roll the pasta to enclose the filling. Transfer the cannelloni, seam side down, to the baking dish(es). Pipe a line of béchamel 1 inch (2.5 cm) wide onto each cannelloni, then top each one with about 1 tablespoon (6 g) of Parmesan and a pinch of pepper flakes.

Bake the cannelloni until the béchamel begins to melt and lightly brown on top, 10 to 15 minutes.

Meanwhile, mix together the romanesco florets, pickled onions, olives, parsley, oil, and vinegar in a small bowl. Taste the mixture, adding salt and pepper until it tastes good to you.

Transfer 2 or 3 cannelloni to each warmed plate if baked in a single dish, or leave in the individual dishes. Top each serving with some of the romanesco salad. Garnish with some pepper flakes if you want a little more heat.

# TRIPE LASAGNA WITH WHOLE WHEAT PASTA

MAKES 8 TO 10
SERVINGS

I've always been adamant that tripe should taste like tripe and not like water. Everyone boils and boils it, removing all of the flavor. But tripe has great flavor. It just needs to be subtle and balanced. If you've never had tripe, this dish is a great introduction.

1¼ pounds (567 g) honeycomb tripe

¼ cup (60 ml) olive oil

½ cup (84 g) finely chopped yellow onion

½ cup (51 g) finely chopped celery

½ cup (70 g) peeled and finely chopped carrot

3 large whole canned San Marzano tomatoes

4 cups (946 ml) whole milk

1½ cups (150 g) grated Parmesan cheese

Kosher salt and freshly ground black pepper

1¾ pounds (794 g) Whole Egg and Whole Wheat Dough (page 29), rolled into sheets a little less than ⅛ inch (3 mm) thick

4 cups (946 ml) béchamel (page 245), warmed

To cook the tripe, bring a large pot of salted water to a boil. Add the tripe and boil, uncovered, at a steady boil for 1½ hours. Remove the pot from the heat and let the tripe cool in the liquid. When the tripe is cool enough to handle, remove it from the liquid and slice it into pieces ½ inch (12 mm) wide. Discard the liquid and set the tripe aside.

Heat the oil in a large saucepan over medium heat. Add the onion, celery, and carrot and sweat the vegetables until they are tender but not browned, 4 to 6 minutes. Add the tomatoes, crushing them with your hand as you add them to the pan. Cook the mixture until the tomatoes begin to break down, 6 to 8 minutes. Pour in the milk, raise the heat to high, and bring the mixture to a boil. Add the tripe, turn down the heat to low, cover, and braise the tripe, stirring now and then, until it is tender and the liquid reduces in volume slightly, about 2 hours. When the mixture is done, it should have the consistency of a *ragù*. At that point, remove the pan from the heat and stir in ½ cup (50 g) of the Parmesan. Taste the *ragù*, adding salt and pepper until it tastes good to you. Let cool until warm and slightly thickened.

Meanwhile, lay a pasta sheet on a lightly floured work surface and trim the edges square. You will be cutting them for a 13 by 9-inch (33 by 23 cm) pan. If you have a different-size pan, cut the pasta to fit the pan. Cut the first pasta sheet into a piece about 30 inches (76 cm) long and 3½ to 4 inches (7.5 to 10 cm) inches wide. Cut a second pasta sheet to the same dimensions, 30 inches (76 cm) long and 3½ to 4 inches (7.5 to 10 cm) wide. Cut the remaining sheets into pieces about 14 inches (35.5 cm) long and 4 inches (10 cm) wide. You should have 6 pieces total. As you work, lightly mist the pasta with water and cover with clean kitchen towels to keep it from drying out.

Have ready a large bowl of ice water. Bring a large pot of salted water to a boil. Working in batches to prevent crowding, drop in the pasta and cover the pot to quickly return the water to a boil. Blanch the pasta for 30 seconds. Using tongs or a spider strainer, transfer each piece to the ice water for about 30 seconds to stop the cooking, then lay the pieces flat on kitchen towels and pat them dry.

Heat the oven to 375°F (190°C). Generously butter a 13 by 9-inch (33 by 23 cm) baking dish. Arrange the two 30-inch (76 cm) lengths of pasta lengthwise and side by side in the prepared baking dish, letting the extra length hang over one edge of the dish. Spoon about one-fourth (about 1 cup/237 ml) of the *ragù* over the pasta, and then spoon about the same amount of béchamel over the *ragù*. Sprinkle with ¼ cup (25 g) of the Parmesan. Top with a layer of two 14-inch (35.5 cm) lengths of pasta, followed by a layer of

*ragù*, a layer of béchamel, and a layer of Parmesan in the same amounts as the first layers. Repeat with another layer of 14-inch (35.5 cm) lengths of pasta, *ragù*, béchamel, and Parmesan. Fold the overhanging pasta over the top and tuck the ends of those lengths over the other ends in the dish to seal the lasagna like a package. Top with a final layer of *ragù*, béchamel, and Parmesan, again in the same amounts as the first layers.

Bake the lasagna until it is golden brown on top, 45 minutes to 1 hour. Remove it from the oven and let it stand for 15 to 20 minutes, then cut it into squares or rectangles. You can also let the whole pan of lasagna cool down, cover it, and refrigerate it for up to 2 days, and then blast each serving of lasagna in a hot oven (500°F/260°C) until warmed through.

# OPEN LASAGNA WITH
# SCAMORZA AND ASPARAGUS

MAKES 6 SERVINGS

The great thing about pasta is that you can play around with it. Make up stuff. Why not use pasta sheets like a pizza crust, layer things on it and bake it? Boom—open lasagna is born. If you can't find smoked *scamorza*, use any good melty cheese with a smoky flavor, like smoked *caciocavallo* or smoked mozzarella.

4 ounces (114 g) Egg Yolk Dough (page 26), rolled into a sheet a little less than ⅛ inch (3 mm) thick

8 ounces (227 g) thick asparagus, trimmed of woody ends

Unsalted butter, for searing cheese

3 ounces (85 g) smoked scamorza cheese, cut into 6 large slices, each about 4 inches (10 cm) square

1 large chunk Parmesan cheese, for shaving

3 fresh mint leaves

2 teaspoons (10 ml) olive oil

1 teaspoon (5 ml) fresh lemon juice

Kosher salt and freshly ground black pepper

Fresh flat-leaf parsley leaves for garnish (optional)

Lay the pasta sheet on a lightly floured work surface and trim the edges square. Cut the pasta into 4-inch (10 cm) squares. You should have 6 usable squares. Use them immediately, or freeze them in a single layer, transfer them to a zipper-lock bag, and freeze them for up to 1 month. Take the pasta straight from the freezer to the boiling pasta water.

Have ready a large bowl of ice water. Bring a large pot of salted water to a boil. Drop in the pasta squares and cover the pot to quickly return the water to a boil. Blanch the pasta for 10 to 20 seconds. Using a spider strainer or tongs, immediately transfer the pasta squares to the ice water to stop the cooking. Lay the squares flat on clean kitchen towels or paper towels and pat them dry.

Heat the oven to 500°F (260°C). Turn on the convection, if possible. Butter 6 individual baking dishes or a small rimmed baking sheet.

Using a mandoline or vegetable peeler, shave the top half of each asparagus spear lengthwise into very thin slices. Reserve the bottom halves of the spears.

Heat a cast-iron skillet over medium-high heat. When it is very hot, grease the pan with a little butter, then, working in

batches if necessary to prevent crowding, add the *scamorza* slices and sear, turning once, until golden brown, 1 to 2 minutes per side. Transfer to a large plate.

Lay a pasta square in each prepared baking dish, or lay all 6 squares in a single layer on the prepared baking sheet, leaving 1 to 2 inches (2.5 to 5 cm) between the squares. Place 1 slice seared cheese on each square. Lay the asparagus slices over the cheese, placing them side by side.

Bake the lasagna until lightly browned, 5 to 6 minutes.

Meanwhile, cut the bottom halves of the asparagus spears on the diagonal into ½-inch (12 mm) pieces. Place the pieces in a bowl. Shave 6 large slices of Parmesan into the bowl. Stack the mint leaves, roll them up lengthwise, and cut crosswise into very thin slices (chiffonade). Add the mint to the bowl along with the oil and lemon juice. Toss the salad gently and then taste it, adding salt and pepper until it tastes good to you.

Transfer each open lasagna to a warmed plate if baked on a baking sheet, or leave in the individual baking dishes. Top each serving with some of the asparagus salad.

# 5

—

# RAVIOLI AND STUFFED PASTA

**WHEN I LIVED IN ITALY, I ALWAYS HEARD STORIES ABOUT THE ORIGIN OF RAVIOLI, AND THE TALES ALWAYS MENTIONED *AVANZA*, OR "LEFTOVERS."** Even now when I visit friends there and they make filled pasta, they talk about how things were years ago in that same town when the peasants waited for scraps from the butcher shop, then boiled all the different meats together, chopped them up, and made ravioli.

I love hearing these stories. And I'm sure many of them are true. But if you read the history books, ravioli are usually linked to festivals, religious ceremonies, and the nobility of the land. Look at Sardinia's *culurgiones* (see page 107). These elaborately hand-formed filled pastas are not something you would make every day. Don't get me wrong, ravioli take to all kinds of leftovers, and they're a great place to experiment. Fish, meat, vegetables, and cheese all have their place. Pasta really lets you spread your wings as a chef. A delicious filling wrapped up in the perfect amount of pasta with just the right condiment can be a religious experience. And yet, in all of my years of making pasta, ravioli are the hardest preparations to communicate to my cooks. For some reason, the formula for perfect ravioli is elusive.

But it shouldn't be. The word that best describes ravioli is *balance*. Whether it's the thickness of the pasta dough, the ratio of filling to pasta, the condiment, or the play of savory, sweet, salty, and rich on the whole plate, it's all about balance. Yes, all pasta dishes need to be balanced, but it's more complex with ravioli because there are more variables. Not only do you have pasta and sauce but also the stuffing.

## RAVIOLI DOUGH

Let's start with the pasta. I will tell you right out of the gate that there's no right or wrong ravioli dough. It's entirely up to you. I use a few different doughs, depending on the filling, the shape, and the traditions of that pasta. However, ravioli are more involved than other pastas, so you might want to get comfortable making a single dough and then experiment with different fillings and sauces for it. Most of the recipes in this chapter call for the basic Egg Yolk Dough (page 26). It works great with a range of fillings, so start there. Once you get confident with the general procedures of filling, cutting, and cooking ravioli, you can start to mix and match fillings and doughs. I say this because each filling and each dough has its own character. When you start playing around, you may need a few extra twists and turns for things to come out right. Let's say you like whole wheat doughs. That's fine, but a whole wheat dough may not fold and hold the same way a white flour dough will because it has less gluten and elasticity.

I roll the dough for stuffed pasta a little thinner than for unstuffed pasta. You are sandwiching a filling between two sheets of dough, and if you look all around that filling, what do you see? Two layers of pasta. The fact is, it takes longer for those doubled-up borders to cook, and that extra time in the boiling water can overcook the filling. In general, thinner is better—especially when you're using a protein-rich egg dough. With a flour-and-water dough, you can go a little thicker because the dough will get tender a little faster.

Thickness is partly determined by your filling. Look at the Ricotta Ravioli (page 81), for example. Ricotta cheese is an amazing filling for stuffed pasta. A little ricotta, some grated nutmeg, and an egg and you're on your way to a delicious stuffing. But cook that ricotta ravioli just 30 seconds too long and the cheese curdles and becomes grainy. Cook it too little and the cheese stays creamy but the pasta is still hard. Have you ever had store-bought cheese ravioli in which the pasta is so thick that you have to cook it for 5 to 7 minutes before it becomes tender? By that time, the cheese is completely curdled and the whole beauty of the pasta is lost. The trick is to make the pasta thin enough so that the dough is perfectly cooked exactly when the cheese inside begins to melt (see photo, opposite).

Different fillings require different dough thicknesses. For a braised meat filling, you can roll the dough a little thicker because the meat won't change texture much with a few more minutes in the pasta water. You might actually want thicker dough for meat fillings, as they tend to weigh more and might rip through thinner dough. That's one reason why I roll the pasta slightly thicker for Doppio Ravioli with Lamb Ragù and Polenta (page 99). But for delicate fillings like raw fish, I go a little thinner. The pasta for Branzino Ravioli with Tomato Butter Sauce (page 87) is just right at about 1⁄32 inch (0.8 mm) thick. Much thicker than that and the doubled-up areas will take so long to cook that the fish inside will be overcooked. Plus, the ravioli won't taste as good. Thick, chewy pasta doesn't go so well with a delicate filling.

## THE PASTA-TO-FILLING RATIO

I'm a big fan of sushi. It's one of those simple preparations where, when done right, everything is in beautiful balance and it moves you. The right amount of rice, the right amount of fish, the perfect bite. It's the same with ravioli. The right amount of pasta, the right amount of filling. Those two elements need to be in balance.

For a lot of chefs, it's the filling that throws a wrench in their game. How much filling should I use? How long do I cook the ravioli? It all depends on the relationship between pasta and filling. Some fillings are rich and flavorful, so a little bit goes a long way. Others are light, so you have to stuff the pasta a little more to keep the dough from overwhelming the filling. For example, on average I use only about 1⁄2 teaspoon

*Left: Perfectly cooked, creamy ricotta filling.*

*Right: Overcooked, grainy ricotta filling.*

(2.5 ml) for chopped raw-fish stuffings. That small amount of fish will cook evenly and quickly. But a big tablespoon (15 ml) in there? The center would stay raw and you'd get a glob of undercooked and overcooked fish in your mouth. On the other hand, if it's a pureed fish stuffing such as *baccalà* (salt cod) with potato and egg, you can spoon in a little more because the filling will be creamy and melt in your mouth. It's very difficult to make general statements like "meat ravioli should be filled more than fish ravioli" or "all cheese ravioli should be large." It depends. Sometimes I like to make small cheese ravioli such as *francobolli* (postage stamps) because that shape works better with a few more ravioli on the plate.

Then again, a half dozen big, round ravioli stuffed with a tablespoon or two (15 or 30 ml) of seasoned ricotta has a different and equally awesome appeal.

The texture of the filling is important, too. If you've got a loose, creamy filling like the pureed peas and *robiola* cheese in Pea Agnolotti with Lardo (page 85), it's good to use a smaller amount with more pasta around it to balance out the overall texture—and so you can put the whole thing in your mouth at once. If you put in too much of a creamy filling and the ravioli is so large you have to cut it to eat it, the filling squirts out before it ever gets to your mouth. With a thicker, denser filling, you can make the ravioli a little larger. Just make sure the filling doesn't eclipse the pasta—or vice versa. All the elements—pasta, filling, and sauce—need to be balanced. Remember, the ravioli as a whole is going into someone's mouth. You are going for the perfect single bite.

## Cheese

Let's go a little deeper into some typical ravioli fillings. Ricotta cheese always works, but you could experiment with almost any cheese. There are so many varieties! In Taleggio Ravioli with Radicchio, Honey, and Walnuts (page 88), I like to mix in a little mascarpone to soften the flavor of the Taleggio and create a very creamy texture. If the cheese is firmer, like *caciocavallo*, I usually grate it and bind it with some egg or bread crumbs or white bread soaked in milk. That way, the filling has some form, but the cheese melts smoothly when the ravioli cooks. However, if the cheese is already soft and melty like Fontina, you could just cover pieces of it between two sheets of pasta and call it a day. When the ravioli are gently boiled, the cheese will melt inside and it will be wonderful pasta. But there's so much more you can do! Keep pungency in mind, too. I love Gorgonzola, but on its own, it would be too strong in ravioli. I prefer to cut Gorgonzola with some ricotta. Play around with mixing together different cheeses. Taleggio and mascarpone, Gruyère and ricotta—choose your favorites. Cheese ravioli are like a four-cheese pizza. Does it really matter what kind is in them? You just know they are going to taste good!

## Meat

Most regions of Italy have some kind of meat-filled pasta. The meat is usually braised, ground, or finely chopped and held together with some egg, Parmesan, and maybe bread crumbs. It's okay to use raw meat, but the ravioli must be cooked much more gently. Overcooking raw meat ravioli can lead to a horrible experience: the meat can dry out and the juices can leak into the pasta and make it soggy. Most of the time, I braise meat for stuffing pasta. I use the vegetables that braise with the meat, too. Just mash them and mix them into the meat as you would for *ragù*. Make the flavors of meat ravioli as simple or as creative as you want. Lamb, rabbit, pork, duck—the choice is yours. Check out Pig's Foot Ravioli with Fennel Pollen (page 96). It's got amazing flavor and texture from the pig's foot. But you could do something similar with pork shoulder and pancetta instead.

## Vegetables

You don't see too many ravioli with raw vegetables inside. The vegetables would leak too much water. There's the rub with vegetables: they're 70 to 95 percent water. I usually roast, sweat, or somehow cook them first, before mixing them with herbs and seasonings. If you puree the vegetables, keep the filling firm by mixing in some bread crumbs, cheese, or bread soaked in milk. Even so, it's a good idea to freeze vegetable ravioli right after you assemble them. Quick freezing will stop the liquid from seeping into the dough.

## Fish

Shellfish and *baccalà* (salt cod) make great ravioli stuffings. I also use branzino and other white fish. But fish is delicate. Handle it gently. For Branzino Ravioli with Tomato Butter Sauce (page 87), I finely chop the raw fish and marinate it briefly in olive oil and herbs. Then between the sheets it goes. When the pasta cooks, it's almost like gently poaching the fish in olive oil inside the ravioli. Fish has subtle flavors, so less is always more when it comes to add-ins. Skip the egg and cheese and go easy on the seasoning. When I bite into fish ravioli, I want to taste the fish. You can enhance that flavor with a beautiful sauce—just don't cover up the taste of the fish itself.

## PRESSING OUT AIR

No matter what filling you drop onto your dough, leave enough room around it to cut out the shape of the ravioli you are making. This seems elementary, but if you're punching out 2-inch (5 cm) rounds and your filling is in ½-inch (12 mm) mounds, you need to leave at least 1 inch (2.5 cm) of space between the mounds of filling. Even more important is pressing out the air. Any air pockets in the dough will bubble up when a ravioli cooks. That bubble will stretch the dough, which then falls back down over the filling when you drain the pasta. That's how you get wrinkly ravioli. You don't want wrinkly ravioli. Press out all the air with your fingers.

## SHAPES

Stuffed pastas are like ski trails at a ski resort. Some are easy, some more challenging. If you're new to ravioli, start on the bunny slope: the Ricotta Ravioli (page 81). The dough is rolled out by hand, the filling is seasoned ricotta, you fold the dough over the filling, and then you punch out rounds with a pasta cutter or cookie cutter. Boom! Once you get comfortable with that procedure, try the intermediate slopes—say, the Fig and Onion Caramelle with Gorgonzola Dolce Fonduta (page 83). For that one, you roll out sheets, cut them into squares, drop filling onto the center of each square, and then twist the pasta around the filling like a candy wrapper. When you become a ravioli-making machine, move up to the double-diamond slope: the Culurgiones with Sweetbreads and Corn (page 107). These handmade Sardinian ravioli are elaborate edible gifts with a teardrop shape and beautifully braided dough on top. All these stuffed pastas are just a sampling of the possibilities. Once you get a feel for balancing pasta and filling, the variety of shapes you can make is limited only by your imagination.

## STORAGE

I store pasta in lots of places all over my kitchens. You'll see fresh pasta like *garganelli* in the refrigerator and extruded pasta like fusilli on drying racks in the dining room or on rimmed baking sheets in the fridge. But for stuffed pasta, I like freezing best. Even if you are going to use the ravioli right away, it's wise to freeze them. I've tried all kinds of storage methods, and I've seen shops in Italy where stuffed pasta sits in the window for hours on end. Let's think about that for a moment. You are putting two sheets of moist dough around a wet filling. If you let ravioli sit for hours at room temperature, there's going to be some evaporation! More often than not, the water in the filling is absorbed by the dough, making the pasta soggy, sticky, and hard to pry off the surface without tearing.

But you can halt the evaporation. Dust the ravioli with flour, put them on a floured rimmed baking sheet, and stick the whole thing in the freezer. Once they're frozen solid, transfer the ravioli to zipper-lock freezer bags, press out the air, seal the bags closed, and keep the ravioli frozen for several weeks. I take my frozen ravioli straight from the freezer to the pasta water, and they don't take any longer to cook.

## EQUIPMENT

You don't need much in the way of special equipment for filled pasta. Some pasta cutters or cookie cutters, a knife, and a cutting wheel do the trick. Pick up a fluted cutting wheel for a nice wavy edge on the ravioli, and a bench scraper, also known as a bench knife, is good for scraping your work surface. But the most important thing is a spray bottle. As you work, a spritz of water now and then

keeps the dough from drying out. Moist dough also seals better when you punch out the ravioli. You want a gentle, even mist—not a shower—so look for a spray bottle with an adjustable nozzle and the finest spray possible. One other tool is handy: a spider strainer. If you don't have one, a slotted spoon will work. That's the easiest way to remove delicate ravioli and other stuffed pastas from the water. And for freezing ravioli, keep a supply of gallon-size zipper-lock bags on hand. The bags also come in handy for piping ravioli fillings onto the pasta if you don't have a pastry bag.

## COOKING

Stuffed pasta cooks a little differently from unfilled pasta. For those noodles, I like the water at a rolling boil. But ravioli tend to knock into one another and split open at a rolling boil, and then out comes the filling. I prefer the water at a low boil. As with other pasta, when the pasta is tender and the filling is heated through, the ravioli should go straight to the pan of sauce or the plate. No cooling or rinsing. Use a spider strainer or slotted spoon, so you can drain the ravioli and keep them intact, transfer them to the pan of sauce or to the plate, and save the pasta water. Pasta water is a great asset. It's like a preseasoned sauce thickener.

## SAUCES

There are no hard and fast rules here. But stuffed pasta does require a more calculated saucing decision because you have the added factor of the filling. Do you float the ravioli in *brodo* to highlight the filling? Just drizzle on some butter and herbs? Make a *crema* of vegetables or cheese? How you sauce depends on the shape and the filling, but rarely do ravioli call for a thick, heavy *ragù* on the plate. The real star is the filling—and its relationship to the pasta. Adding a heavy sauce would mask the perfect marriage that you worked so hard to create. And the worst thing that can happen to a marriage is to get into a threesome—figuratively speaking!

# RICOTTA RAVIOLI

MAKES 4 TO 6
SERVINGS

Here's a simple, round ricotta ravioli you can make from start to finish in less than an hour. I like to roll this dough the old-school way: by hand into a circle or square rather than into sheets with a machine roller. Either way, keep this ravioli out of the freezer. If you freeze a plain ricotta filling, it will get grainy. To keep it creamy, use the ravioli right after you make them. You could also refrigerate them for up to a day.

DOUGH SWAP I like the chew of this stone-ground wheat dough against the creaminess of the ricotta, but if you want a richer mouthfeel, use Egg Yolk Dough (page 26).

2 cups (1 lb/454 g) ricotta impastata cheese (see page 241)

1 teaspoon (3 g) kosher salt

½ teaspoon (1 g) freshly grated nutmeg

⅛ teaspoon (0.3 g) freshly ground black pepper, plus some for garnish

1 egg, beaten

8 ounces (227 g) Whole Egg, Bread Flour, and Stone-Ground Wheat Dough (page 29)

½ cup (114 g) unsalted butter, melted

½ cup (50 g) grated Parmesan cheese

In a bowl, mix together the ricotta, salt, nutmeg, pepper, and egg with a spoon.

Cut the dough in half and lay it on a lightly floured work surface. Roll out half of the dough into an 18-inch (45 cm) square between ⅟₁₆ (1.5 mm) and ⅟₃₂ inch (0.8 mm) thick. Starting about 2 inches (5 cm) from the edge of the dough, drop 1¾-inch (4.5 cm) balls of filling (about 1½ tablespoons/ 21 g) in a row that goes from one edge of the square to the opposite edge, leaving about 1 inch (2.5 cm) between the balls. Lightly mist the dough with water to keep it from drying out and to help create a good seal. Fold the 2-inch (5 cm) edge of dough over the filling. Using a round cutter 2 inches (5 cm) in diameter, punch out ravioli along the row. The ravioli should be very full and mounded and have almost no border of dough. Cut off the scraps and save them for another use. Continue dropping the filling

in rows, folding the dough over the filling, and punching out ravioli. Repeat with the remaining dough and filling. As the ravioli are formed, transfer them to floured rimmed baking sheets. You should have about 24 ravioli. Cover the ravioli and use them within 1 hour or refrigerate them for up to 8 hours. Avoid freezing the ravioli because the ricotta filling will become grainy.

Bring a large pot of salted water to a boil. Drop in the ravioli and cover the pot to quickly return the water to a low boil. Gently cook the ravioli until they are tender but still a little chewy when bitten, 3 to 5 minutes. The filling should look smooth and creamy; if it is grainy, the ravioli are overcooked. Using a spider strainer or slotted spoon, drain the ravioli, letting them drip-dry for a moment. Arrange the ravioli on warmed plates and drizzle on the melted butter. Sprinkle with some Parmesan and a few grinds of pepper.

# FIG AND ONION CARAMELLE WITH GORGONZOLA DOLCE FONDUTA

MAKES 8 SERVINGS

Figs and blue cheese love each other. But go easy on the cheese. Too much pungency can ruin this dish. I prefer a mild Gorgonzola here. And for the sweet fig and onion filling, *caramelle* is the perfect shape. With twists of pasta on either edge of the filling, these ravioli resemble wrapped caramel candies.

DOUGH SWAP For another layer of flavor, use Cocoa Dough (page 145). The slight bitterness harmonizes well with the sweet figs, onions, and cheese.

2 tablespoons (30 ml) olive oil

2 yellow onions, sliced into half-moons

12 ounces (340 g) ripe Mission figs (about 16 figs), stemmed and halved lengthwise

2 sprigs rosemary

2 tablespoons (30 g) unsalted butter, cut into small pieces

½ cup (50 g) grated Parmesan cheese

Kosher salt and freshly ground black pepper

12 ounces (340 g) Egg Yolk Dough (page 26), rolled into sheets about ⅟₃₂ inch (0.8 mm) thick

⅓ cup (78 ml) heavy cream

5 ounces (142 g) Gorgonzola dolce cheese, crumbled

Best-quality extra-virgin olive oil, for drizzling

Heat the olive oil a large, deep sauté pan over medium-high heat. When hot, add the onions, shaking the pan to distribute the hot oil. Lower the heat to medium and cook the onions, stirring occasionally, until they shed their water and go from translucent to light golden brown to deep caramel brown, 25 to 35 minutes. Stir in a little water now and then if necessary to keep the onions from burning on the bottom. You should end up with about ½ cup caramelized onions. Scrape the onions into a food processor or blender.

Heat the same pan over high heat until it is smoking hot. Add the figs, cut side down, and then the rosemary, slipping the sprigs among the figs. Sear the figs until they are very soft and caramelized golden brown, 3 to 5 minutes. Add the butter and shake the pan until it melts and is evenly distributed. Discard the rosemary, and then transfer the contents of the pan to the processor or blender along with the Parmesan. Puree the fig-onion mixture until smooth, stopping to scrape down the container once or twice (it will be thick). Taste the mixture, adding salt and pepper until it tastes good to you. Transfer the filling to a zipper-lock bag or pastry bag, seal closed, and refrigerate it for at least 1 hour or up to 2 days.

Lay a pasta sheet on a lightly floured work surface and trim the ends square. Lightly mist the dough with water to keep it from drying out, and then cut the dough into 2-inch (5 cm) squares. Snip a corner from the bag of filling and pipe ½-inch (12 mm) balls of filling near the bottom of each square. Wet your fingers and moisten the corners of a square. Fold the bottom of the pasta over the filling so the edge just covers the filling, then continue folding until the filling is enclosed and the filled pasta forms a small rectangle. Gently twist the ends of the dough like a candy wrapper and pinch the edges to seal (see photos, page 84). Repeat with the remaining pasta and filling. As the *caramelle* are formed, transfer them to floured rimmed baking sheets. You should have about 200 *caramelle*.

Cover the *caramelle* and refrigerate them for up to 2 hours, or freeze them in a single layer on floured rimmed baking sheets, transfer them to zipper-lock bags, and freeze them for up to 2 weeks. Take the pasta straight from the freezer to the boiling pasta water.

CONTINUED

Bring a large pot of salted water to a boil. Working in batches to prevent crowding, drop in the *caramelle* and cover the pot to quickly return the water to a low boil. Gently cook the *caramelle* until they are tender but still a little chewy when bitten, 4 to 5 minutes.

Meanwhile, bring the cream to a boil in a small saucepan. Remove the pan from the heat and whisk in the Gorgonzola until it melts and the fonduta is smooth. Keep it warm over the lowest possible heat.

Spoon a pool of the fonduta onto each warmed plate. Using a spider strainer or slotted spoon, drain the *caramelle*, letting them drip-dry for a moment. Arrange them on the fonduta. Grind some black pepper over each serving and drizzle some olive oil around the plates.

# PEA AGNOLOTTI WITH LARDO

**MAKES 6 SERVINGS**

Winter, spring, summer, and fall—I make agnolotti every season. People love the rectangular shape and the fillings are countless, from beets and cheese to corn and squash. In the spring, sweet peas are perfect. *Lardo* adds a burst of salt and fat to finish the dish. If you can't get your hands on *lardo*, use thinly sliced pancetta instead.

DOUGH SWAP For especially tender ravioli, use Rich Egg Yolk Dough (page 29), or for a little more chew, use Whole Egg and Yolk Dough (page 29).

1½ cups (220 g) shelled green peas (from about 3 pounds/1.4 kg peas in their pod)

4 ounces (112 g) robiola cheese

Kosher salt and freshly ground black pepper

½ egg (beat a whole egg, then pour out half)

8 ounces (227 g) Egg Yolk Dough (page 26), rolled into sheets about ⅛₂ inch (0.8 mm) thick

½ cup (114 g) unsalted butter

¼ cup (25 g) grated Parmesan cheese

2 ounces (57 g) lardo, sliced paper-thin

Have ready a bowl of ice water. Bring a pot of water to a boil. Drop in the peas and blanch them until they are bright green, about 30 seconds. Drain the peas and transfer them to the ice water to stop the cooking. Drain again and transfer them to a food processor. Add the cheese and puree the mixture until it is very smooth, about 1 minute. Taste it, adding salt and pepper until it tastes good to you. Add the egg and process until blended. Spoon the filling into a zipper-lock bag, seal closed, and refrigerate it for at least 1 hour or up to 1 day.

Lay a pasta sheet on a lightly floured work surface. Snip a corner from the bag of filling and pipe ½-inch (12 mm) balls of filling in two rows along the length of the sheet, leaving a 1½-inch (4 cm) margin around each ball. Cut the pasta sheet in half lengthwise between the rows of filling to make two long sheets. Lightly mist the dough with water to keep it from drying out and to help create a good seal. Fold the outside edge of the dough over to cover the filling, and then roll the sheet of pasta over itself again. Press out the air around each ball of filling, starting at one end of the sheet and working your way to the opposite end. Place a finger gently on the filling to create a dimple, and then cut between the balls of filling, preferably with a fluted cutter, to create rectangular agnolotti. Repeat the process with the remaining pasta dough and filling. As the agnolotti are

formed, transfer them to floured rimmed baking sheets. You should have 75 to 100 agnolotti.

Cover the agnolotti and use them within 1 hour or refrigerate them for up to 8 hours. You can also freeze the agnolotti in a single layer, transfer them to zipper-lock bags, and freeze them for up to 2 weeks. Take the agnolotti right from the freezer to the boiling pasta water.

Bring a large pot of salted water to a boil. Working in batches to prevent crowding, drop in the agnolotti and cover the pot to return the water quickly to a low boil. Gently cook the agnolotti until they are tender but still a little chewy when bitten, 1 to 2 minutes.

Meanwhile, melt the butter in a large, deep sauté pan over medium heat. Add 1 cup (237 ml) of the pasta water and stir like crazy until the liquid is blended and emulsified, 1 to 2 minutes. Using a spider strainer or slotted spoon, drain the agnolotti and transfer them directly to the pan of sauce. Gently toss and stir until pasta and sauce become one thing in the pan, adding a little more pasta water if necessary to create a creamy sauce.

Dish out the agnolotti onto warmed plates and garnish with the Parmesan and *lardo*.

# BRANZINO RAVIOLI WITH TOMATO BUTTER SAUCE

MAKES 6 TO 8
SERVINGS

Fish ravioli? You'll be amazed. It's light, beautiful, and easy. Just use fatty fish and the filling will bind itself together without any egg or bread crumbs. I like to fillet a couple of whole branzino, but you can use 1 pound (454 g) skinless branzino fillets or even salmon, yellowtail, or tuna belly. For the tomatoes, use whatever you have on hand, canned or fresh. Tomato *concassé* (see page 150) is even better.

DOUGH SWAP This dish is all about subtlety—not big flavors. An herb dough like Basil Dough (page 145) would be perfect.

1 pound (454 g) skinless branzino fillets, very finely chopped (about 3 cups total)

3 tablespoons (45 ml) extra-virgin olive oil

4 teaspoons (5 g) chopped fresh thyme, plus 6 sprigs

Kosher salt and freshly ground black pepper

12 ounces (340 g) Egg Yolk Dough (page 26), rolled into sheets about 1/32 inch (0.8 mm) thick

6 tablespoons (85 g) unsalted butter

3 canned whole San Marzano tomatoes

1½ teaspoons (3 g) grated lemon zest

Mix together the branzino, oil, and chopped thyme in a bowl. Season the mixture with salt and pepper, and then let it stand for 15 to 30 minutes to marinate. Transfer to a pastry bag, if you like.

Lay a pasta sheet on a lightly floured work surface and trim the edges square. Cut the sheet in half lengthwise, then pipe or spoon ½- to ¾-inch (12 mm to 2 cm) balls of filling down the entire length of each strip, leaving a 1½-inch (4 cm) margin around each ball. Lightly mist the dough with water to keep it from drying out and to help create a good seal. Fold the long edge of the pasta closest to you over a row of filling. Fold the opposite long edge over the other row of filling. Use your fingers to press out the air around each ball of filling. Using a round cutter 1¾ to 2 inches (4.5 to 5 cm) in diameter, cut out half-moons by positioning the cutter halfway over the filling. Repeat the process with the remaining pasta and filling. As the ravioli are formed, transfer them to floured rimmed baking sheets. You should have 80 to 90 ravioli.

Cover the ravioli and use them within 1 hour or refrigerate them for up to 4 hours. You can also freeze the ravioli in a single layer, transfer them to zipper-lock bags, and freeze

them for up to 2 weeks. Take the ravioli right from the freezer to the boiling pasta water.

Bring a large pot of salted water to a boil. Working in batches to prevent crowding, drop in the ravioli and cover the pot to quickly return the water to a low boil. Gently cook the ravioli until they are tender but still a little chewy when bitten, 4 to 5 minutes.

Meanwhile, melt the butter in a large, deep sauté pan over medium heat. Add the tomatoes, crushing them with your hands as you drop them into the pan. Add the thyme sprigs and ¾ cup (177 ml) of the pasta water and cook the mixture until it reduces in volume slightly, 2 to 3 minutes. Using a spider strainer or slotted spoon, drain the ravioli and transfer them directly to the pan of sauce. Toss gently until the sauce gets creamy and coats the pasta, 1 to 2 minutes. Taste the sauce, adding salt and pepper until it tastes good to you. Remove the pan from the heat and keep the pasta moving until pasta and sauce become one thing in the pan.

Dish out the pasta onto warmed plates, arranging the ravioli nicely on each plate. Garnish with the lemon zest.

# TALEGGIO RAVIOLI WITH RADICCHIO, HONEY, AND WALNUTS

MAKES 4 SERVINGS

This dish came about one fall, after serving a cheese plate featuring Taleggio accompanied with shaved radicchio, walnuts, and honey as condiments. I thought . . . hmm . . . maybe we can put all of this together in one dish. It worked perfectly.

DOUGH SWAP I would stick to softer doughs here. Chestnut Dough (page 145) would be awesome. It would be like serving a cheese plate with chestnut bread.

7 ounces (200 g) Taleggio cheese

½ cup (120 g) mascarpone cheese

Kosher salt and freshly ground black pepper

1 egg

8 ounces (227 g) Egg Yolk Dough (page 26), rolled into sheets about ⅟₃₂ inch (0.8 mm) thick

2 tablespoons (15 g) walnuts

1 tablespoon (15 ml) olive oil

2 tablespoons (21 g) finely chopped yellow onion

3 cups (110 g) julienned radicchio

1 tablespoon (15 ml) honey, plus some for drizzling

Combine the Taleggio and mascarpone in a food processor and puree until the cheeses are smooth. Taste the mixture, adding salt and pepper until it tastes good to you. Add the egg and process until blended. Spoon the filling into a zipper-lock bag, seal closed, and refrigerate it for at least 1 hour or up to 2 days.

Lay a pasta sheet on a lightly floured work surface and trim the edges square. Fold the sheet in half crosswise and cut a small notch at the fold to mark the center of the sheet. Unfold the sheet so it lies flat again. Snip a corner from the bag of filling and pipe ¾-inch (2 cm) balls of filling in two rows along half the length of the sheet, leaving a 1½-inch (4 cm) margin between the balls and stopping about 1½-inches (4 cm) from the center mark of the sheet. Lightly mist the dough with water to keep it from drying out and to help create a good seal. Lift up the empty side of the sheet and fold it over the balls of filling. Use your fingers to press out the air around each ball. Using a round cutter (preferably fluted) 1½ to 2 inches (4 to 5 cm) in diameter, punch out ravioli along the rows. Repeat with the remaining dough and filling. As the ravioli are formed, transfer them to floured rimmed baking sheets. You should have 30 to 40 ravioli.

Cover the ravioli and use them within 1 hour, or freeze them in a single layer on a floured rimmed baking sheet,

transfer them to a zipper-lock bag, and freeze them for up to 2 weeks. Take the pasta straight from the freezer to the boiling pasta water.

Bring a large pot of salted water to a boil. Working in batches to prevent crowding, drop in the ravioli and cover the pot to quickly return the water to a low boil. Gently cook the ravioli until they are tender but still a little chewy when bitten, 4 to 5 minutes.

Meanwhile, toast the walnuts in a large, dry sauté pan over medium heat, shaking the pan now and then, until fragrant, 2 to 3 minutes. Transfer the nuts to a cutting board and chop them. Heat the oil in the same pan over medium heat. When the oil is hot, add the onion and sweat it until it is soft but not browned, 3 to 4 minutes. Add the radicchio and cook it until it is tender but still a little crunchy, 3 to 4 minutes. Stir in the honey.

Dish out the radicchio mixture onto warmed plates, placing it to the side of each plate. Using a spider strainer or slotted spoon, drain the ravioli, letting them drip-dry for a moment. Arrange the drained ravioli on the other side of each plate. Drizzle the ravioli with honey and sprinkle with the walnuts.

# RAMP RAVIOLI WITH RICOTTA AND LEMON ZEST

MAKES 6 SERVINGS

Ramp season only lasts for about a month in Pennsylvania, and this ravioli is what I look forward to most during that time. It's probably one of the best things that chef Brad Spence came up with during his tenure at Vetri. The ravioli are half-moons, and the ricotta is whipped and piped onto the plates under the ravioli. Brown butter and Parmesan go on top. Simple and perfect.

DOUGH SWAP The ramps need to shine here, but Chive Dough (page 145) or Parsley Dough (page 143) would complement them nicely.

1½ pounds (680 g) ramps, stems and greens separated

3 tablespoons (45 ml) olive oil

1 tablespoon (15 ml) grapeseed or canola oil

½ cup (22 g) fresh bread crumbs (1 slice bread pulsed in a food processor)

¼ cup (25 g) grated Parmesan cheese, plus some for garnish

Kosher salt and freshly ground black pepper

1 egg

12 ounces (340 g) Egg Yolk Dough (page 26), rolled into sheets about 1⁄32 inch (0.8 mm) thick

½ cup (113 g) ricotta impastata cheese (see page 241)

6 tablespoons (85 g) unsalted butter

Grated zest of ½ lemon

Julienne enough of the ramp stems and greens to equal ¼ cup (40 g) fine strips. Set the strips aside. Heat 2 tablespoons (30 ml) of the olive oil in a large sauté pan over medium-low heat. Add the remaining ramp stems (but not the greens) and cook, stirring now and then, until the stems are very tender but not browned, 6 to 8 minutes. Scrape the ramp stems into a food processor.

Add the grapeseed oil to the pan and place over medium-high heat. When the oil is hot, add the ramp greens and cook them just until they wilt, 1 to 2 minutes. Scrape the greens into the food processor. Puree the ramps until they are relatively smooth, and then add the bread crumbs and Parmesan and process until blended. Taste the filling, adding salt and pepper until it tastes good to you. Add the egg and process until blended. Spoon the filling into a zipper-lock bag, seal closed, and use it within 1 hour or refrigerate it for up to 1 day.

Lay a pasta sheet on a lightly floured work surface and trim the edges square. Snip a corner off the bag of filling and, starting at each of the long edges, pipe ½-inch (12 mm) balls of filling in two rows down the entire length of the sheet, leaving a 1½-inch (4 cm) margin around each ball of filling (3 inches/7.5 cm total between rows). Lightly mist the dough with water to keep it from drying out and to help create a good seal. Fold the long edge of the pasta closest to you over one row of filling. Fold the opposite long edge over the other row of filling. Use your fingers to press out the air around each ball of filling. Using a round cutter (preferably fluted) 2 to 2½ inches (5 to 6 cm) in diameter, cut out half-moons by positioning the cutter halfway over the filling. Repeat the process with the remaining pasta and filling. As the ravioli are formed, transfer them to floured rimmed baking sheets. You should have 50 to 60 ravioli.

Cover the ravioli and use them within 1 hour or refrigerate them for up to 4 hours. You can also freeze the ravioli in a single layer, transfer them to zipper-lock bags, and freeze them for up to 2 weeks. Take the pasta straight from the freezer to the boiling pasta water.

Puree the ricotta and the remaining 1 tablespoon (15 ml) olive oil in a small food processor until light and fluffy, about 2 minutes. Taste the mixture, adding salt and pepper until it tastes good to you. Spoon the whipped ricotta into a zipper-lock bag, seal closed, and refrigerate until needed.

Melt the butter in a sauté pan over medium heat and cook until it turns golden yellow and the milk solids fall to the bottom of the pan and turn golden brown, 6 to 8 minutes. Add the reserved julienned ramp stems and greens; they should frizzle up in 1 to 2 minutes. Keep warm over low heat.

Bring a large pot of salted water to a boil. Working in batches to prevent crowding, drop in the ravioli and cover the pot to quickly return the water to a low boil. Gently cook the ravioli until they are tender but still a little chewy when bitten, 4 to 5 minutes.

Meanwhile, pipe a thin stripe of whipped ricotta—about 1 inch (2.5 cm) wide—down the center of 6 warmed pasta plates. Using a spider strainer or slotted spoon, drain the ravioli and let them drip-dry for a moment. Arrange the ravioli over the stripe of ricotta and garnish each serving with about 1 tablespoon (6 g) Parmesan. Spoon the brown butter mixture over the top. Garnish the servings with the lemon zest.

# LARDO CAPPELLETTI WITH FAVA CREMA AND PECORINO

MAKES 4 TO 6
SERVINGS

In some Italian restaurants, *lardo* seems to be the new butter. One day I had it whipped on crusty toast and thought it would make a great ravioli filling. Instead of cured *lardo*, I ground fatback and pancetta in a food processor along with coriander, cinnamon, nutmeg, and cloves—the same seasonings used to cure *lardo*. It was fantastic. The warming spices seemed to call for shaping the pasta into *cappelletti*, which are popular on Christmas Day in central Italy. *Cappelletti* means "little hats," and they resemble tortellini but are larger and contain more filling. To take it over the top, add a few thin strips of *lardo* along with the pecorino.

DOUGH SWAP For a little more bite, use the Whole Egg and Yolk Dough (page 29) and roll it just a bit thicker.

6 ounces (170 g) pancetta, finely chopped

6 ounces (170 g) pork fatback, finely chopped

1 teaspoon (3 g) kosher salt, plus a little more for seasoning

⅛ teaspoon (0.3 g) freshly ground black pepper, plus some for garnish

Pinch of ground coriander

Pinch of ground cinnamon

Pinch of freshly grated nutmeg

Pinch of ground cloves

12 ounces (340 g) Egg Yolk Dough (page 26), rolled into sheets about 1/32 inch (0.8 mm) thick

1½ pounds (680 g) young fava beans in the pod

⅔ cup (158 ml) extra-virgin olive oil, plus more for drizzling

2 teaspoons (10 ml) sherry vinegar

¼ cup (42 g) finely chopped yellow onion

1 small chunk pecorino cheese, for grating

In a bowl, stir together the pancetta, fatback, salt, pepper, coriander, cinnamon, nutmeg, and cloves. Spread the mixture in a single layer on a small rimmed baking sheet or cutting board and freeze the mixture until it is very cold, about 20 minutes. Put the blade of a food processor in the freezer at the same time.

Fit the food processor with the cold blade and process the cold meat mixture until it is smooth, scraping down the sides a few times. It should become a thick, pale pink paste, and you should have about ¾ cup. Spoon the filling into a zipper-lock bag, seal closed, and use it immediately or refrigerate it for up to 2 days.

Lay a pasta sheet on a lightly floured work surface and trim the edges square. Snip a corner from the bag of filling and, starting at each of the long edges, pipe ½-inch (12 mm) balls of filling in two rows down the entire length of the sheet, leaving a 1½-inch (4 cm) margin around each ball of filling

(3 inches/7.5 cm total between rows). Lightly mist the dough with water to keep it from drying out and to help create a good seal. Fold the long edge of the pasta closest to you over one row of filling. Fold the opposite long edge over the other row of filling. Use your fingers to press out air around each ball of filling. Using a round cutter (preferably fluted) 2 to 2½ inches (5 to 6 cm) in diameter, cut out half-moons by positioning the cutter halfway over the filling. Take the two pointed ends of each cutout and pinch them together around the straight side of the filling to make a cone shape resembling a little hat. Dab with a little water between the points to seal (see photos, page 95). Repeat with the remaining pasta and filling. As the *cappelletti* are formed, transfer them to floured rimmed baking sheets. You should have 50 to 60 *cappelletti*.

CONTINUED

Cover the *cappelletti* and use them within 1 hour or refrigerate them for up to 4 hours. You can also freeze them in a single layer, transfer them to zipper-lock bags, and freeze them for up to 2 weeks. Take the pasta straight from the freezer to the boiling pasta water.

Have ready a bowl of ice water. Bring a large pot of salted water to a boil. Shell the fava beans, discard the pods, and blanch the beans in the boiling water for 1 minute. Using a spider strainer or slotted spoon, transfer the beans to the ice water to stop the cooking. Pinch open the pale green skin on each bean and pop out the bright green fava. You should have about 1½ cups (170 g) peeled favas. In a small bowl, toss ½ cup (57 g) of the favas with 1 tablespoon (15 ml) of the oil and 1 teaspoon (5 ml) of the vinegar. Taste the salad, adding salt and pepper until it tastes good to you. Use the salad within 2 hours or cover it and refrigerate for up 6 hours.

Put the beaker of a blender in the freezer. Meanwhile, heat 1 tablespoon (15 ml) of the oil in a sauté pan over medium-low heat. Add the onion and cook it, stirring now and then, until it is soft but not browned, 3 to 4 minutes. There should be no color on the onion. Add the remaining 1 cup (113 g) favas and enough water to barely come to the top of the ingredients. Turn up the heat to high, and as soon as the water simmers, remove the pan from the heat. Pour the mixture into the chilled blender beaker, stirring to cool it down.

When cooled, puree the mixture, adding the remaining ½ cup plus 2 teaspoons (128 ml) oil through the opening in the lid, until the mixture is smooth and emulsified, 1 to 2 minutes. Add the remaining 1 teaspoon (5 ml) vinegar and blend until incorporated. Taste the *crema*, adding salt, pepper, and additional vinegar until it tastes good to you. The *crema* should be bright green and very smooth, and you should have about 1½ cups (355 ml). Use it within 1 hour or refrigerate it in an airtight container for up to 1 day.

Bring a large pot of salted water to a boil. Working in batches to prevent crowding, drop in the *cappelletti* and cover the pot to quickly return the water to a low boil. Gently cook the *cappelletti* until they are tender but still a little chewy when bitten, 2 to 3 minutes. Using a spider strainer, drain the pasta by transferring it to a clean kitchen towel.

Meanwhile, heat the fava *crema* in a small saucepan over low heat until it is warm, but do not let it simmer. Smear a few tablespoons (45 to 60 ml) of warm *crema* on each plate and place 10 to 15 *cappelletti* over the *crema*. Spoon the fava bean salad over the *cappelletti*, and then grate pecorino over each serving. Garnish with a grind or two of pepper and a drizzle of olive oil.

# DOPPIO RAVIOLI WITH LAMB AND POLENTA

MAKES 6 TO 8
SERVINGS

I love the idea of two complementary flavors in one ravioli. Lamb and polenta is just one combination. Use your imagination to come up with other types of double ravioli. For the cheese here, I like Calcagno, a firm, white cheese made from the milk of sheep that graze on wild herbs and grasses on the hillsides of Sardinia. The cheeses are sent to Salerno Province on the Italian mainland, where they are aged in the caves of the Madaio family. If you can't find it, substitute another firm, flaky aged pecorino. And for the lamb, hind shanks work great. Each one weighs a bit more than a pound, and they're less expensive than shanks cut for osso buco.

DOUGH SWAP Whole Egg, Bread Flour, and Stone-Ground Wheat Dough (page 29) would work nicely here. The bite in that dough would match both the lamb and the polenta.

### LAMB RAGÙ AND FILLING

2 lamb hind shanks (about 1¼ lb (567 g) each)

Kosher salt and freshly ground black pepper

Tipo 00 or all-purpose flour, for dusting

2 tablespoons (28 g) unsalted butter

1 yellow onion, coarsely chopped

1 large carrot, peeled and coarsely chopped

2 celery stalks, coarsely chopped

1½ cups (355 ml) dry red wine

⅓ cup (37 g) grated Calcagno cheese

1 tablespoon (4 g) chopped mixed fresh herbs (flat-leaf parsley, rosemary, and thyme are nice)

1 egg, beaten

### POLENTA FILLING

½ cup (80 g) polenta (page 247)

¼ cup (59 g) mascarpone cheese

¼ cup (25 g) grated Parmesan cheese

Kosher salt and freshly ground black pepper

1 egg

12 ounces (340 g) Egg Yolk Dough (page 26), rolled into sheets between ¹⁄₁₆ inch and ¹⁄₃₂ inch (1.5 and 0.8 mm) thick

½ cup (120 ml) veal stock (page 242)

2 tablespoons (28 g) unsalted butter

Grated Parmesan cheese, for garnish

To make the lamb *ragù*, heat the oven to 350°F (175°C). Remove and discard any sinew from the lamb shanks. Season them all over with salt and pepper, and then dust them with flour, shaking off the excess. Melt the butter in a Dutch oven over medium-high heat. When it is hot and bubbly, add the shanks and sear them until they are deeply browned all over, 10 to 12 minutes total. Transfer the shanks to a plate.

Lower the heat to medium, add the onion, carrot, and celery, and cook the vegetables, stirring occasionally, until they are deeply browned, 6 to 8 minutes. Pour in the wine, raise the heat to high, bring the wine to a boil, and boil until reduced by about half, 6 to 8 minutes. Return the shanks to the pot and add enough water to come three-fourths of the way up the sides of the shanks. Bring the liquid to a boil over high heat, then turn down the heat to low, cover, and braise the lamb in the oven until the meat is so tender that it easily pulls off the bone, 2 to 3 hours.

CONTINUED

Remove the pan from the oven and let the contents cool in the pan. When they are cool enough to handle, remove 1 shank and set it aside for the filling. Remove the second shank, pull the meat from the bone, and shred or chop the meat into bite-size pieces. Discard the gristle, fat, and bone. Pass the vegetables and braising liquid through a food mill fitted with the large die, or using short pulses, pulse them in a food processor just until the vegetables are finely chopped but not pureed. If the resulting mixture is thin and watery, return it to the pan and boil it until it has reduced to a thick consistency similar to that of tomato sauce.

Add the shredded meat to the pan, mix with the braising mixture, and then taste the *ragù*, adding salt and pepper to taste. You should have about 3 cups (710 ml) *ragù*. Use the *ragù* within 2 hours or transfer it to an airtight container and refrigerate it for up to 3 days or freeze it for up to 1 month.

To make the lamb filling, remove the meat from the reserved shank and discard the gristle, fat, and bones. Grind the meat with a meat grinder fitted with the small die, capturing it in a bowl. Alternatively, using short pulses, chop the meat in a food processor just until it is finely chopped but not pureed, then transfer it to a bowl. Mix in the cheese and herbs and then taste the mixture, adding salt and pepper until it tastes good to you. If the mixture seems dry, blend in some of the *ragù* liquid to moisten it. Stir in the egg. You should have about 2 cups of filling. Spoon the filling into a zipper-lock bag or pastry bag, seal closed, and refrigerate it for 1 hour or up to 2 days.

To make the polenta filling, combine the polenta, mascarpone, and 2 tablespoons (12 g) of the Parmesan in a food processor and process until combined. Taste the filling, adding salt and pepper until it tastes good to you. Add the egg and process until blended. Spoon the mixture into a zipper-lock bag or pastry bag, seal closed, and refrigerate it for at least 1 hour or up to 2 days.

Lay a pasta sheet on a lightly floured work surface and trim the edges square. Fold the sheet in half crosswise and cut a small notch at the fold to mark the center of the sheet. Unfold the sheet so it lies flat again. Snip a corner from each bag of filling and pipe the fillings in columns ¼ inch (6 mm) wide and about 3 inches (8 cm) long along the length of the sheet, alternating the fillings and leaving a ½ inch (12 mm) margin around each column. Pipe the same number of lamb-filling columns as polenta-filling columns and stop the columns about 1 inch (2.5 cm) from the center mark. Lightly mist the dough with water to keep it from drying out and to help create a good seal. Lift up the empty side of the sheet and fold it over to cover the fillings. Use a dowel or a clean round pencil to firmly press between each column of filling and neaten up the columns. Press the dowel across the end of the columns to seal, making the filling about 3 inches (7.5 cm) long. Using a fluted cutting wheel, cut along the same areas you just sealed with the dowel. Then cut between every second column of filling. Each ravioli should measure 3 by 2 inches (7.5 by 5 cm) and have two columns of filling. Repeat with the remaining pasta and fillings. As the ravioli are formed, transfer them to floured rimmed baking sheets. You should have 35 to 45 ravioli.

Cover the ravioli and use them within 1 hour. You can also refrigerate them for up to 4 hours, or freeze them in a single layer until frozen solid, transfer them to zipper-lock bags, and freeze them for up to 2 weeks. Take the pasta straight from the freezer to the boiling pasta water.

Bring a large pot of salted water to a boil. Working in batches to prevent crowding, drop in the ravioli and cover the pot to quickly return the water to a low boil. Gently cook the ravioli until they are tender but still a little chewy when bitten, 3 to 4 minutes.

Meanwhile, divide the stock between two large, deep sauté pans over medium heat. Add 1 tablespoon (15 g) butter and ¼ cup (60 ml) pasta water to each pan and cook until reduced and thickened, 2 to 3 minutes. Using a spider strainer or slotted spoon, drain the ravioli as you transfer them to the pans. Toss gently, and then divide the *ragù* evenly between the pans and cook until the sauce reduces slightly and coats the pasta, 2 to 3 minutes. Remove the pans from the heat and add 1 tablespoon Parmesan to each pan. Keep the pasta moving until pasta and sauce become one thing in the pan.

Dish out the pasta onto warmed plates, arranging them nicely on the plate. Garnish with Parmesan.

# STUFFED PAPPARDELLE WITH FOIE GRAS TERRINE AND ONION MARMALADE

MAKES 6 TO 8
SERVINGS

This ravioli was a Paolo Begnini invention. He's the chef at Osteria della Brughiera in a small town in Bergamo Province in Lombardy. When I came back from Italy with Jeff Michaud, the chef at Osteria in Philadelphia, we were both screaming, "This is the coolest thing ever!" We made this dish at Vetri for a year after our return. It's ridiculously rich, so you can't eat it every day. But every once in a while, it's unbelievable. Note that a whole foie gras will come with two lobes for a total weight of about 2 pounds (907 g). Separate the lobes and use the smaller one for this recipe. Or use both, adjusting the salt and sugar amounts for the total weight. You can keep the foie gras terrine in the freezer for 2 months.

DOUGH SWAP I wouldn't touch this one. It's just right.

### FOIE GRAS TERRINE

1 small lobe foie gras (about 12 oz/340 g)

Kosher salt, 1.8 percent of the weight of the foie gras (for 12 oz foie gras, that's 2⅛ teaspoons/0.22 oz/6.2 g)

Sugar, 1 percent of the weight of the foie gras (for 12 oz foie gras, that's ¾ teaspoon/0.12 oz/3.4 g)

### ONION MARMALADE

4 tablespoons (57 g) unsalted butter

4 Spanish onions, thinly sliced into half-moons

Kosher salt

### PARMESAN FILLING

1 cup (100 g) grated Parmesan cheese

½ cup (118 ml) heavy cream

4 to 5 tablespoons (27 to 34 g) plain dried bread crumbs

Kosher salt and freshly ground black pepper

1 egg, beaten

12 ounces (340 g) Egg Yolk Dough (page 26), rolled into sheets about ⅟₃₂ inch (0.8 mm) thick

½ cup (114 g) unsalted butter

Grated Parmesan cheese, for garnish

To make the terrine, heat the oven to 350°F (175°C). Line a 13 by 4 by 4-inch (33 by 10 by 10 cm) terrine mold or a 9 by 5 by 3-inch (23 by 13 by 7.5 cm) loaf pan with parchment paper, with enough hanging over the edges to cover the terrine.

You need to remove the veins from the foie gras because they are tough and chewy. First, let the liver stand at room temperature for 15 minutes to allow it to soften up. Spread a large sheet of plastic wrap on a work surface and set the lobe vertically on the plastic. Using a pairing knife, remove any visible veins and the membrane from the outside of the lobe. Remove any green bile. Slowly and gently open up and spread apart the lobe from the top to bottom to find the primary vein, which runs from the top to the bottom.

Dig with your fingers, gently pushing the liver and spreading it out like butter to find the vein. When you find it, spread the liver a little more on either side of the large vein to reveal the small veins running off it like branches on a tree. Once all the veins are exposed, use a paring knife or your fingers to pick up the large vein from one end and gradually pull it and the attached branches away from the liver, gently tugging it and scraping it out but leaving the liver on the plastic. Discard all the veins. Dig a little deeper to make sure you have removed every last vein. The foie gras may look ruined, but don't worry. You will rebuild it. Season it all over with the salt and sugar, and then reshape it into a semiflat disk resembling its original shape, using the plastic wrap to help reshape it if needed.

CONTINUED

Transfer the foie gras to an ovenproof sauté pan or rimmed baking sheet and warm it in the oven until it reaches an internal temperature of 90°F (32°C), 3 to 4 minutes. Remove the foie gras from the melted fat in the pan (discard the fat) and transfer it to the prepared mold, using the parchment paper to form it into a neat cylinder about 3 inches (7.5 cm) in diameter. If it has completely disintegrated in the pan, you can reemulsify it by pureeing it in a food processor, and then pour it into the prepared mold. Cover the foie gras with the overhanging parchment and then top it with a heavy weight to compact it. Freeze the terrine until solid, at least 3 hours. The foie gras can be kept wrapped in the parchment in a zipper-lock bag in the freezer for up to 2 months.

To make the marmalade, melt the butter in a large, deep sauté pan over medium heat. Add the onions and salt and toss the onions to coat them with the butter. Cook the onions slowly, stirring occasionally, until they shed their water and go from translucent to light golden brown to deep caramel brown and are almost disintegrated, 45 minutes to 1 hour. Stir in a little water now and then if necessary to keep the onions from burning on the bottom. Taste the marmalade, adding salt until it tastes good to you. You should have about ¾ cup onion marmalade. Use it within 4 hours or transfer it to an airtight container and refrigerate it for up to 1 week.

To make the Parmesan filling, whisk together the Parmesan and cream in a bowl; the mixture will look soupy. Stir in 4 tablespoons (27 g) of the bread crumbs. At this point, the mixture should look like a creamy paste. If it still looks soupy, add more bread crumbs, just 1 teaspoon (2.2 g) at a time, to thicken it a bit. Taste the filling, adding salt and pepper until it tastes good to you. Stir in the egg. Spoon the filling into a zipper-lock bag, seal closed, and use it within 1 hour or refrigerate it for up to 1 day.

Lay a pasta sheet on a lightly floured work surface and trim the edges square. Fold the sheet in half crosswise and cut a small notch at the fold to mark the center of the sheet.

Unfold the sheet so it lies flat again. Snip a corner from the bag of filling and pipe columns of the filling ½ inch (12 mm) wide crosswise on the sheet, leaving a ½-inch (12 mm) margin between the columns and stopping about 1 inch (2.5 cm) from the center mark. Lightly mist the dough with water to keep it from drying out and to help create a good seal. Lift up the empty side of the sheet and fold it over to cover the filling. Press a dowel or clean round pencil between and against the filling to neaten up the columns. Using a knife or fluted cutting wheel, cut between the columns of filling to make ravioli about 4 inches (10 cm) long and 1½ inches (4 cm) wide. Each ravioli should resemble a piece of stuffed *pappardelle*. Repeat with the remaining pasta and filling. As the ravioli are formed, transfer them to floured rimmed baking sheets. You should have about 30 ravioli.

Cover the ravioli and use them within 1 hour. You can also refrigerate them for up to 3 hours, or freeze them in a single layer until frozen solid, transfer them to zipper-lock bags, and freeze them for up to 2 weeks. Take the pasta straight from the freezer to the boiling pasta water.

Melt the butter in a large, deep sauté pan over medium heat. Cook the butter until it turns golden brown, 6 to 8 minutes, and then stir in ½ cup of the onion marmalade. Reserve the remaining marmalade for another use.

Meanwhile, bring a large pot of salted water to a boil. Drop in the ravioli and cover the pot to quickly return the water to a low boil. Gently cook the ravioli until they are tender but still a little chewy when bitten, 2 to 3 minutes. Using a spider strainer or slotted spoon, drain the ravioli, letting them drip-dry for a moment, then arrange them nicely on warmed plates.

Garnish the servings with the Parmesan and spoon the hot onion marmalade over the top. Using a Microplane or other fine-rasp grater, generously shave the frozen terrine over the pasta.

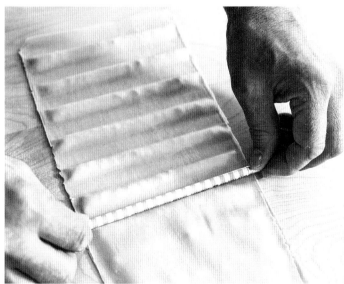

# CULURGIONES WITH SWEETBREADS AND CORN

MAKES 6 TO 8
SERVINGS

If you look up this pasta, you'll find all sorts of spellings. They're all correct. That's just how Italy is. No one wants to tell others that they can't do something their own way! *Culurgiones* come from Sardinia, where local cooks sculpt dough into elaborate breads for weddings and other celebrations. They look like stuffed teardrops with a series of folds or braids over the top. Traditionally they are filled with potatoes, but in the summer, I like to use pureed corn. A mixture of fresh corn kernels and crispy sweetbreads makes a nice condiment, too. But try different fillings. The important thing is that the filling not be too loose. It has to have some body to ensure the *culurgiones* hold their shape. For help with the braiding technique, check out some videos online.

DOUGH SWAP Unlike most other ravioli doughs, this one is a semolina dough. There's no egg, and the protein in the semolina makes the dough sturdy enough to be shaped. You could, however, flavor this dough with some minced fresh flat-leaf parsley or basil.

### FILLING

1 tablespoon (15 g) unsalted butter

3 ears corn, shucked and kernels cut from cobs

2 ounces (57 g) Chevrot (cave-aged French goat cheese) or Montrachet cheese

2 tablespoons (13 g) grated Parmesan cheese

2 tablespoons (14 g) plain dried bread crumbs

Kosher salt and freshly ground black pepper

1 egg

1 pound (454 g) Culurgione Dough (page 29), rolled into sheets about 1/16 inch (1.5 mm) thick

### SWEETBREADS

6 ounces (170 g) veal sweetbreads, preferably thymus

Kosher salt and freshly ground black pepper

¾ cup (170 g) unsalted butter

3 ears corn, shucked and kernels cut from cobs

3 ounces (85 g) pecorino al tartufo cheese (truffle pecorino)

2 tablespoons (6 g) thinly sliced fresh chives (optional)

To make the filling, melt the butter in a large sauté pan over medium-high heat. Add the corn kernels and cook, stirring occasionally, until tender and lightly browned, 4 to 6 minutes. Transfer the mixture to a food processor, add the Chevrot and Parmesan, and process the mixture, scraping down the sides once or twice, until it is very smooth, 2 to 3 minutes. Add the bread crumbs and process until blended, then taste the filling, adding salt and pepper until it tastes good to you. Add the egg and process until blended. Spoon the filling into a zipper-lock bag, seal closed, and refrigerate it for at least 1 hour or up to 2 days.

Lay a pasta sheet on a lightly floured work surface. Using a round cutter 3 to 4 inches (7.5 to 10 cm) in diameter, cut the dough into circles. Snip a corner from the bag of filling and squeeze about 1 tablespoon (15 ml) of the filling into the center of each circle. To shape each pasta, pick up the circle of dough and filling and hold it in one hand like a taco. To make the folding easier, rest the bottom of the taco on the side of your middle finger and hold the two sides of the taco gently between your thumb and index finger. At the open end of

CONTINUED

the taco opposite your palm, pinch the dough together near the bottom where the dough curves upward to form the taco shape. Pinch hard so the dough gets thinner. Now, hold that pinched piece between your thumb and index finger and push the dough directly toward the center of the filling just enough to make the taco curve out on each side. From the top, it should look sort of like a pointy bracket—one of these: }. Take the pinched point of dough and press it into one curve of that bracket, right into the rounded part. Pinch those two pieces of dough together to form a new pinched piece. Then stretch that new thinner piece into the opposite curved part, starting to seal in the filling. Now, push the pinched piece toward the center of the filling again to make the remaining part of the taco curve out on each side like a pointy bracket. Repeat the previous steps and continue pushing, pinching, stretching, and tucking the dough to opposite sides, working your way to the other end of the taco. When you reach the other end, pinch and twist the dough into a point. When finished, each filled pasta should have a teardrop shape that is round at the end where you started, pointed at the end where you finished, and the top should look braided. Repeat with the remaining pasta dough and filling. As the *culurgiones* are formed, transfer them in a single layer to floured rimmed baking sheets. You should have 25 to 30 *culurgiones*.

Cover the *culurgiones* and use them within 1 hour. You can also refrigerate them for up to 4 hours, or freeze them in a single layer until frozen solid, transfer them to zipper-lock bags, and freeze them for up to 2 weeks. Take the pasta straight from the freezer to the boiling pasta water.

To prepare the sweetbreads, rinse them in cold water, then soak them in a bowl of ice water for 10 minutes. Drain them, pat dry, and carefully remove the outer membrane and sinew. Finely chop the sweetbreads and season them all over with salt and pepper. Set them aside, or if not using them within 5 to 10 minutes, cover and refrigerate them for up to 2 hours. (Organ meats spoil easily, so it is important to keep the sweetbreads cold right up until you cook them.)

Melt the butter in a large sauté pan over medium heat. Add the corn and sweetbreads and cook until they are both nicely browned, 8 to 10 minutes. Remove the pan from the heat and cover it to keep the corn and sweetbreads warm.

Meanwhile, bring a large pot of salted water to a boil. Working in batches to prevent crowding, drop in the *culurgiones* and cover the pot to quickly return the water to a low boil. Gently cook the *culurgiones* until they are tender but still a little chewy when bitten, 2 to 3 minutes. Using a spider strainer or slotted spoon, drain the *culurgiones*, letting them drip-dry for a moment, and arrange them attractively on warmed plates.

Grate the pecorino over the *culurgiones*, and then spoon the corn and sweetbread mixture over the top. Garnish with the chives.

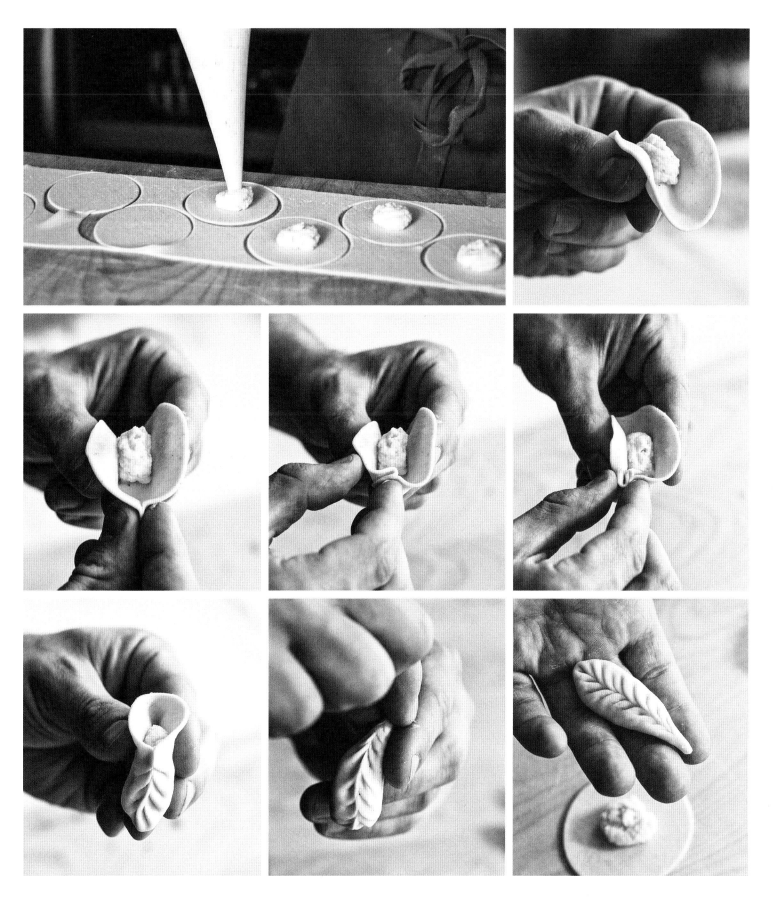

# 6

—

# EXTRUDED AND
# DRIED PASTA

**THE SETARO PASTA FACTORY BLENDS RIGHT INTO THE OTHER BUILDINGS
IN THE TOWN OF TORRE ANNUNZIATA IN SOUTHERN ITALY.** It's an
unassuming stone structure with a blue awning. But inside, some of the
best dried pastas in the world is made. You've got Mount Vesuvius on one
side of town and the Tyrrhenian Sea on the other. Between the volcano and
the water, this part of the province of Naples has the perfect temperature,
humidity, and airflow for drying pasta. In the late 1800s, the area was home
to over two hundred pasta factories, and the nearby town of Gragnano was
dubbed the Pasta Capital of Europe. Then the industrial revolution gradually
forced all the *pastifici* in Torre Annunziata to close—all except one: Setaro.

"How long do you dry the pasta?" I ask Vincenzo Setaro. "*Essiccazione,*"
he replies, "the drying . . . seventy-two to one hundred and twenty hours.
There's no recipe." Of course there is no recipe. Just like everything else in
Italy, it depends! And that's what makes it so beautiful. Making dried pasta
is not an exact science.

Things change. At different times of year, the air is wetter or drier; the flour bought from one place is different from the flour purchased somewhere else. There are many variables. You just have to be aware. "Australian wheat in the winter, Canadian in the summer," Vincenzo says. "And the rest, Italian." Vincenzo talks with vigor and *orgoglio* (pride), like he's told this story a thousand times. Even though it's the twenty-first century with new technology everywhere, Vincenzo is a craftsman. He wants his craft of making dried pasta to live on for generations. The factory uses the same pasta extruder it started with in the 1930s, and the pasta is still packed by hand. However, some things have changed. In the old days, the pasta was dried outside in the sun, but with the growth of industry, the air became polluted, so special rooms were built to replicate the outside temperature and humidity conditions. That is pretty amazing. These are the people we need to celebrate—pasta artisans, small farmers, seed savers. They keep their craft sacred and don't compromise the best things about it.

Setaro is just one of the great artisanal pasta companies in Italy. Afeltra is another, along with Martelli, Benedetto Cavalieri, and Latini. There are dozens of them. They're all a little different, depending on the flour they use and how they dry the pasta. That's the trick. Dried pasta is just flour and water. There is no real recipe. But the way it's dried—slow or fast, with heat or without—gives the pasta a different texture, a different mouthfeel when it's cooked. In researching this book, I visited pasta factories in both Italy and the United States, tasted dozens of different brands, read books and papers on commercial pasta drying, and consulted with food scientists to try and answer one simple question: does it matter what brand of dried pasta you buy?

## SEMOLINA

I can say now, there is a difference—a very big difference—and it's mostly in the bite of the pasta. A lot of that bite comes from the way the pasta is dried, but some comes from the flour itself. Almost all dried pasta is made with 100 percent high-protein durum wheat. In Italy, it's the law. The word *durum* is Latin for "hard," and that hard wheat not only helps dried noodles hold their shape but is also what gives dried pasta its chew. Durum flour is made by grinding durum

wheat, but the special flour used for most dried pasta is milled from only the yellow endosperm of durum wheat. Coarsely ground and granular, it's called *semolino* in Italian or semolina in English and has about 12 percent protein, which is pretty high among wheat flours.

High-protein durum wheat grows all over the world and grows best in warm, dry climates. Southern Italy has that climate—but not all year long. That's why Vincenzo Setaro buys some of his semolina from Australia in the winter. It's fresh from Australia at that time of year. He buys from Canada in the summer because it's fresher from Canada at that time of year. As I explained in the Wheat Flour chapter, freshness matters with wheat flour. So does seasonality. Some Italian pasta makers even buy semolina from the United States at certain times of year. There may very well be American wheat in your favorite brand of Italian pasta. Quality is not measured by the location of the pasta factory but by the freshness of the flour, because the fresher the flour, the better tasting the pasta.

## MIXING SEMOLINA DOUGH

The way semolina dough is mixed, extruded, and dried also have a big effect on pasta quality. We're talking mostly about texture here. To get the texture right, semolina needs time to hydrate after it is mixed with water. Mixing also develops some gluten. The protein in the flour starts to form a gluten network that gives the pasta its strength. For more details on gluten in pasta dough, check out the discussion that begins on page 13. I mix my semolina doughs for a total of 20 to 25 minutes to fully hydrate the dough and develop some gluten. How much water do I add? It depends. Variables like the time of year, the climate in the room, and even the shape of the pasta play a role. In my base recipe the water is about 30 percent of the weight of the semolina. But in the summer in Philadelphia, it's very humid, so I may need less water. In the winter, the air is dry, so I may need more. Short, fat shapes like rigatoni need less water because the extruder holes are bigger, and it's easier to press the dough through the holes. Long, thin shapes like spaghetti need a little more water so the dough can easily squeeze through the smaller extruder holes. As Vincenzo says, "there is no recipe."

## EXTRUDING SEMOLINA DOUGH

As semolina dough gets extruded, the gluten network gets stronger. The auger turns, the dough gets pressed through an extrusion plate, and the sheer force compresses and strengthens the gluten. Most artisanal pasta makers use traditional bronze extrusion plates or dies. Bronze dies rough up the surface of the noodle and make the pasta more porous. That means more starch can come out of the pasta when it cooks and more liquid can go in. It's not just tradition. Bronze dies make better pasta because that extra starch helps the pasta and sauce come together more completely. Sure, modern Teflon dies are cheaper, lighter, and easier to clean. But they create slicker pasta and the sauce doesn't stick to it as easily. That's one of the big differences between industrial and artisanal pasta. Look on the package to see if the pasta maker extrudes with bronze dies. Or, look at the surface of the pasta itself. Is the pasta supersmooth and glassy looking? Those are signs of Teflon dies. Is it rough and opaque? Then bronze dies were probably used. If you're extruding pasta at home, you'll get the best quality from a machine with bronze dies. The tabletop models from Arcobaleno (see Sources, page 249) do a great job.

Keep in mind that extruding dough through a machine creates friction, which generates heat and warms up the dough. You might notice that a large batch of dough begins with a nice dusting of semolina on the noodles as they are extruded, but by the end of the batch the noodles look wetter and feel stickier. That's because the dough is warming up, especially if you use metal (bronze) extrusion plates. We tested the temperature of a few batches and, after mixing, the dough tends to register around 85°F (29°C), but when the last of the noodles are extruded, the dough temperature can rise to nearly 100°F (38°C). To keep the dough and noodles from warming up too much and getting sticky in the machine, I like to chill both the extrusion plates and the dough in the fridge before extruding. I also use cold water and mix the semolina and water in a cold stainless steel bowl for about 10 minutes, and then chill the dough in the bowl for 15 minutes. Once the dough is chilled, mix it for another 10 to 15 minutes, then extrude it through the cold extruder plate. With chilled dough, you should get a nice dusting of semolina on all the noodles without sticking.

## THE DRYING PROCESS

Most people think that extruded pasta means dried pasta. Not so. Extruded pasta is just that: fresh pasta that has been pressed through an extruder to create different shapes. You don't have to dry it. Extruded pasta still has more bite than fresh egg pasta because of the hard semolina and the extrusion process. But drying is entirely optional. Drying the pasta makes it last longer in storage and creates an even firmer texture. But you don't want it to crack. To prevent cracking, you have to regulate the humidity and the temperature—preferably to replicate those perfect climatic conditions between Mount Vesuvius and the Tyrrhenian Sea.

Vincenzo Setaro dries his pasta for three to five days with a relatively low amount of heat, 104°F to 113°F (40°C to 45°C), depending on the time of year and the temperature outside. Barilla, the world's largest pasta manufacturer, speeds up that process with higher heat. Their pasta dries for seven to ten hours starting at 131°F to 149°F (55°C to 65°C) and increasing the temperature to a maximum of 183°F (84°C), depending on the shape of the pasta. Setaro and Barilla represent the two extremes of low-heat-dried pasta and high-heat-dried pasta. You'll also find every variation of time and temperature in between. The Benedetto Cavalieri family makes excellent pasta that is dried for slightly less time than Setaro's, one to two days, with slightly higher heat, a maximum of 130°F (54°C). In America, the Severino family makes high-quality artisan pasta with no heat at all—just the ambient room temperature of about 72°F (22°C). The question I ask is: what does slow drying or quick drying do to the pasta?

To find an answer, I tasted dozens of pastas, from Italian-made ones like Afeltra and Benedetto Cavalieri to American-made ones like Barilla and Severino. I can tell you that, regardless of brand, the pastas that are dried slowly with low heat taste better to me. They have a definite bite when you break the pasta between your teeth, but then the noodles dissolve easily and get creamy in your mouth. That creamy texture blends with the sauce and tastes incredible. It's one of the things that I love most about pasta! On the other hand, quick-dried pastas tend to feel more rubbery between your teeth. They almost snap when you bite into them, even when cooked past the al dente stage. They don't seem to get as creamy. I'm a chef. I go by what I taste, see, and feel. But I wanted to find out the science behind these different textures. I read several books and articles on commercial pasta making and cereal science. They all seemed to support my theory that pasta dried at higher temperatures develops a firmer texture, a texture that doesn't get as creamy when the pasta is cooked.

To help confirm my theory, I contacted Nathan Myrhvold and asked him, "What is the difference between pasta dried at low temperatures and pasta dried at high temperatures?" Nathan is the genius behind the book *Modernist Cuisine: The Art and Science of Cooking*, and he and his team of food researchers went above and beyond to answer the question. They gathered research, conducted experiments, and sent me microscopic photographs—beautiful, amazing images! They helped paint for me a much clearer picture of the difference between artisanal pasta and industrial pasta.

If you know how proteins behave when they are heated, that helps to explain it. Just like the proteins in eggs or meat, the proteins in wheat firm up when they are heated. Each protein first denatures, or unravels. This causes individual proteins to expose many more bonding sites to other proteins. Many unwound proteins then come together to form a larger, stronger web. The result is a firm protein network. It's like when you cook scrambled eggs. The eggs coagulate and get firm. And you know how scrambled eggs get a rubbery texture if the heat is too high and they cook too fast? That's because the protein network starts to go overboard with polymerization. Larissa Zhou, a food scientist who works with Nathan Myhrvold, explained it like this: Individual proteins are called monomers, and when you heat them, they unwind, bond to other unwound proteins, and form a conglomerate of proteins known as a polymer. If you increase the temperature, the higher heat makes the polymer network stronger. In the scrambled eggs example, if you cook the eggs too fast, they end up with a more rubbery, less creamy texture.

It's the same principle with pasta. But wheat also contains a lot of starch, and the really interesting thing is what happens to the starch. As the wheat protein polymerizes, the starch granules get caught in the protein network. Shown on page 116 are images of raw and cooked pastas (10 minutes in boiling

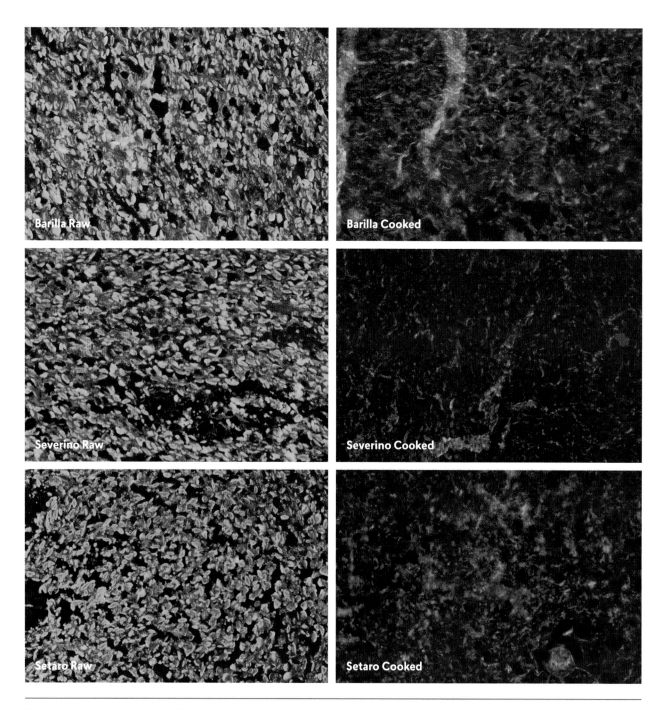

*Light microscopy of three brands of dried pasta (raw and cooked) shows the protein network (red) and starch granules (green). A moderately low drying temperature results in pasta with a protein network that is less dense and more evenly distributed among the starch.*

water) as seen under the microscope. Larissa explains what you see in the images: "We cut Setaro, Barilla, and Severino pasta with a cryotome (which is like a tiny, cooled meat slicer, and is mostly used to cut human and animal tissues for biological research), stained the protein and starch with different fluorescent dyes, and looked at them under the microscope.

The drying temperature determines how much protein polymerization takes place. As the heated proteins in wheat bind together, the starch granules get caught in the resulting network. During cooking, starch absorbs water, bursts, and turns into a continuous paste where individual granules are no longer visible. This turns pasta from dry and brittle to soft and creamy. A very tight protein network, however, prevents water from reaching the starch. We see this in the Barilla spaghetti, where the red areas are much more developed in the raw form. The pasta has a "snap," even after cooking. On the other hand, a very loose protein network isn't ideal either. The Severino pasta is dried at relatively low temperatures, which leaves the network not quite strong enough to hold the whole thing together after cooking. Although the cooked pasta has good texture, it is not as creamy as the Setaro. Setaro is in the sweet spot when it comes to drying temperature. Its gluten network becomes strong enough to hold the starch granules together but stays loose enough to allow water to get to the starch. After cooking, the result is just the right mix of creamy and al dente."

That creamy yet al dente texture is what I love so much when I'm eating a great dish of pasta. There are certainly other factors at play here, including the type of semolina, its protein content, and the specific humidity and convection (airflow) techniques employed by each pasta factory during the drying process. We primarily analyzed the drying temperature, which plays a large role. But Larissa and I did consult several sources to confirm our findings, including the well-respected cereal scientist R. Carl Hoseney, and they appear to agree with the lab work she conducted. Now, I'm not saying that high-heat-dried pasta is bad. It's just different. If you look in my cupboards at home, you'll find some Barilla, which is great for casual dinners with the family. If I'm stepping it up a bit, I'll go for Severino because I think it has a better mouthfeel. But when I'm in the mood for something really special, I'll choose Setaro, Benedetto Cavalieri, or another artisanal pasta from Italy.

## DRYING PASTA AT HOME

Of course, I had to apply everything I learned to the way I dry my pasta. I started playing around more with humidity and temperature. Think about water and your body. Water wants to evaporate, especially in a hot, dry environment. When it's summertime in Arizona, you sweat, but the water evaporates right off your skin. To stay hydrated, you have to take in more water. If you don't, your skin gets dry. Even when it's cold out, like in the winter in Philadelphia, if the humidity is low and you don't take in water, your skin dries and cracks; hence chapped lips. It's the same principle with drying pasta. Put it in a low-humidity environment—whether it's warm or cold—and the water in the pasta wants to evaporate. If it evaporates too quickly, the pasta dries too fast and cracks.

The trick is regulating the humidity so the pasta dries slowly and doesn't crack. The easiest way to do this at home is to put the pasta in the fridge. The temperature is low, about 40°F (4°C), and refrigerators have a low to moderate amount of humidity, about 30 percent on average. Just place your extruded pasta on wire racks that will fit in your refrigerator and you can dry it there, uncovered, for several days. The pasta will gradually get drier and harder. I like the texture best after two to three days in the fridge. It has a good bite but isn't brittle.

For even more bite, you need some heat and a little more humidity to keep the pasta from drying too fast. At home, I use a small humidifier set up under a milk crate. I put the pasta rack on the crate and cover the whole thing with a big cardboard box to trap the moisture. I set the humidity to about 75 percent and keep the heat at warm room temperature, about 73°F (23°C). This setup sits in my living room and the pasta dries in thirty-two to thirty-six hours. After that, I bag it up and it keeps for weeks at room temperature. When cooked, these home-dried noodles have beautiful bite, the starch comes out easily when cooked, and the pasta marries with the sauce, creating that incredible creamy texture. Artisanal pasta at home!

## COOKING AND SAUCING

And that brings us to cooking. Boiling dried pasta is very similar to boiling fresh pasta. It just takes longer. Check out the procedures for boiling fresh pasta on page 25. Here's the cheat sheet: use plenty of water, salt the water, and stir now and then to prevent sticking. Simple, right? To drain the pasta, I like to use a spider strainer or tongs and pull the pasta right from the water. Even simpler than a colander! Drain the pasta when it's slightly underdone. It will finish cooking in the sauce. That finishing step is the single most important procedure. That's when the marriage of pasta and sauce happens. As you stir, toss, or shake, the pasta absorbs liquid from the sauce. The sauce absorbs starch from the pasta. And the two emulsify. They become one. And, of course, the better the pasta, the more starch there is on the surface, and the better the emulsification—the better the final dish. The end result should always be a sauce that literally clings to the pasta. A tomato sauce that leaks tomato water under the noodles is *spaghetti al pomodoro* gone awry. A *ragù* that pools its liquid under the pasta has not been emulsified correctly. Here's the best test: when you eat a dish of perfectly cooked pasta with a perfectly emulsified sauce and that has the right ratio of sauce to pasta, you are left with a perfectly empty bowl after your last perfect bite. No extra sauce, no extra pasta. Just empty.

The magic is in the mixing. If you're already skilled at tossing ingredients in a sauté pan, just rapidly toss and flip the pasta and sauce back and forth about twenty times right in the pan. The two should become one. You can also use a thin pasta fork. A thick fork or even tongs can steal too much sauce from the pasta. Go thin. That allows you to stir quickly and forcefully without breaking the pasta. I have a pasta fork that I've used for twenty years. It's my tool of tools and it cooked virtually every pasta dish that went out of Vetri for the first ten years!

## PUTTING TOGETHER SAUCES AND SHAPES

As I've said in other chapters, many different pastas go with many different sauces. Putting a certain pasta with a certain sauce is really a matter of tradition and personal preference. Sure, there are better combinations than others. A *ragù* with big pieces of meat won't get caught inside long, thin strands of spaghetti. But I've successfully served a meat *ragù* with both short and long pasta. You can't just say "chunky sauces go with short pasta and smooth sauces go with long pasta." Look at Spaghetti with Pepper Ragù (page 123). The pepper pieces make it a "chunky" *ragù*, and it works perfectly with long spaghetti. But you could also use short rigatoni. Both pastas work. Or check out Stuffed Paccheri with Octopus Ragù and Caciocavallo Fondue (page 131). This dish blows all "rules" right out of the water! It has two sauces, one chunky and one smooth. It has fat, short pasta (*paccheri*), and it pairs fish with cheese! You take one bite of that dish and tell me it isn't delicious. Rules be damned.

Yes, traditions are behind the combinations that people have come to know and love in Italian cuisine. That's where the rules come in. Many of those marriages were born of necessity, created by housewives who struggled to feed their

families and came up with interesting ways to turn everyday ingredients into something new to eat. *Trenette* with *pesto alla genovese* was not created in a restaurant. It was born in the homes of Ligurians using the local sauce of basil, pine nuts, and olive oil, with some potatoes and green beans cooked along with the pasta. But does it always have to be served that way? No. The dish has evolved over time. Some cooks use the shorter *trofie* pasta in place of the longer *trenette*. Does the smooth sauce still work with the shorter pasta? Of course it does. Or consider *tortellini en brodo*. That pasta has been boiled in broth—not water—and served in a bowl of broth since the late 1500s when Bartolomeo Scappi started making the dish for Pope Pius V. But today some Italians serve tortellini in broth, some serve it with sauce.

The big question is, how far can you go with innovation? Where do you draw the line? All I can say is, keep yourself informed. Try not to stray too far from tradition. If you cross the line, you'll know . . . because the Italians will laugh at you! When I worked in Italy, Americans would come into the restaurant and order cappuccino with their dessert. Back in the kitchen, the cooks would all laugh. The servers would get angry, and some would even refuse to serve cappuccino with dessert. They'd say, "How can you possibly have milk after your meal? Crazy Americans!" If a diner asked for angel hair pasta with tomato sauce, the same thing would happen. "Everyone knows that angel hair is too thin for sauce. You can break it up and put it in soup, but that's it. Ugh," the servers would mumble, walking away from the table distraught over the request. "Some people just don't know how to eat."

You have to love Italians for the passion they have for food. It gives all of us a lot more to talk about at the table! Are some of my pastas traditional? Absolutely yes. My Spaghetti with Tomato and Basil Sauce (page 124) is about as traditional as you can get. Others, like Cockscomb Pasta with Duck Ragù, Juniper, and Castelmagno (page 134), push the boundaries a little more. But all of the combinations make sense. And they all taste delicious.

# EXTRUDED SEMOLINA DOUGH

**MAKES ABOUT
1 POUND (454 G)**

This dough is just semolina and water. The trick is to get the dough to the consistency of damp sand. Between 25 and 30 percent hydration is ideal for most pasta extruders. That means that the weight of the added water is 25 to 30 percent of the weight of the semolina. Dough with this hydration level was tested successfully on several professional and consumer pasta extruders. The smaller machines are less powerful, so they need a little extra water to help the dough get through the extruder. Once the pasta is extruded, you can dry it in the refrigerator or with a humidifier and some heat. As with my basic fresh pasta dough, the total weight of the mixture weighs more than a pound, but after mixing, extruding, and drying, the recipe yields about 1 pound (454 g) of usable pasta.

2¾ cups plus 1½ tablespoons (475 g) semolina, plus some for dusting

½ cup to ½ cup plus 2 tablespoons (118 to 142 ml) cold water

Refrigerate the extruder plate for 1 hour before extruding. Refrigerate a stainless steel mixing bowl as well. When both are chilled, put the semolina in the bowl and start mixing with a fork, spoon, your fingers, or a machine. Slowly drizzle in ½ cup (118 ml) of the cold water. Mix for 10 minutes, then refrigerate the mixture for 15 minutes so it can fully hydrate without warming up too much. If using a stand mixer for extruding, stir the chilled mixture by hand for another 10 minutes. If using a combo pasta mixer-extruder machine, put the chilled mixture in the machine and mix in the machine for another 10 minutes. After mixing, the mixture should resemble damp sand rather than come together in a ball of dough. Pinch a little between your fingers; it should stick together when pinched. If it doesn't, add a little more cold water, 1 tablespoon (15 ml) at a time, just until it can be pinched into clumps here and there. The amount of water you need to add depends on the humidity in the air. On dry days in the winter, you may need to add more water. On humid days in the summer, you may need less water. The mixture should look very dry—like clumpy, buttered bread crumbs. Too dry is better than too wet; if the dough is too wet or too warm, it will stick in the machine and gum up the works. If using a stand-mixer attachment, you will need to add slightly more water than if using a more powerful extruder. At this point, you could cover and refrigerate the dough for up to 1 day.

Fit your pasta extruder or stand-mixer attachment with the chilled extruder plate needed for your pasta shape. If using a pasta extruder, set it to medium speed. If using a stand mixer, with the machine running on medium speed, feed the dough into the hopper in marble-size clumps, using a pushing tool to push the clumps into the auger, being careful not to overload it. As the pasta is extruded, cut it into the lengths appropriate for the recipe you are making and immediately dust the pasta with semolina to prevent sticking. If the pasta does not extrude easily, gradually mix more water into the dough 1 tablespoon at a time.

Dry the pasta by placing it on wire racks that will fit in your refrigerator (coil long pasta like spaghetti and *bucatini* into nests) and refrigerate it uncovered for at least 8 hours or up to 4 days. The pasta will get drier and harder as it sits. For most recipes, the texture is perfect after 2 days in the refrigerator. Two-day-old pasta will cook in about 4 minutes in salted boiling water.

For drier pasta that keeps a little longer and has a little more bite, you need more heat and humidity. You can set up a small room humidifier, put a large milk crate over the humidifier, set your pasta rack on the crate, and then cover the whole thing with a cardboard box to trap the humidity. I've used this method to dry short shapes like rigatoni with 75 percent humidity at room temperature (about 70°F/21°C).

It takes about 36 hours, but then the pasta can be kept in an airtight container at room temperature for 4 to 6 weeks.

**FARRO SEMOLINA DOUGH** *Farro* has a protein content similar to durum wheat semolina. This dough tastes best with freshly milled *farro*. Just grind *farro* as you would whole wheat flour and sieve it so that it is pretty fine—a little finer than the semolina—or, to be exact, through a #35 sieve. It's a great dough for a hearty meat *ragù*. Mix 1⅔ cups (200 g) *farro* flour, 1 cup plus 3 tablespoons (200 g) semolina, and ½ cup (118 ml) cold water as directed in Extruded Semolina Dough. Makes about 1 pound (454 g).

**LORIGHITTAS SEMOLINA DOUGH** *Lorighittas* are Sardinian pasta shapes formed by twisting spaghetti into small rope-like rings. The dough calls for a little more water so that it can be easily twisted by hand. Follow the directions for Extruded Semolina Dough but add ⅔ cup (158 ml) cold water. Makes about 1 pound (454 g).

**RED WINE SEMOLINA DOUGH** This dough comes out bright red and slightly acidic from the wine. The color dulls a little when the pasta is boiled, but the wine flavor remains. Pair this dough with any sauce that goes with red wine. Pour 1¼ cups (296 ml) dry red wine into a saucepan and bring to a boil over high heat. Boil the wine until reduced by about half (about ⅔ cup/158 ml). Remove from the heat and let cool to room temperature. Use in place of the water in Extruded Semolina Dough and proceed as directed. Makes about 1 pound (454 g).

**SAFFRON SEMOLINA DOUGH** Here's a recipe for the most aromatic, golden orange dough you've ever seen. It's an amazing partner for fish and vegetables. Steep ¾ teaspoon (0.6 g) saffron threads in ½ cup (118 ml) water overnight. Use in place of the water in Extruded Semolina Dough and proceed as directed. Makes about 1 pound (454 g).

**SQUID INK SEMOLINA DOUGH** You want black dough? You got it. More important, you get a briny, mineral-like taste of the ocean that goes perfectly with seafood sauces. The ink stains everything, so handle it carefully (don't worry, it's not permanent ink so your hands, pasta machine, and countertop will come clean). Mix together 2 tablespoons (30 ml) squid ink and ½ cup (118 ml) cold water. Use in place of the water in Extruded Semolina Dough and proceed as directed. Makes about 1 pound (454 g).

**SWEET PEA SEMOLINA DOUGH** I love this dough with lamb sauces. The sweet flavor of fresh green peas and the bright green color make lamb taste even more delicious. Blanch ½ cup (73 g) shelled green peas in boiling water until they are tender, about 1 minute, and then transfer them to a bowl of ice water to stop the cooking. Transfer the peas to a kitchen towel and pat them dry. Combine the peas and ½ cup (40 g) packed fresh flat-leaf parsley leaves in a food processor or blender, turn on the machine, and drizzle in just enough cold water for the mixture to puree to the consistency of heavy cream. The puree should be bright green and measure about ½ cup (118 ml). Use in place of the water in Extruded Semolina Dough and proceed as directed. Makes about 1 pound (454 g).

**WHOLE WHEAT SEMOLINA DOUGH** The extra bit of chew you get here from the whole wheat flour goes well with shellfish. An unlikely couple, I know, but try it for yourself in Whole Wheat Spaghetti with Olive Oil–Braised Octopus (page 168). Combine 1¾ cups plus 2 tablespoons (317 g) semolina, 1 cup plus 2 tablespoons (135 g) whole wheat flour, and ½ cup (118 ml) cold water and proceed as directed in Extruded Semolina Dough. Makes about 1 pound (454 g).

# SPAGHETTI WITH PEPPER RAGÙ

MAKES 4 SERVINGS

My farmer, Ian Brendle, walked into the restaurant one day with boxes and boxes of new peppers he'd grown. He asked if we could use them, and initially we didn't have a clue. But then it came to us. This is a simple dish, but the mix of peppers makes it special. If you use only one kind of pepper, the *ragù* won't have the same complexity.

PASTA SWAP Linguine or rigatoni would work well here.

12 ounces (340) Extruded Semolina Dough (page 120)

Semolina, for dusting

¾ cup (177 ml) extra-virgin olive oil

2 cloves garlic, smashed

8 ounces (227 g) Anaheim peppers, stemmed, seeded, and cut into ¼-inch (6 mm) pieces (about 1¾ cups/112 g)

8 ounces (227 g) poblano peppers, stemmed, seeded, and cut into ¼-inch (6 mm) pieces (about 1¾ cups/112 g)

8 ounces (227 g) red Fresno peppers, stemmed, seeded, and cut into ¼-inch (6 mm) pieces (about 1¾ cups/112 g)

8 ounces (227 g) Italian long, hot (frying) peppers, stemmed, seeded and cut into ¼-inch pieces (about 1¾ cups/112 g)

½ cup (50 g) grated Parmesan cheese, plus some for garnish

Kosher salt and freshly ground black pepper

Fit your pasta extruder or stand-mixer attachment with the chilled spaghetti plate. If using a pasta extruder, set it to medium speed. If using a stand mixer, with the machine running on medium speed, feed the dough into the hopper in marble-size clumps, using a pushing tool to push the clumps into the auger, being careful not to overload it. As the pasta is extruded, cut it into 9-inch (23 cm) lengths and immediately dust it with semolina to prevent sticking.

Dry the pasta by placing it on wire racks that will fit in your refrigerator and refrigerate it uncovered for at least 8 hours or up to 4 days. The pasta will get drier and harder as it sits. I like the texture after 2 days in the refrigerator. For more bite, dry the pasta with a humidifier as described on page 120, and then store it in an airtight container at room temperature for up to 1 month.

Bring a large pot of salted water to a boil. Drop in the spaghetti, cover the pot to quickly return the water to a boil, and cook the pasta until it is tender but still a little chewy when bitten, 4 to 6 minutes (8 to 10 minutes for fully dried boxed pasta). Drain the pasta and reserve the pasta water.

Meanwhile, heat the oil and garlic in a large, deep sauté pan over medium-high heat. When the oil is hot, add all of the peppers and cook them, stirring now and then, until they are very tender and lightly browned, 8 to 10 minutes. Add 1½ cups (355 ml) of the pasta water and cook the sauce until it thickens slightly, 4 to 5 minutes. Remove and discard the garlic.

Add the drained pasta to the pan and toss until the sauce gets creamy and coats the pasta, 1 to 2 minutes, adding more pasta water if necessary to create a creamy sauce. Remove the pan from the heat and stir in the Parmesan. Keep the pasta moving until the cheese melts and pasta and sauce become one thing in the pan. Taste it, adding salt and pepper until it tastes good to you.

Dish out the pasta onto warmed plates and garnish with Parmesan.

# SPAGHETTI WITH TOMATO AND BASIL SAUCE

MAKES 4 SERVINGS

For this dish, I actually don't like to use Parmesan on top. I like it fresh and clean so you can really taste the tomato and basil. It's one of those dishes where if anything is just a little off, the whole dish is ruined. Use the best canned tomatoes and olive oil you can get, and be sure to emulsify the oil and pasta water to create a creamy sauce.

PASTA SWAP I would substitute bucatini for the spaghetti any day.

12 ounces (340 g) Extruded Semolina Dough (page 120)

Semolina, for dusting

¼ cup (60 ml) extra-virgin olive oil

1 clove garlic, smashed

1 cup (240 g) whole canned San Marzano tomatoes

¼ teaspoon (0.5 g) red pepper flakes

Kosher salt and freshly ground black pepper

10 fresh basil leaves, torn into pieces

Fit your pasta extruder or stand-mixer attachment with the chilled spaghetti plate. If using a pasta extruder, set it to medium speed. If using a stand mixer, with the machine running on medium speed, feed the dough into the hopper in marble-size clumps, using a pushing tool to push the clumps into the auger, being careful not to overload it. As the pasta is extruded, cut it into 9-inch (23 cm) lengths and immediately dust it with semolina to prevent sticking.

Dry the pasta by placing it on wire racks that will fit in your refrigerator and refrigerate it uncovered for at least 8 hours or up to 4 days. The pasta will get drier and harder as it sits. I like the texture after 2 days in the refrigerator. For more bite, dry the pasta with a humidifier as described on page 120, and then store it in an airtight container at room temperature for up to 1 month.

Heat the oil and garlic in a large, deep sauté pan over medium heat. Keep the heat on medium so you don't burn the garlic. A little brown is okay. After about 2 minutes, add the tomatoes, crushing them with your hands as you add them to the pan. Lower the heat to medium-low and cook, stirring occasionally, for about 10 minutes. You want the tomatoes cooked—not with a raw tomato flavor; there's a big difference.

Bring a large pot of salted water to a boil. Drop in the spaghetti and cover the pot to quickly return the water to a boil. Cook the pasta until it is tender but still a little chewy when bitten, 4 to 6 minutes (8 to 10 minutes for fully dried boxed pasta). Drain the pasta and reserve the pasta water.

Add the drained pasta to the pan along with ½ cup (118 ml) of the pasta water. Cook and toss the pasta and sauce together over medium-high heat until the sauce reduces in volume slightly, gets creamy, and coats the pasta. Keep the pasta moving until pasta and sauce become one thing in the pan. Taste it, adding salt and pepper until it tastes good to you but is slightly underseasoned. Add the basil leaves and toss again.

Dish out the pasta onto warmed plates and garnish with salt and pepper.

# FUSILLI WITH PUTTANESCA SAUCE

MAKES 4 TO 6
SERVINGS

Like Spaghetti with Tomato and Basil Sauce (opposite), I prefer this sauce without a garnish of Parmesan so that I can taste all the elements—the briny olives and capers, the savory anchovies, and the red pepper flakes. But if you like a little cheese, who's going to stop you?

PASTA SWAP Any short pasta like penne or rigatoni can stand in for the fusilli. I even make this with spaghetti or linguine now and then.

14 ounces (397 g) Extruded Semolina Dough (page 120)

Semolina, for dusting

½ cup (118 ml) olive oil

1 clove garlic, smashed

8 salt-packed anchovies (about 1¾ oz/50 g), rinsed, filleted and tails removed

1 can (14 oz/397 g) whole San Marzano tomatoes

¾ cup (120 g) halved and pitted Gaeta or similar black olives

⅓ cup (50 g) drained small capers

Pinch of red pepper flakes

Kosher salt

Fit your pasta extruder or stand-mixer attachment with the chilled fusilli plate. If using a pasta extruder, set it to medium speed. If using a stand mixer, with the machine running on medium speed, feed the dough into the hopper in marble-size clumps, using a pushing tool to push the clumps into the auger, being careful not to overload it. As the pasta is extruded, cut it into 2-inch (5 cm) lengths and immediately dust it with semolina to prevent sticking.

Dry the pasta by placing it on wire racks that will fit in your refrigerator and refrigerate it uncovered for at least 8 hours or up to 4 days. The pasta will get drier and harder as it sits. I like the texture after 2 days in the refrigerator. For more bite, dry the pasta with a humidifier as described on page 120, and then store it in an airtight container at room temperature for up to 1 month.

Bring a large pot of salted water to a boil. Drop in the fusilli, cover the pot to quickly return the water to a boil, and cook the pasta until it is tender but still a little chewy when bitten, 4 to 6 minutes (8 to 10 minutes for fully dried boxed pasta). Drain the pasta and reserve the pasta water.

Meanwhile, heat the oil and garlic in a large, deep sauté pan over medium heat. Add the anchovies and cook them until they fall apart, 2 to 3 minutes. Add the tomatoes, crushing them with your hand as you add them to the pan. Cook the tomatoes, stirring now and then, until they begin to break down, about 4 minutes. Add the olives and capers and continue to cook, stirring now and then, for 2 minutes. Stir in the pepper flakes.

Add the drained pasta to the pan and toss, stirring vigorously until the sauce gets somewhat creamy and coats the pasta, 2 to 3 minutes. Add a little pasta water if necessary to create a creamy sauce. Keep the pasta moving until pasta and sauce become one thing in the pan. Taste it, adding salt until it tastes good to you; the ingredients are already fairly salty, so you may not need much. Remove and discard the garlic.

Dish out the pasta onto warmed plates.

# BUCATINI WITH ALMOND PESTO

MAKES 4 TO 6
SERVINGS

This dish pays tribute to Han Chiang, the chef at Han Dynasty in Philadelphia. Brad Spence, the chef at Amis, eats lunch there regularly, and one week he was devouring the cold sesame noodles. Seduced by the creaminess of the sauce, he thought to himself, we could do some kind of a creamy nut pesto on pasta and spice it up a little. Thanks for the inspiration, Han!

PASTA SWAP With the heavy pesto, you need a chewy pasta that holds up well. Both spaghetti and linguine will work.

1 pound (454 g) Extruded Semolina Dough (page 120)

Semolina, for dusting

1¼ cups (179 g) skin-on almonds

2 cloves garlic

½ cup plus 1 tablespoon (133 ml) extra-virgin olive oil

Kosher salt

1 jalapeño pepper, stemmed and thinly sliced

1 cup (100 g) grated Parmesan cheese

Fit your pasta extruder or stand-mixer attachment with the chilled *bucatini* plate. If using a pasta extruder, set it to medium speed. If using a stand mixer, with the machine running on medium speed, feed the dough into the hopper in marble-size clumps, using a pushing tool to push the clumps into the auger, being careful not to overload it. As the pasta is extruded, cut it into 9-inch (23 cm) lengths and immediately dust it with semolina to prevent sticking.

Dry the pasta by placing it on wire racks that will fit in your refrigerator and refrigerate it uncovered for at least 8 hours or up to 4 days. The pasta will get drier and harder as it sits. I like the texture after 2 days in the refrigerator. For more bite, dry the pasta with a humidifier as described on page 120, and then store it in an airtight container at room temperature for up to 1 month.

Toast the almonds in a large, deep sauté pan over medium heat, shaking the pan now and then, until they are fragrant, 3 to 4 minutes. Transfer 1 cup (145 g) of the almonds to a blender or food processor. Chop the remaining ¼ cup (36 g) almonds with a knife and set them aside. Add 1 clove garlic and ¼ cup (60 ml) of the oil to the blender or processor. Turn on the machine and drizzle in another ¼ cup (60 ml) of the oil, blending until the pesto is relatively smooth. Taste the pesto, adding salt until it tastes good to you.

Bring a large pot of salted water to a boil. Drop in the *bucatini*, cover the pot to quickly return the water to a boil, and cook the pasta until it is tender but still a little chewy when bitten, 4 to 5 minutes (8 to 10 minutes for fully dried boxed pasta). Drain the pasta and reserve the pasta water.

Meanwhile, heat the remaining 1 tablespoon oil over medium heat in the pan used to toast the almonds. Thinly slice the remaining garlic clove and add it to the pan along with the jalapeño. Cook, stirring occasionally, until the garlic is golden brown, 4 to 5 minutes.

Add 1 cup (237 ml) of the pasta water to the pan, swirling the water and scraping up any browned bits on the pan bottom. Add the drained pasta and the almond pesto and toss until the sauce reduces slightly, gets creamy, and coats the pasta, about 1 minute. Remove the pan from the heat and add ½ cup (50 g) of the Parmesan. Keep the pasta moving until the cheese melts and pasta and sauce become one thing in the pan. Taste it, adding salt until it tastes good to you.

Dish out the pasta onto warmed plates and garnish with the remaining ½ cup (50 g) Parmesan and the reserved almonds.

# STUFFED PACCHERI WITH OCTOPUS RAGÙ AND CACIOCAVALLO FONDUE

MAKES 6 SERVINGS

Here we go: cheese with seafood again. Yes, it works. The *caciocavallo* fondue—salty, savory, and smooth—is great with the meaty octopus *ragù*. The cool thing is that we take a pasta that's normally tossed with sauce and stuff it with *ragù* instead. The short, fat tubes of *paccheri* will stand upright on the plate with the *ragù* inside, and the creamy fondue rests underneath.

PASTA SWAP If you don't want to make *paccheri*, you can buy good-quality boxed *paccheri*. Or, you can use large shells, stuffing them with the octopus *ragù* as directed.

6 ounces (170 g) Extruded Semolina Dough (page 120)

Semolina, for dusting

1 (1½ to 2 lb/680 to 907 g) octopus

Rock salt, for cleaning octopus

2 tablespoons (21 g) finely chopped yellow onion

2 tablespoons (16 g) peeled and finely chopped carrot

2 tablespoons (13 g) finely chopped celery

1 cup (237 ml) water

Kosher salt and freshly ground black pepper

2 bunches Swiss chard (about 1¼ lb/567 g total)

1 tablespoon (15 ml) extra-virgin olive oil

¼ cup (42 g) finely chopped white onion

1 cup (237 ml) heavy cream

1 cup (113 g) shredded caciocavallo cheese

1 tablespoon (4 g) chopped fresh flat-leaf parsley

Fit your pasta extruder or stand-mixer attachment with the chilled *paccheri* plate. If using a pasta extruder, set it to medium speed. If using a stand mixer, with the machine running on medium speed, feed the dough into the hopper in marble-size clumps, using a pushing tool to push the clumps into the auger, being careful not to overload it. As the pasta is extruded, cut it into 2-inch (5 cm) lengths and immediately dust it with semolina to prevent sticking. You should have 18 to 24 *paccheri*.

Dry the pasta by placing it on wire racks that will fit in your refrigerator and refrigerate it uncovered for at least 8 hours or up to 4 days. The pasta will get drier and harder as it sits. I like the texture after 2 days in the refrigerator. For more bite, dry the pasta with a humidifier as described on page 120 and then store it in an airtight container at room temperature for up to 1 month.

To clean the octopus, insert your fingers into the body and turn it inside out. Scrape away and discard the ink sac and other innards, and then rinse the body well. Turn the body

right side out. Remove and discard the eyes and black mouth, or beak, located at the center where the tentacles meet the body. Scrub the tentacles very well with rock salt, rinse, and repeat until you are sure the tentacles are clean. Scrubbing with salt also breaks down the muscle fibers a bit to make the octopus more tender. Measure out 1¼ pounds (567 g) octopus.

Fit a meat grinder with the large die and grind the octopus into a saucepan. (You can instead finely chop the octopus in a food processor using short pulses. Just make sure you don't make octopus puree.) Add the yellow onion, carrot, celery, and ½ cup (118 ml) of the water to the pan and bring the mixture to a simmer over medium-high heat. Turn down the heat to a very gentle simmer and cook the octopus until it is tender and the liquid has reduced by about two-thirds, about 1 hour. Taste the mixture, adding salt and pepper until it tastes good to you. Set aside.

CONTINUED

Remove the chard leaves from the stems and coarsely chop the leaves (reserve the stems for another use or discard). Heat the oil in a large, deep sauté pan over medium heat and add the white onion and chard. Cover and sweat the vegetables, lifting and turning the chard leaves with tongs now and then, until the onion is soft and the chard has wilted, 4 to 5 minutes. Add the remaining ½ cup (118 ml) water, cover the pan, and braise the chard over low heat until it is very tender and most of the liquid has evaporated, 25 to 30 minutes. Stir the octopus *ragù* into the chard in the sauté pan. Keep the mixture warm over low heat.

Bring a large pot of salted water to a boil. Drop in the *paccheri*, cover the pot to quickly return the water to a boil, and cook the pasta until it is tender but still a little chewy when bitten, 4 to 6 minutes (8 to 10 minutes for fully dried boxed pasta).

Meanwhile, bring the cream to a simmer in a small saucepan over medium heat. Whisk in the cheese until it is melted and smooth. Keep the fondue warm over the lowest possible heat.

Drain the *paccheri*, add it to the pan of *ragù*, and toss gently. Use a small spoon to stuff each noodle with about 2 table-spoons (30 ml) of the *ragù*.

Spoon a pool of fondue onto each of 6 warmed plates. Arrange 3 or 4 stuffed *paccheri* on each plate and garnish with the parsley.

# RIGATONI WITH SCORPION FISH

MAKES ABOUT 6
SERVINGS

Scorpion fish, often considered bycatch or "trash fish," makes this a very special plate of pasta. It's a tough fish to find. But make the effort and you won't be sorry. Scorpion fish bones also make the best fish stock (page 243). If you can't find scorpion fish, monkfish makes a good substitute.

**PASTA SWAP** I used to use *paccheri* for this dish, so that would be my first choice for a substitute.

1¼ pounds (567 g) Extruded Semolina Dough (page 120)

Semolina, for dusting

1 cup (237 ml) extra-virgin olive oil

½ yellow onion, finely chopped

1 clove garlic, smashed

1 pint (283 g) cherry or grape tomatoes, halved lengthwise

2 canned whole San Marzano tomatoes

2 cups (473 ml) fish stock (page 243), preferably made with scorpion fish bones

8 ounces (227 g) scorpion fish fillets, skinned and finely chopped

Pinch of red pepper flakes

1 tablespoon (4 g) chopped fresh flat-leaf parsley

Fit your pasta extruder or stand-mixer attachment with the chilled rigatoni plate. If using a pasta extruder, set it to medium speed. If using a stand mixer, with the machine running on medium speed, feed the dough into the hopper in marble-size clumps, using a pushing tool to push the clumps into the auger, being careful not to overload it. As the pasta is extruded, cut it into 1½-inch (4 cm) lengths and immediately dust it with semolina to prevent sticking.

Dry the pasta by placing it on wire racks that will fit in your refrigerator and refrigerate it uncovered for at least 8 hours or up to 4 days. The pasta will get drier and harder as it sits. I like the texture after 2 days in the refrigerator. For more bite, dry the pasta with a humidifier as described on page 120, and then store it in an airtight container at room temperature for up to 1 month.

Bring a large pot of salted water to a boil. Drop in the rigatoni, cover the pot to quickly return the water to a boil, and cook the pasta until it is tender but still a little chewy when bitten, 4 to 5 minutes (8 to 10 minutes for fully dried boxed pasta). Drain the pasta and reserve the pasta water.

Meanwhile, heat the oil in a large, deep sauté pan over medium heat. Add the onion and garlic and cook, stirring occasionally, until they are tender, about 4 minutes. Add the cherry tomatoes and cook until the tomatoes soften and start to fall apart, 6 to 8 minutes. Add the canned tomatoes, crushing them with your hand as you add them to the pan. Continue cooking, stirring a few times, until the canned tomatoes break down, 4 to 5 minutes. Add the stock, bring the liquid to a simmer, and simmer for 3 to 4 minutes.

Remove and discard the garlic. Add the fish, pepper flakes, parsley, and drained pasta to the pan, tossing until the sauce reduces slightly, gets creamy, and coats the pasta, 3 to 4 minutes, adding a little pasta water if necessary to create a creamy sauce. Keep the pasta moving until the fish turns white and the pasta and sauce become one thing in the pan. Taste it, adding salt and pepper until it tastes good to you.

Dish out the pasta onto warmed plates.

# COCKSCOMB PASTA WITH DUCK RAGÙ, JUNIPER, AND CASTELMAGNO

MAKES 4 TO 6
SERVINGS

The pasta here is a store-bought shape that resembles the fleshy top of a rooster's head. To match it, I usually make the *ragù* with goose. But a goose weighs about 10 pounds (4.5 kg) and makes a ton of *ragù*. So I simplified the recipe for home cooks by using duck instead. Of course, if you're serving a crowd, go for the goose! D'Artagnan (see Sources, page 249) sells geese if you can't find one from your local farmer.

PASTA SWAP You could easily sub a long strand pasta like fettuccine or tagliatelle.

1 duck (about 5 lb/2.25 kg)

Kosher salt and freshly ground black pepper

½ red onion, cut into large pieces

1 small carrot, peeled and cut into large pieces

3 celery stalks, cut into large pieces

1 cup (237 ml) dry red wine

8 juniper berries

1 small clove garlic, smashed

3 to 4 cups (710 to 946 ml) duck stock (page 242)

8 ounces (227 g) store-bought cockscomb pasta (creste di gallo)

2 tablespoons (28 g) unsalted butter

6 ounces (170 g) Castelmagno cheese, grated (about 1½ cups), plus some for garnish

Remove the giblets from the duck and reserve them for another use. Cut the leg-thigh portions from the duck by pulling each leg away from the body, bending the leg to find the hip joint, and then driving your knife straight through the joint. Remove the breasts by cutting slits on either side of the breastbone and then working the knife carefully around the rib cage, keeping the knife against bone at all times and pulling the breast away from the carcass. Reserve the carcass to make duck stock.

Separate the legs from the thighs by driving a cleaver straight through the joint. Cut the breasts in half. Season the duck pieces all over with salt and pepper, and then place them, skin side down, in a single layer, in a large, deep braising pan (or 2 pans, if necessary). Slowly cook the duck over medium-low heat, turning the pieces now and then, until all of the fat is rendered out and the skin is golden brown, 35 to 40 minutes.

Transfer the duck pieces to a plate. Strain and reserve the rendered fat for another purpose (it will keep frozen for 8 to 10 months—duck fat is great for frying potatoes!).

Heat the oven to 300°F (150°C). Return the pan to medium heat, add the onion, carrot, and celery, and sweat the vegetables until they are soft but not browned, 4 to 6 minutes. Add the wine and simmer until the liquid has reduced by about half. Tie the juniper and garlic in a cheesecloth bundle and add the bundle to the pan along with the duck pieces. Add enough stock to come about three-fourths of the way up the sides of the duck pieces, cover the pan, and braise the duck in the oven until it is very tender, about 1½ hours.

Remove the pan from the oven and let the duck cool in the pan. When the duck pieces are cool enough to handle, pull the meat from the bones, discarding the skin and bones. Set the meat aside. Remove and discard the cheesecloth bundle. Skim off any excess fat from the surface of the braising liquid and then pass the vegetables and liquid through a food mill fitted with the medium die, or pulse them briefly in a food processor just until the vegetables are very coarsely chopped. The *ragù* should be somewhat chunky. Return the meat to the *ragù*, and then taste the mixture, adding salt and pepper until it tastes good to you. If the *ragù* is watery, return it to the pan and simmer over medium heat until it is somewhat thick. Use within 1 hour or refrigerate in an airtight container for up to 4 days or freeze for up to 1 month.

Bring a large pot of salted water to a boil. Drop in the pasta, cover the pot to quickly return the water to a boil, and cook the pasta until it is tender but still a little chewy when bitten, 8 to 10 minutes. Drain the pasta and reserve the pasta water.

Heat the *ragù* in a large, deep sauté pan over medium heat. Add the drained pasta and the butter, tossing until the sauce reduces slightly, gets creamy, and coats the pasta, 3 to 4 minutes. Add a little pasta water if necessary to create a creamy sauce. Remove the pan from the heat and stir in the cheese until it melts into the sauce. Keep the pasta moving until pasta and sauce become one thing in the pan. Taste it, adding salt and pepper until it tastes good to you.

Dish out the pasta onto warmed plates and garnish with a little more Castelmagno.

# 7

---

# PLAYING WITH FLAVOR

**VETRI OCCUPIES THE ORIGINAL SPACE OF LE BEC FIN.** Once hailed as the best French restaurant in America, Le Bec Fin eventually moved to another space in Philadelphia, but then closed its doors for good in the summer of 2013. After forty years in business, the chef, Georges Perrier, was so influential in the city that I decided to transform Vetri back into the original Le Bec Fin for three nights shortly after the restaurant was shuttered. Not just a simple pop-up—I really wanted to turn back the clock and relive the glory days of French cuisine in America. Our servers wore tuxedos and our chefs wore toques. We served everything from caviar and escargots to crab galette, fillet of beef, and Grand Marnier soufflé. Courses came to the tables in gleaming silver cloches. It was magical. The food, service, and ambience reminded everyone of what perfect French dining used to be.

The most amazing part was cooking alongside Georges Perrier in the kitchen. I had never trained with a real French chef before. It was my chance to learn from a true *saucier*. French cooking is based on its sauces, and Georges told me they were always his first love. He was like poetry in motion. Special orders came in, and he made sauces to order *à la minute*. For a guest who didn't eat beef, Georges whipped up squab *salmis*. He made the dish in about ten minutes, using stock, Madeira, and the bird's liver for the sauce. The whole kitchen staff watched in amazement, then he turned to me and said, "Taste this fucking sauce. I'll show you how to make a squab *salmis*!" It was fantastic. His *salmis* displayed an expert understanding of how to carefully layer flavors and balance them on the plate.

After that night, I saw pasta in a new light. I hate it when cooks say, "Let's make a green pasta. It will look good against the protein." "Green is not a flavor," I always tell them. "What matters is what it will taste like." When you think about it, building flavors in a dish of pasta is similar to building flavors in a pan sauce or a ragout. For those preparations, you first sear the meat to create a layer of deep, savory flavor. Then you add wine, vegetables, and aromatics to the pan—more layers. Maybe some stock—another layer. When the sauce or ragout is done, it has one harmonious taste with multiple layers of flavor. It's the same with a dish of pasta. You layer flavors from the noodles to the condiment, always making sure that the flavors work together.

The great thing about pasta is that it's an open book. You can flavor it almost any way you like. Wheat flour tastes mild and earthy, sometimes with mineral and floral notes. You can build on that flavor base with any number of different flours, ground nuts, powdered spices, chopped herbs, pureed vegetables, and even wine. For me, combining flavors isn't rocket science. Ingredients that grow at the same time of year tend to taste good together, so seasonality matters. But sometimes I just go to the slam-dunk combinations that everyone knows and loves. Lemon and fish. Peas and mint. Wine and cheese. You would never hesitate to put these flavors together. Why not pull one of those flavors out and put it right into the pasta? Instead of adding lemon to the fish, you can put it in the noodles. That's how I came up with Lemon Fettuccine with Scallops (page 151). Simple. I love wine and cheese together. I thought, let's make a pasta dish out

of that combination. The only groundbreaking thing about Red Wine Spaghetti with Crunchy Vegetables and Roquefort (page 170) is that the wine is in the pasta. It's just a little twist.

When you start thinking like this, you'll come up with all kinds of ways to flavor pasta dough. It works for both fresh Egg Yolk Dough (page 26) and Extruded Semolina Dough (page 120). Semolina dough is just semolina and water, so the easiest thing is to replace the water with another flavored liquid. Try saffron-infused water or squid ink. You can also replace some of the semolina with different flours like whole wheat flour or, one of my favorites, *farro* flour. Almond flour gives pasta a sweeter, nuttier taste. Cocoa powder adds a note of bitterness.

## A FEW GUIDELINES

Herbs are the easiest flavoring to add to pasta dough. You can add them directly to the dough with no other changes to the recipe. I like to blanch and shock them first to bring out their color. And if the herb has a really strong aroma, like basil or mint, I mix it with some parsley so it doesn't dominate. To make herb-flecked pasta, just chop up the herbs and mix them in with the other ingredients. For a more uniform flavor and color, puree the herbs with some liquid from the recipe.

Ground spices can also go right into the pasta dough in place of a little of the flour. I usually use 5 to 8 tablespoons of spice per kilogram (2 pounds, 2 ounces) of flour, depending on the strength of the spice.

The real challenge is switching out liquids and flours. These changes can alter the very structure of the dough. In egg dough, the liquid is typically some combination of eggs, oil, and water. You can substitute other liquids, but think about what you are replacing. Eggs contain protein and fat; oil is fat. When making substitutions for them you need to maintain the overall protein and fat content in the mix to get a similar texture in the pasta. If you replace the water and whole eggs with egg yolks and a flavored liquid like red wine, that could mean adding more protein in the form of higher-protein flour. As a starting point, keep in mind that my homemade egg yolk pasta is about 38 percent water, 38 percent carbohydrate, 11 percent protein, and 13 percent fat by weight. Dried semolina pasta is about 12 percent water, 74 percent carbohydrate,

13 percent protein, and 1 percent fat. Use this as a guide and swap in different ingredients, pushing the percentages up or down just a little.

Swapping out flours is a slightly different ballgame. As I've discussed earlier, wheat flour contains gluten proteins that get stronger when mixed with water. So-called strong flours develop more gluten and create sturdier doughs. "Weak" flours create delicate doughs. For details, see Wheat Flour Characteristics on page 16. No matter what type of flour you use in fresh egg dough, you'll always need enough strength and elasticity for the dough to be rolled out. So if you want to make whole wheat pasta dough, you might try to replace the total amount of flour in Egg Yolk Dough (page 26) with whole wheat flour. But whole wheat dough isn't as elastic as dough made with tipo 00 flour. And whole wheat flour includes the bran and germ, so it will absorb more liquid. This isn't to say you can't make whole wheat dough. Of course you can! You just have to fine-tune the total amount of protein and liquid. My solution? Whole eggs instead of egg yolks. The additional egg whites add the protein and liquid needed because of the whole wheat flour. Taste for yourself in Whole Egg and Whole Wheat Dough (page 29). This dough also makes more rustic-tasting pasta because whole wheat flour is coarsely ground, while double-zero flour is ground superfine. Coarseness is another consideration when switching flours.

You can use nonwheat flours and powders, too. But try to balance the overall protein content in the mix. Otherwise, the dough may not have enough structure to be rolled out. As an experiment, try making chestnut pasta dough with just chestnut flour: replace the weight of the flours in Egg Yolk Dough (page 26) with the same weight of chestnut flour.

## Protein in Nonwheat Flours and Powders

Gluten protein is one of the components in wheat pasta that gives the dough its structure and elasticity. The nonwheat ingredients listed below do not contain any gluten. But they do contain protein, which also contributes to the texture of the pasta. When substituting flours, use the chart below to help balance the overall protein and fat content of the pasta dough you are making.

| FLOUR OR POWDER | PROTEIN % BY WEIGHT | FAT % BY WEIGHT | CARBOHYDRATE % BY WEIGHT |
|---|---|---|---|
| Pistachio | 20 | 45 | 28 |
| Cocoa | 18 | 13 | 58 |
| Oat | 15 | 9 | 66 |
| Buckwheat | 13 | 3 | 70 |
| Cornmeal | 7 | 4 | 77 |
| Chestnut | 4 | 3 | 76 |

Source: USDA National Nutritional Database for Standard Reference

You'll find that the dough won't hold together. It will be too crumbly because chestnut flour has only 4 percent protein and zero gluten, while the flours called for in the base recipe average 12 percent protein and have moderate gluten strength. The solution is to use equal parts chestnut flour and tipo 00 or all-purpose flour, and just a little less semolina. The tipo 00 flour and the semolina are adding protein. I also like to use a mix of whole eggs and egg yolks for additional protein in the form of egg whites. Taste the results for yourself in the Chestnut Dough (page 145) used to make Chestnut Tagliolini with Sweetbread Ragù (page 158).

I like to think of nonwheat flours and powders as additional flavors—not the foundation of the dough. Whenever you add a nonwheat flour or powder, bear in mind all of the other characteristics brought to the dough by that ingredient. It's not just flavor. For instance, I love pistachios and wanted to make pasta with them. I ground them with some of the flour from my basic egg dough recipe and worked the pistachio "flour" into the dough. But pistachios also contain fat, and fat surrounds gluten proteins in dough, which weakens the gluten network and makes the dough softer. I couldn't use too much pistachio flour because the dough would get too soft. So to get the pistachio flavor I was going for, I replaced the olive oil in my recipe with pistachio oil.

You can see how tricky it gets once you start swapping in this for that. But don't let that stop you! You should be able to flavor pasta any way you want. Just remember that pasta dough is made of flour and water and maybe some eggs. Those ingredients bring protein, starch (carbohydrate), fat, and water to the dough. If you can use other ingredients to bring those same elements into the dough in similar percentages, go for it.

Or, just explore the recipes in this chapter and throughout the book. These tried-and-true combinations result from years of trial and error. Use them as a starting point to create flavored pastas of your own. Play with different ingredients and have some fun with it—just like Georges Perrier building and layering flavors in his saucepan!

# PARSLEY DOUGH

**MAKES ABOUT 1 POUND (454 G)**

This recipe is similar to the basic Egg Yolk Dough (page 26) but with a little more flour and egg to bind up the herbs. Like that dough, it makes enough for 4 sheets of pasta that are 5 to 6 inches (13 to 15 cm) wide, each 4 to 5 feet (1.3 to 1.5 m) long if rolled to 1⁄32-inch (0.8 mm) thickness; 3 to 4 feet (1 to 1.3 m) long if rolled to 1⁄16-inch (1.5 mm) thickness; and 2 to 3 feet (61 cm to 1 m) long if rolled to 1⁄8-inch (3 mm) thickness. That's enough to make about 80 four-inch (10 cm) squares for cannelloni or lasagna, 95 two-inch (5 cm) squares for ravioli, or 150 one-inch (2.5 cm) squares for ravioli. The total weight of the mixture is more than a pound, but the recipe yields about 1 pound (454 g) of usable dough.

½ cup (40 g) packed fresh flat-leaf parsley leaves

1 tablespoon (15 ml) extra-virgin olive oil

1¼ cups (188 g) tipo 00 flour, or 1½ cups (188 g) all-purpose flour, plus some for dusting

½ cup (62.5 g) durum flour

10 egg yolks

Have ready a bowl of ice water. Bring a large pot of water to a boil. Add the parsley and blanch it until it is bright green, about 15 seconds. Using a spider strainer or slotted spoon, immediately transfer the parsley to the ice water to stop the cooking. For a dough with a deep green color, reserve about ¼ cup (60 ml) of the blanching water and let it cool. When the parsley is cooled, remove it from the ice water and shake off the excess water. Transfer the parsley to a blender, small food processor, or mortar and pestle, add the oil and 1 tablespoon (15 ml) fresh water—or 1 tablespoon (15 ml) of the blanching water—and puree the mixture until smooth. The finer you puree the parsley, the fewer specks you'll have in the pasta.

Transfer the parsley puree to a stand mixer fitted with the paddle attachment and add both flours and the egg yolks. Or, mix the flours on a work surface, make a well in the center, then add the egg yolks and parsley puree, mixing with your fingers. Mix on medium speed for 2 to 3 minutes, adding fresh water or the cooled blanching water, 1 tablespoon (15 ml) at a time, until the dough comes together. You should only need 1 to 3 tablespoons of water.

Turn the dough out onto a lightly floured work surface and knead it until it feels silky and smooth, about 5 minutes, kneading in a little flour if necessary to keep the dough from

sticking. The dough is ready if when you stretch it with your hands, it gently pulls back into place.

Shape the dough into a ball, then flatten the ball into a disk. Cover and set aside for at least 30 minutes or wrap it in plastic wrap and refrigerate it for up to 3 days. You can also freeze it for up to 3 months. Thaw the dough overnight in the refrigerator before using it. Alternatively, thaw it in a microwave oven on 50 percent power in 5-second increments, just until cool to the touch.

To roll out the dough, cut it into 4 equal pieces. If you have a very long work surface, you can cut the dough into fewer pieces. Let the pieces sit, covered, at room temperature for 10 minutes if chilled. The dough should be cool but not cold. Shape each piece into an oval wide enough to fit the width of your pasta roller. Lightly flour your work surface and set the pasta roller to its widest setting. Lightly flour 1 piece of dough, pass it through the roller, and then lightly dust the rolled dough with flour, brushing off the excess with your hands. Pass the dusted dough through the widest setting again. Set the roller to the next narrowest setting and pass the dough through, dusting again with flour and brushing off the excess. Pass once again through the roller.

CONTINUED

Fold the dough in half lengthwise over itself and cut about ¼ inch (6 mm) off both corners at the fold. This folding and cutting helps to create an evenly wide sheet of dough. Continue passing the dough once or twice through each progressively narrower setting. For thicker pasta like *corzetti*, *chitarra*, *pappardelle*, fettuccine, and tagliatelle, you generally want to roll the dough about ⅛ inch (3 mm) thick—setting 2 or 3 on a KitchenAid attachment—or about as thick as a thick cotton bedsheet. For sheet pastas like lasagna and cannelloni, you want to roll it a little thinner, just less than ⅛ inch (2 mm) thick, and for *rotolo* thinner still, about 1⁄16 inch (1.5 mm) thick–setting 4 or 5 on a KitchenAid attachment or about as thick as a thin cotton bedsheet. For ravioli, you want to roll the pasta a little thinner, to about 1⁄32 inch (0.8 mm) thick or setting 6 or 7 on a KitchenAid; ravioli sheets should generally be thin enough to read a newspaper through. As you roll and each sheet gets longer and more delicate, drape the sheet over the backs of your hands to easily feed it through the roller. You should end up with a sheet 2 to 5 feet (61 cm to 1.5 m) long, 5 to 6 inches (13 to 15 cm) wide, and ⅛ to 1⁄32 inch (3 to 0.8 mm) thick, depending on your roller and the pasta you are making.

To cut the pasta sheet into the pasta shape for the dish you are making, lay it on a lightly floured work surface and use a cutting wheel or knife, or use the cutter attachment on the pasta machine. If you want to hold the pasta after cutting it, dust it with flour, cover it, and refrigerate it for a few hours, or freeze it in a single layer, transfer the frozen pasta to a zipper-lock bag, and freeze it for up to 1 month. Take the pasta straight from the freezer to the boiling pasta water.

BASIL DOUGH Replace all of the parsley with basil and proceed as directed for Parsley Dough. Makes about 1 pound (454 g).

BUCKWHEAT DOUGH Use ½ cup (77.5 g) tipo 00 flour or ½ cup plus 2 tablespoons (77.5 g) all-purpose flour, ½ cup plus 2 tablespoons (77.5 g) buckwheat flour, ½ cup plus 1 tablespoon (70 g) durum flour, 10 egg yolks, and 1 tablespoon (15 ml) extra-virgin olive oil. Proceed as directed for Parsley Dough, adding the oil along with the egg yolks. Makes about 1 pound (454 g).

CHESTNUT DOUGH Use ¾ cup plus 1 tablespoon (125 g) tipo 00 or 1 cup (125 g) all-purpose flour, 1 cup plus 3 tablespoons (125 g) chestnut flour, ⅔ cup (113 g) semolina, 3 egg yolks, 3 whole eggs, and 1 tablespoon (15 ml) extra-virgin olive oil. Proceed as directed for Parsley Dough, adding the oil along with the egg yolks. Makes about 1¼ pounds (567 g).

CHIVE DOUGH Replace all of the parsley with chives and proceed as directed for Parsley Dough. Makes about 1 pound (454 g).

COCOA DOUGH Use ¾ cup (113 g) tipo 00 flour or ¾ cup plus 2½ tablespoons (113 g) all-purpose flour, 7 tablespoons (57 g) additional all-purpose flour, ⅔ cup (57 g) cocoa powder, 7 tablespoons (71 g) semolina, 9 eggs, and 1 tablespoon (15 ml) extra-virgin olive oil. Proceed as directed for Parsley Dough, adding the oil along with the egg yolks. You'll need a little extra water here. Makes about 1½ pounds (680 g).

LEMON DOUGH Omit the parsley, add the grated zest of 1 lemon and the olive oil along with the egg yolks, and proceed as directed for Parsley Dough. For Lemon-Herb Dough, keep some combination of herbs and add the lemon zest along with the yolks. Makes about 1 pound (454 g).

MINT DOUGH Replace half of the parsley with fresh mint leaves and proceed as directed for Parsley Dough. I like to use half parsley and half mint to cut the strong flavor of the mint. But if you want a strong mint flavor, replace all of the parsley with mint. Makes about 1 pound (454 g).

ORANGE DOUGH Omit the parsley, add the grated zest of ½ orange and the olive oil along with the egg yolks, and proceed as directed for Parsley Dough. For Orange-Herb Dough, keep some combination of herbs and add the orange zest along with the yolks. Makes about 1 pound (454 g).

PIMENTÓN DOUGH Use 1½ cups (187.5 g) durum flour, ⅓ cup plus 1½ tablespoons (62.5 g) tipo 00 flour or ½ cup (62.5 g) all-purpose flour, 5¼ teaspoons (12 g) pimentón (smoked paprika), 10 egg yolks, and 1 teaspoon (5 ml) olive oil. Proceed as directed for Parsley Dough, adding the oil along with the egg yolks. Makes about 1 pound (454 g).

PISTACHIO DOUGH Combine 1½ cups (8 ounces/227 g) shelled and peeled pistachios (preferably Sicilian) and ½ cup (76 g) tipo 00 flour or ½ cup plus 1½ tablespoons (76 g) all-purpose flour in a food processor and process until extremely fine, about 5 minutes. Pass the mixture through a tamis or fine-mesh sieve over a large bowl, scraping the bottom of the tamis or sieve to capture all of the pistachio flour. Discard any clumpy solids. Measure out 62.5 g (about ½ cup) pistachio flour and combine with 1¾ cups (215 g) durum flour, 1¼ cups plus 3 tablespoons (215 g) tipo 00 or 1¾ cups (215 g) all-purpose flour, 6 egg yolks, 1 whole egg, and 1 tablespoon (15 ml) pistachio oil. Proceed as directed for Parsley Dough. You'll need a little extra water here. The dough is a little oily, so if you roll it with a machine roller, you may need to roll it by hand a few times first. Makes about 1½ pounds (680 g).

# MINT PAPPARDELLE WITH MORELS

**MAKES 4 SERVINGS**

Fresh mint with earthy mushrooms is a mind-blowing combination. Use morels, black trumpets, or whatever rich-tasting mushrooms you can find. Whichever type you choose, the pairing should open the door to many other herb-mushroom combinations. Basil Dough (page 145) or Chive Dough (page 145) works well with mushrooms, too. Mint can be strong, so, as you will see in the dough recipe, I like to cut it with a little parsley to balance the flavors. You can toss a little fresh mint and parsley into the pan, too.

PASTA SWAP Spaghetti, linguine, bucatini, or any long pasta fits right in here.

8 ounces (227 g) Mint Dough (page 145), rolled into sheets about ⅛ inch (3 mm) thick

Tipo 00 flour or all-purpose flour, for dusting

1 tablespoon (15 ml) olive oil

½ cup plus 1 teaspoon (119 g) unsalted butter

¼ cup (21 g) finely chopped white onion

1 small clove garlic, smashed

8 ounces (227 g) morel mushrooms, cleaned

Kosher salt and freshly ground black pepper

½ cup (50 g) grated Parmesan cheese

Lay a pasta sheet on a lightly floured work surface and trim the edges square. Cut the sheet crosswise into strips a little less than 1 inch (2.5 cm) wide, preferably with a fluted cutter, to make *pappardelle*. Dust the *pappardelle* with flour and repeat with the remaining dough. Use the *pappardelle* within 1 hour or freeze it in an airtight container for up to 3 days. Take the pasta straight from the freezer to the boiling pasta water.

Heat the oil and 1 teaspoon (5 g) of the butter in a large, deep sauté pan over medium heat. When the butter melts, add the onion and garlic and sweat them until the onion is soft but not browned, 4 to 5 minutes. Add the mushrooms and cook until they soften, 4 to 5 minutes. Taste the mixture, adding salt and pepper until it tastes good to you. Remove and discard the garlic. Keep the mixture warm.

Bring a large pot of salted water to a bowl. Drop in the *pappardelle* and cover the pot to quickly return the water to a boil. Cook the pasta until it is tender but still a little chewy when bitten, about 2 minutes. Using a spider strainer or tongs, drain the pasta by transferring it to the pan of mushrooms. Reserve the pasta water.

Add the remaining ½ cup (114 g) butter, in pieces, to the pan along with 1 cup (237 ml) of the reserved pasta water, tossing over medium heat until the sauce reduces slightly, gets creamy, and coats the pasta, 1 to 2 minutes. Add a little more pasta water if necessary to create a creamy sauce. Remove the pan from the heat and stir in ¼ cup (25 g) of the Parmesan. Keep the pasta moving until pasta and sauce become one thing in the pan. Taste it, adding salt and pepper until it tastes good to you.

Dish out the pasta onto warmed plates and garnish with the remaining Parmesan.

# SAFFRON FUSILLI WITH LOBSTER AND LEEKS

MAKES 3 OR 4
SERVINGS

Have you ever had that popular cold pasta salad with lobster, tomato, and parsley? I never liked it. Here's an improvement on the combination, one with a little more finesse. Make sure you get female lobsters with their roe. The roe is dark green, almost black—not to be mistaken for the lighter green tomalley. The roe turns red when cooked, and that's part of what makes this dish special.

PASTA SWAP Use any other short shape you might see in a pasta salad, like small shells.

8 ounces (227 g) Saffron Semolina Dough (page 121)

Semolina, for dusting

2 live female lobsters (about 1½ lb/680 g each)

½ cup (114 g) unsalted butter, at room temperature

1 large, ripe tomato

1 leek, white and light green parts only, thinly sliced into half-moons

2 tablespoons (30 ml) Pernod

⅛ teaspoon (0.1 g) saffron threads

4 small sprigs herbs (basil, oregano, or flat-leaf parsley)

Kosher salt and freshly ground black pepper

Fit your pasta extruder or stand-mixer attachment with the chilled fusilli plate. If using a pasta extruder, set it to medium speed. If using a stand mixer, with the machine running on medium speed, feed the dough into the hopper in marble-size clumps, using a pushing tool to push the clumps into the auger, being careful not to overload it. As the pasta is extruded, cut it into 2-inch (5 cm) lengths and immediately dust it with semolina to prevent sticking.

Dry the pasta by placing it on wire racks that will fit in your refrigerator and refrigerate it uncovered for at least 8 hours or up to 4 days. The pasta will get drier and harder as it sits. The texture is perfect after 2 days in the refrigerator.

Have ready a bowl of ice water. Bring a large pot of water to a boil. To prepare the live lobsters for cooking as painlessly as possible, put 1 lobster on a cutting board and uncurl the tail so the lobster is flat against the board. Position the tip of a chef's knife just behind the head and press down firmly until the knife tip reaches the cutting board, then bring the blade down between the eyes to finish the cut. Repeat with the second lobster. Add the lobsters to the boiling water and blanch for 30 seconds. Using tongs,

immediately transfer the lobsters to the ice water to stop the cooking. Reserve the water in the pot.

Remove the meat from the lobster shells and cut into bite-size pieces. Reserve the dark green lobster roe (coral) that lies near the tail. You can refrigerate the blanched lobster meat in an airtight container for up 4 hours.

Transfer the lobster roe (about 2 tablespoons) and 6 table-spoons (85 g) of the butter to a small food processor and process until the mixture is smooth. You can also make this lobster butter with a fork and a strong arm. Use the lobster butter within 1 hour or refrigerate it in an airtight container for up to 4 hours.

Return the large pot of water to a boil and replenish the ice in the ice water. Using a small, sharp knife, score an X in the skin on the bottom of the tomato. Blanch the tomato in the boiling water until the skin begins to split and curl back a little from the X, 30 to 60 seconds. Using a slotted spoon, immediately transfer the tomato to the ice water and let it stand until cooled, a minute or two. Starting at the X, peel

CONTINUED

the skin from the tomato and discard it. Cut the tomato in half through its equator, turn each half cut side down over a bowl, and squeeze gently to remove the seeds and gel (you can use your fingers or the tip of a knife to help dig out the seeds and gel). Discard the contents of the bowl. Cut out the core from each tomato half, then finely dice the tomato. This preparation is called tomato *concassé*. Set the tomato *concassé* aside. Reserve the water in the pot.

Heat the remaining 2 tablespoons (28 g) butter in a large, deep sauté pan over medium-low heat. Add the leek and sweat it until it is soft but not browned, about 10 minutes. Add the Pernod and saffron threads and cook until the liquid evaporates, 4 to 5 minutes.

Meanwhile, return the large pot of water to a boil and salt it for pasta. Drop in the fusilli, cover the pot to quickly return the water to a boil, and cook the pasta until it is tender but still a little chewy when bitten, 4 to 5 minutes. Using a spider strainer or slotted spoon, drain the pasta by transferring it to the pan of sauce. Reserve the pasta water.

Add the tomato *concassé*, lobster meat, lobster butter, and herbs to the pan. Toss over medium heat until the sauce gets creamy and coats the pasta, 1 to 2 minutes, adding a little pasta water if necessary to create a creamy sauce. Keep the pasta moving until pasta and sauce become one thing in the pan. Taste it, adding salt and pepper until it tastes good to you.

Dish out the pasta onto warmed plates.

# LEMON FETTUCCINE WITH SCALLOPS

MAKES 6 SERVINGS

You can make versions of this dish with all sorts of seafood and various citrus pastas like lemon, orange, or lime. Use seafood that can be just warmed through like crab meat, shrimp, lobster meat, shucked clams or mussels, or white fish such as monkfish. Try shrimp and orange pasta—the combination works great.

PASTA SWAP You need a long, delicate pasta here. Linguine or pappardelle would work.

1 pound (454 g) sea scallops, preferably unsoaked diver scallops, diced

40 fresh basil leaves (about ½ cup packed/22 g), cut into chiffonade

1 cup (237 ml) extra-virgin olive oil

Kosher salt and freshly ground black pepper

½ Vidalia onion, halved lengthwise and thinly sliced crosswise

8 canned whole San Marzano tomatoes

1 pound (454 g) Lemon Dough (page 145), rolled into sheets about ⅛ inch (3 mm) thick

Stir together the scallops, basil, and all but 2 tablespoons (30 ml) of the oil in a large bowl. Taste the mixture, adding salt and pepper until it tastes good to you (scallops are one of the safest shellfish to eat raw). Cover and marinate the mixture at room temperature for at least 1 hour or in the refrigerator for up to 4 hours.

Heat the remaining 2 tablespoons (30 ml) oil in a large, deep sauté pan over medium heat. Add the onion and sweat it until tender but not browned, about 10 minutes. Add the tomatoes, crushing them with your hand as you add them to the pan. Turn down the heat to low and cook, stirring occasionally until the flavors have blended and the tomatoes lose their canned taste, about 40 minutes. Taste the sauce, adding salt and pepper until it tastes good to you. Use the sauce within 1 hour or refrigerate it in an airtight container for up to 3 days.

Lay a pasta sheet on a lightly floured work surface and trim the edges square. Cut the sheet into 9-inch (23 cm) lengths. Fit your stand mixer or pasta machine with the fettuccine cutter and set it to medium speed. Feed 1 length of dough at a time through the cutter, dusting the dough lightly with flour as it is cut into strands. Coil the fettuccine into nests and set them on a floured rimmed baking sheet. Repeat

with the remaining sheets. Use the fettuccine within 1 hour or freeze it in an airtight container for up to 3 days. Take the pasta straight from the freezer to the boiling pasta water, adding 30 seconds or so to the cooking time.

Bring a large pot of salted water to a boil. Drop in the fettuccine, cover the pot to quickly return the water to a boil, and cook the pasta until it is tender but still a little chewy when bitten, 3 to 4 minutes. Using a spider strainer or slotted spoon, drain the pasta by transferring it to the pan of tomato sauce. Reserve the pasta water.

Add 1 cup (237 ml) of the pasta water and the scallop mixture to the pan and cook over medium heat, tossing until the sauce reduces slightly, becomes creamy, and coats the pasta, 2 to 3 minutes. Keep the pasta moving until pasta and sauce become one thing in the pan. Taste it, adding salt and pepper until it tastes good to you.

Dish out the pasta onto warmed plates.

# PISTACHIO FETTUCCINE
# WITH ARTICHOKES

MAKES 4 SERVINGS

Years ago, I made this dish over and over. It was so good. But I never wrote down a recipe. I made it again recently, but this time I wrote down the proportions for the pasta made with ground pistachios and pistachio oil. It tasted just like I remembered it.

PASTA SWAP Thinner *tagliolini* works well, or use plain fettuccine instead of pistachio.

8 ounces (227 g) Pistachio Dough (page 145), rolled into sheets about ⅛ inch (3 mm) thick

2 tablespoons (30 ml) fresh lemon juice

2 cups (473 ml) water

8 baby artichokes

½ cup (114 g) unsalted butter

¼ cup (60 ml) pistachio oil

⅔ cup (67 g) grated Parmesan cheese

Kosher salt and ground black pepper

¼ cup (38 g) shelled, peeled, and chopped pistachios, preferably Sicilian

Lay a pasta sheet on a lightly floured work surface and trim the edges square. Cut the sheet into 9-inch (23 cm) lengths. Fit your stand mixer or pasta machine with the fettuccine cutter and set it to medium speed. Feed 1 length of dough at a time through the cutter, dusting the dough lightly with flour as it is cut into strands. Coil the fettuccine into nests and set them on a floured rimmed baking sheet. Repeat with the remaining sheets. Use the fettuccine within 1 hour or freeze it in an airtight container for up to 3 days. Take the pasta right from the freezer to the boiling pasta water, adding 30 seconds or so to the cooking time.

Combine the lemon juice and water in a bowl. Working with 1 artichoke at a time, snap off and discard all of the fibrous outer leaves. Using a paring knife, trim the artichoke until you are left with only pale yellow leaves in a bullet shape about 1 inch by ½ inch (2.5 by 1 cm) in size. As each artichoke is trimmed, drop it into the lemon water to keep it from browning. When all of the artichokes have been trimmed, lift them from the water, quarter them lengthwise for a rustic effect (as shown in the photo) or chop them into ¼-inch (6 mm) pieces for a more refined effect, and return the pieces to the lemon water.

Bring a large pot of salted water to a boil. Drop in the fettuccine, cover the pot to quickly return the water to a boil, and cook the pasta until it is tender but still a little chewy when bitten, 3 to 4 minutes.

Meanwhile, melt the butter in a large, deep sauté pan over medium heat. Drain the artichokes and add them to the pan along with 2 cups (473 ml) of the pasta water. Simmer the mixture until the artichokes are tender, about 5 minutes.

Using a spider strainer or slotted spoon, drain the pasta by transferring it to the pan with the artichokes. Add the pistachio oil and toss over medium heat until the sauce reduces slightly, gets creamy, and coats the pasta, 2 to 3 minutes. Remove the pan from the heat and add ½ cup (50 g) of the Parmesan. Keep the pasta moving until pasta and sauce become one thing in the pan. Taste it, adding salt and pepper until it tastes good to you.

Dish out the pasta onto warmed plates and garnish with the remaining Parmesan and the pistachios.

# PIMENTÓN LINGUINE WITH BABY OCTOPUS, JAMÓN BROTH, AND MARCONA ALMONDS

I like making chorizo *salumi* and enjoy Spanish dishes using *pata negra* (cured Ibérico ham). I thought, why not make spaghetti with *pimentón* (Spanish smoked paprika)? Then, the dish just fell into place. The ham broth is made with a leftover Ibérico ham bone. You can ask a local Spanish restaurant for one after they've cut all the ham from the bone. Just bend the lower part of the leg and cut through the knee joint. You only need the lower leg bone to make the broth, which is then used to simmer the pasta instead of plain water. Or, you can make the broth with a leftover ham bone from a baked ham.

PASTA SWAP You can cut this dough into fettuccine or *pappardelle* instead.

1 Ibérico ham bone, cut through the knee joint

1¼ pounds (567 g) baby octopuses

Rock salt, for cleaning octopuses

1 cup plus 2 tablespoons (267 ml) olive oil

½ cup (118 ml) sparkling mineral water, preferably San Pellegrino

½ small clove garlic, smashed

8 ounces (227 g) Pimentón Dough (page 145), rolled into sheets about ⅛ inch (3 mm) thick

2 tablespoons (8 g) chopped fresh flat-leaf parsley

Kosher salt and freshly ground black pepper

2 tablespoons (20 g) Marcona almonds, chopped

Place the lower portion of the ham bone in a large pot; reserve the other bone for another use or discard. You will need a pot that is at least 12 inches (30 cm) in diameter. A deep, heavy roasting pan or braising pan will also work. Add water to cover the bone. Bring the water to a simmer over medium heat, turn down the heat to low, and gently simmer the bone for 12 hours. Remove the pot from the heat and let the bone cool to room temperature in the liquid. Discard the bone and strain the broth through a fine-mesh sieve. Use the ham broth within a few hours, refrigerate it in an air-tight container for up to 3 days, or freeze it for up to 1 month.

To clean the octopuses, insert your fingers into the bodies and turn them inside out. Scrape away and discard the ink sacs and other innards, and then rinse the bodies well. Turn the bodies right side out. Remove and discard the eyes and black mouth, or beak, located at the center where the tentacles meet the body. Scrub the tentacles very well with rock salt, rinse, and repeat until you are sure the tentacles are clean. This breaks down the muscle fibers a bit so the octopuses become more tender. Set the octopuses aside.

Place the heads and tentacles in a pot just big enough to accommodate them. Add 1 cup (237 ml) of the olive oil, the sparkling water, and the garlic. Bring the liquid to 180°F (82°C) over medium-high heat, then lower the heat to maintain a steady temperature of 180°F (82°C). Braise the octopuses uncovered at 180°F (82°C) until they are tender, about 1½ hours.

Remove the pan from the heat and let the octopuses cool in the liquid. Once they are cool, transfer the octopuses to a cutting board and chop them into bite-size pieces. Reserve the braising liquid.

Lay a pasta sheet on a lightly floured work surface and trim the edges square. Cut the sheet into 9-inch (23 cm) lengths.

CONTINUED

# CHESTNUT TAGLIOLINI WITH SWEETBREAD RAGÙ

MAKES 4 SERVINGS

A visit to Strand Book Store in New York City inspired this dish. I was looking at books from the Renaissance that had all these pictures of people eating noodles with different kinds of *ragù*. A few leaps of the mind later, this dish was born.

PASTA SWAP Any long pasta like fettuccine, spaghetti, or even *pappardelle* works with this *ragù*.

1 pound (454 g) Chestnut Dough (page 145), rolled into sheets about ⅛ inch (3 mm) thick

8 ounces (225 g) veal sweetbreads, preferably thymus

Kosher salt and freshly ground black pepper

Tipo 00 or all-purpose flour, for dusting sweetbreads

¼ cup (60 ml) olive oil

1 clove garlic, smashed

½ cup (114 g) unsalted butter

1 sprig thyme, plus 3 tablespoons (8 g) fresh thyme leaves

2 cups (473 ml) veal stock (page 242)

1 cup (100 g) grated Parmesan cheese, plus some for garnish (optional)

Lay a pasta sheet on a lightly floured work surface and trim the edges square. Cut the sheets into 10-inch (25 cm) lengths. Fold each length in half lengthwise over itself, then fold in half lengthwise again. Julienne each folded piece crosswise into thin strips about ⅛ inch (3 mm) wide. You should end up with long strands that resemble square spaghetti. Dust the strands with flour and place them in nests on a floured rimmed baking sheet. Repeat with the remaining dough. Use the *tagliolini* within 1 hour or freeze it in an airtight container for up to 3 days. Take the pasta straight from the freezer to the boiling pasta water.

Rinse the sweetbreads in cold water, then soak them in a bowl of ice water for 10 minutes. (Organs spoil easily, so it's important to keep the sweetbreads cold right up until you cook them.) Drain them, pat dry, and carefully remove the outer membrane and sinew. Cut the sweetbreads into ½-inch (12 mm) pieces. Season them all over with salt and pepper, then dust them with flour, gently shaking off the excess. You want to remove as much flour as possible.

Heat the oil in a large, deep sauté pan over medium heat. Add the garlic and cook it until it is golden, 2 to 3 minutes. Remove and discard the garlic, and then add 2 tablespoons of the butter and the thyme sprig. When the butter is foamy, add the sweetbreads and cook them, turning them a few times, until they are crispy on all sides, 10 to 12 minutes. Pour in 1 cup (237 ml) of the stock, bring it to a simmer, and simmer until reduced by about half and thickened into a sauce, 6 to 8 minutes more. Remove and discard the thyme sprig. Use the *ragù* within 1 hour or refrigerate it in an airtight container for up to 1 day.

Bring a large pot of salted water to a boil. Drop in the *tagliolini* and cover the pot to quickly return the water to a boil. Cook the pasta until it is tender but still a little chewy when bitten, 3 to 4 minutes. Drain the pasta and reserve the pasta water.

Add the remaining 1 cup stock, 4 tablespoons of the remaining butter, and 1 cup (237 ml) of the pasta water to the sweetbread *ragù*. Simmer the mixture until it has reduced by about one-third and starts to thicken, 5 to 6 minutes. Add the drained pasta and toss until the sauce reduces a little more, gets creamy, and coats the pasta, 1 to 2 minutes. Remove the pan from the heat and add the thyme leaves, the remaining 2 tablespoons butter, and the Parmesan, tossing until the cheese melts and pasta and sauce become one thing in the pan, about a minute. Taste it, adding salt and pepper until it tastes good to you.

Dish out onto warmed plates and garnish with Parmesan.

# COCOA FETTUCCINE
# WITH VENISON RAGÙ

MAKES 8 SERVINGS

A little cocoa in a game *ragù* helps to calm down any gamey taste in the meat. Here, I put the cocoa in the pasta instead. I usually make this *ragù* with a whole venison leg that weighs about 10 pounds (4.5 kg). But you need a big pan to cook the whole leg, so we tested this recipe with smaller venison shanks. They worked perfectly. You could also use venison shoulder.

PASTA SWAP Chestnut Dough (page 145) tastes delicious here, or try the Farro Semolina Dough (page 121), extruded into strands such as spaghetti.

4 pounds (1.8 kg) bone-in venison shanks or shoulder

Kosher salt and freshly ground black pepper

Tipo 00 flour or all-purpose flour, for dusting venison

2 tablespoons (30 ml) grapeseed or canola oil

4 carrots, peeled and cut into large pieces

2 celery stalks, cut into large pieces

1 large yellow onion, cut into large pieces

½ cup (114 g) unsalted butter

½ cup (118 ml) olive oil

Grated zest and juice of 2 small lemons

1 pound (454 g) Cocoa Dough (page 145), rolled into sheets about ⅛ inch (3 mm) thick

½ cup (50 g) grated Parmesan cheese

Heat the oven to 200°F (95°C), or to 160°F (70°C) if it can be set that low. Season the venison all over with salt and pepper, and then dust it with flour, shaking off the excess. Heat the oil over medium-high heat in a large Dutch oven or in a flameproof roasting pan big enough to accommodate the venison. Add the venison and cook it, turning it as each side is browned, until it is deeply browned all over, 8 to 10 minutes. Transfer the venison to a large plate and set it aside.

Turn down the heat to medium, add the carrots, celery, and onion to the pan, and cook, stirring now and then, until nicely browned, about 5 minutes. Return the venison to the pan and pour in enough water to come about three-fourths of the way up the sides of the venison. Cover the pan (with aluminum foil if you don't have a lid) and braise the meat in the oven until it is so tender that the meat pulls easily off the bone, 7 to 8 hours.

Remove the pan from the oven and transfer the venison to a cutting board. When the venison is cool enough to handle, pick the meat from the bones, discarding the bones. Shred or chop the meat into bite-size pieces and set aside.

Pass the vegetables and braising liquid through a food mill fitted with the medium die, or pulse them briefly in a food processor just until the vegetables are coarsely chopped. Return the *ragù* to the pan; if it looks watery, simmer it over medium-low heat until it is somewhat thick. Stir in the meat and reheat gently over medium-low heat. Taste the mixture, adding salt and pepper until it tastes good to you. Use the *ragù* within 1 hour or refrigerate it in an airtight container for up to 1 week.

Lay a pasta sheet on a lightly floured work surface and trim the edges square. Cut the sheet into 9-inch (23 cm) lengths. Fit your stand mixer or pasta machine with the fettuccine cutter and set it to medium speed. Feed 1 length of dough at a time through the cutter, dusting the dough lightly with flour as it is cut into strands. Form the fettuccine into nests and set them on a floured rimmed baking sheet. Repeat with the remaining dough. Use the fettuccine within 1 hour or freeze it in an airtight container for up to 3 days. Take the pasta straight from the freezer to the boiling pasta water, adding 30 seconds or so to the cooking time.

Bring a large pot of salted water to a boil. Drop in the fettuccine, in batches if necessary to prevent crowding, and cover the pot to quickly return the water to a boil. Cook the pasta until it is tender but still a little chewy when bitten, 2 to 3 minutes.

Meanwhile, heat 4 to 5 cups (1 to 1.2 L) of the *ragù* in a large, deep sauté pan (or 2 pans if necessary) over medium heat. Reserve any remaining *ragù* for another use; it can be frozen for up to 1 month. Using a spider strainer or slotted spoon, drain the pasta by transferring it to the pan of *ragù*. Reserve

the pasta water. Add the butter, oil, and lemon zest and juice to the pan, tossing the mixture until the sauce reduces slightly, gets creamy, and coats the pasta, 1 to 2 minutes. Add a little pasta water if necessary to create a creamy sauce. Remove the pan(s) from the heat and keep the pasta moving until pasta and sauce become one thing in the pan(s). Taste it, adding salt and pepper until it tastes good to you.

Dish out the pasta onto warmed plates and garnish with the Parmesan.

# SAFFRON GNOCCHI SARDI WITH BONE MARROW

**MAKES 4 SERVINGS**

Bouillabaisse inspired this combination. Butter, fennel, saffron, orange—I can't get enough of those flavors. And the bone marrow ties them all together. You'll need about 2 pounds (907 g) veal marrowbones. Slide out the marrow as directed in the marrowbone stock on page 242 and then use the bones to make the stock.

**PASTA SWAP** Saffron Semolina Dough is important to the flavor in this dish, but it can be shaped into short pasta. Try fusilli or rigatoni.

8 ounces (227 g) Saffron Semolina Dough (page 121)

Semolina, for dusting

6 ounces (170 g) fennel bulbs, trimmed

1 tablespoon (14 g) unsalted butter

3 ounces (85 g) bone marrow, finely chopped

1½ teaspoons (1 g) saffron threads

1½ to 2 cups (355 to 473 ml) marrowbone stock (page 242)

1 tablespoon (4 g) julienned or chopped fresh basil or flat-leaf parsley

1½ teaspoons (3 g) grated orange zest

½ cup (50 g) grated Parmesan cheese, plus some for garnish

Kosher salt and freshly ground black pepper

Fit your pasta extruder or stand-mixer attachment with the gnocchi sardi (malloreddus) plate. Set the extruder to medium speed; if using a stand-mixer attachment, feed the dough into the extruder in marble-size clumps, using a pushing tool to push the clumps through the extruder. The first few clumps may come out uneven; just throw them away. Continue gradually dropping marble-size clumps into the extruder and pushing them through, being careful not to overload it. As the pasta is extruded, cut it into ¾-inch (2 cm) lengths and immediately dust it with semolina to prevent sticking.

You can also shape the pasta by hand. Form the dough into a ball, adding a little water if necessary, then cut the ball into a few pieces. On a lightly floured work surface, roll each piece into a rope ¼ inch (6 mm) in diameter, then cut each rope crosswise into ¼-inch (6 mm) pieces. Roll each piece on a grooved gnocchi board or on the back of fork tines to create a ridged oval shape similar to, though a little shorter than, *cavatelli*.

Dry the pasta by placing it on wire racks that will fit in your refrigerator and refrigerate it uncovered for at least 8 hours or up to 4 days. The pasta will get drier and harder as it sits. The texture is perfect after 2 days in the refrigerator.

Bring a large pot of salted water to a boil. Drop in the gnocchi sardi and cover the pot to quickly return the water to a boil. Cook the pasta until it is tender but still a little chewy when bitten, 6 to 8 minutes.

Meanwhile, shave the fennel into thin strips, preferably on a mandoline—even a handheld one. Heat the butter in a large, deep sauté pan over medium heat. Add the fennel and sweat it until it is tender but not browned, 4 to 6 minutes.

Using a spider strainer or slotted spoon, drain the pasta by transferring it to the pan. Add the bone marrow, saffron, 1½ cups (355 ml) of the stock, the basil, and the orange zest to the pan. Toss over medium heat until the sauce reduces slightly, gets creamy, and coats the pasta, 2 to 3 minutes. If necessary, add the remaining ½ cup (118 ml) stock to create a creamy sauce. Remove the pan from the heat, stir in the Parmesan, and keep the pasta moving until the cheese melts and the pasta and sauce become one thing in the pan. Taste it, adding salt and pepper until it tastes good to you.

Dish out onto warmed plates and garnish with Parmesan.

# SWEET PEA MALLOREDDUS WITH LAMB RAGÙ AND MINT

**MAKES 6 SERVINGS**

Some of my flavor combinations push the boundaries, but most of them are pretty classic. Lamb, peas, and mint taste awesome together, and there's no need to mess with that combination. But you could switch around what appears here. The peas are in the dough in this recipe, but you could make Mint Dough (page 145) instead.

**PASTA SWAP** Try fusilli or spaghetti or any shape you might pair with Bolognese sauce.

1 pound (454 g) Sweet Pea Semolina Dough (page 121)

Semolina, for dusting

1 pound (454 g) boneless lamb shoulder, cut into 1-inch (2.5 cm) pieces

2 ounces (57 g) pork fatback, cut into 1-inch (2.5 cm) pieces

2 sprigs thyme

2 sprigs rosemary

2 sprigs flat-leaf parsley

4 sprigs mint

1 teaspoon (2 g) black peppercorns

1 teaspoon (3 g) coriander seeds

2 cloves garlic

Kosher salt and freshly ground black pepper

1 tablespoon (15 ml) grapeseed or canola oil

1 cup (168 g) minced Spanish onion

½ cup (76 g) peeled and minced carrot

1½ cups (355 ml) dry red wine

½ cup (118 ml) tomato puree

½ cup (73 g) shelled green peas

4 tablespoons (57 g) unsalted butter

½ cup (50) grated Parmesan cheese

2 tablespoons (3 g) chopped fresh mint

Fit your pasta extruder or stand-mixer attachment with the malloreddus (gnocchi sardi) plate. Set the extruder to medium speed; if using a stand-mixer attachment, feed the dough into the extruder in marble-size clumps, using a pushing tool to push the clumps through the extruder. The first few clumps may come out uneven; just throw them away. Continue gradually dropping marble-size clumps into the extruder and pushing them through, being careful not to overload it. As the pasta is extruded, cut it into ¾-inch (2 cm) lengths and immediately dust it with semolina to prevent sticking.

You can also shape the pasta by hand. Form the dough into a ball, adding a little water if necessary, then cut the ball into a few pieces. On a lightly floured work surface, roll each piece into a rope ¼ inch (6 mm) in diameter, then cut each rope crosswise into ¼-inch (6 mm) pieces. Roll each piece on a grooved gnocchi board or the back of fork tines to create a ridged oval shape similar to, though a little shorter than, *cavatelli*.

Dry the pasta by placing it on wire racks that will fit in your refrigerator and refrigerate it uncovered for at least 8 hours or up to 4 days. The pasta will get drier and harder as it sits. The texture is perfect after 2 days in the refrigerator.

Put a bowl and all of the parts of a meat grinder in the freezer for 20 minutes. Put the lamb and fatback in a single layer on a rimmed baking sheet and freeze until very cold, about 20 minutes.

Grind the lamb and fatback on the medium die of the meat grinder into the cold bowl. Season with salt and pepper and stir to mix in the seasonings.

Tie the herb sprigs, peppercorns, coriander seeds, and garlic cloves in a cheesecloth bundle.

Heat a large, deep sauté pan over medium-high heat. When hot, add the oil, swirling to coat the pan. Add the meat mixture and let it cook undisturbed until the meat is deeply browned on the bottom, 3 to 4 minutes. Scrape up and stir the meat, continuing to cook until it is browned all over, another 2 to 3 minutes. Add the onion and carrot and cook, stirring occasionally, until the vegetables are lightly browned, 3 to 4 minutes. Pour in the wine and deglaze the pan, scraping up any browned bits on the pan bottom. Boil over high heat until the wine nearly evaporates, 5 to 6 minutes, then add the tomato puree and cheesecloth bundle. Turn down the heat to low, cover, and gently simmer the meat until it is extremely tender, 1½ to 2 hours. The *ragù* should be mostly meat with barely any liquid left in the pan. Taste it, adding salt and pepper until it tastes good to you. Use within 2 hours or cover and refrigerate in an airtight container for up to 3 days.

Have ready a bowl of ice water. Bring a small saucepan filled with water to a boil. Drop the peas into the boiling water and blanch them until they are bright green, about 30 seconds. Using a spider strainer or slotted spoon, immediately transfer the peas to the ice water to stop the cooking. Let the peas stand in the ice water until you are ready to use them.

Bring a large pot of salted water to a boil. Drop in the pasta and cover the pot to quickly return the water to a boil. Cook the pasta until it is tender but still a little chewy when bitten, 3 to 4 minutes.

Meanwhile, using a spider strainer or slotted spoon, transfer the blanched peas to the *ragù* and stir until heated through, 1 to 2 minutes.

Using the spider strainer or slotted spoon, drain the pasta by transferring it to the *ragù*. Reserve the pasta water. Add ½ cup (118 ml) of the pasta water and the butter to the pan and stir until the sauce reduces slightly, gets creamy, and coats the pasta, 1 to 2 minutes. Remove the pan from the heat and stir in ¼ cup (25 g) of the Parmesan. Keep the pasta moving until the cheese melts and the pasta and sauce become one thing in the pan. Taste it, adding salt and pepper until it tastes good to you.

Dish out the pasta onto warmed plates and garnish with the remaining Parmesan and the mint.

# SQUID INK LINGUINE WITH UNI AND CRAB

MAKES 3 OR 4 SERVINGS

*Uni* (sea urchin) has an incredible texture. It makes a creamy sauce and almost behaves like fat in a dish, even though it's actually pretty low in fat. But you have to be careful: as with fat, too much is not a good thing. Look for West Coast *uni*; it's bigger and creamier than East Coast *uni*.

PASTA SWAP Spaghetti or *bucatini* would be good, but keep it flavored with squid ink. The black pasta and orange sauce help make this dish what it is.

12 ounces (340 g) Squid Ink Semolina Dough (page 121)

Semolina, for dusting

16 pieces cleaned uni (about 10 oz/283 g or ¾ cup)

6 tablespoons (90 ml) olive oil

3 tablespoons (28 g) peeled and minced carrot

3 tablespoons (20 g) minced celery

3 tablespoons (32 g) minced yellow onion

3 ounces (85 g) jumbo lump crabmeat, picked over to remove any shells and cartilage

2 tablespoons (6 g) chopped fresh chives

1 tablespoon (15 ml) fresh lemon juice

Kosher salt and freshly ground black pepper

Fit your pasta extruder or stand-mixer attachment with the linguine plate. Set the extruder to medium speed; if using a stand-mixer attachment, feed the dough into the extruder in marble-size clumps, using a pushing tool to push the clumps through the extruder. The first few clumps may come out uneven; just throw them away. Continue gradually dropping marble-size clumps into the extruder and pushing them through, being careful not to overload it. As the pasta is extruded, cut it into 9-inch (23 cm) lengths and immediately dust it with semolina to prevent sticking.

Dry the pasta by placing it on wire racks that will fit in your refrigerator and refrigerate it uncovered for at least 8 hours or up to 4 days. The pasta will get drier and harder as it sits. The texture is perfect after 2 days in the refrigerator.

Bring a large pot of salted water to a boil. Drop in the linguine and cover the pot to quickly return the water to a boil. Cook until the pasta is tender yet firm, 4 to 5 minutes.

Meanwhile, mash the *uni* in a mortar with a pestle or process in a food processor until coarsely pureed. Heat the oil in a large, deep sauté pan over medium heat. When the oil is hot, add the carrot, celery, and onion and cook, stirring occasionally, for 30 seconds.

Using a spider strainer or slotted spoon, drain the pasta by transferring it to the pan. Reserve the pasta water. Add the *uni*, crabmeat, chives, lemon juice, and ½ cup (118 ml) of the pasta water to the pan and toss and stir until the sauce reduces slightly, gets creamy, and coats the pasta, 1 to 2 minutes. Keep the pasta moving until pasta and sauce become one thing in the pan. Taste it, adding salt and pepper until it tastes good to you.

Dish out the pasta onto warmed plates.

# WHOLE WHEAT SPAGHETTI WITH OLIVE OIL–BRAISED OCTOPUS

**MAKES 4 SERVINGS**

Stefano Arrigoni, the owner of Osteria della Brughiera restaurant in Villa d'Almè, near Bergamo, told me that the aroma of wheat goes great with octopus. I had to try it, and he was absolutely right. See for yourself. It's a simple dish, so every ingredient counts. Even the mineral water used to braise the octopus adds to the briny, mineral flavor.

PASTA SWAP Use any whole wheat pasta here, such as the Farro Semolina Dough (page 121) extruded into spaghetti or *bucatini*. Or use Whole Egg and Whole Wheat Dough (page 29) and cut it into fettuccine.

8 ounces (227 g) Whole Wheat Semolina Dough (page 121)

Semolina, for dusting

1½ pounds (680 g) octopus

Rock salt, for cleaning octopus

1 cup (237 ml) olive oil

½ cup (118 ml) sparkling mineral water, preferably San Pellegrino, or more if needed

1 small clove garlic, smashed

1 to 2 tablespoons (15 to 30 ml) fresh lemon juice

Kosher salt and freshly ground black pepper

Fit your pasta extruder or stand-mixer attachment with the spaghetti plate. Set the extruder to medium speed; if using a stand-mixer attachment, feed the dough into the extruder in marble-size clumps, using a pushing tool to push the clumps through the extruder. The first few clumps may come out uneven; just throw them away. Continue gradually dropping marble-size clumps into the extruder and pushing them through, being careful not to overload it. As the pasta is extruded, cut it into 9-inch (23 cm) lengths and immediately dust it with semolina to prevent sticking.

Dry the pasta by placing it on wire racks that will fit in your refrigerator and refrigerate it uncovered for at least 8 hours or up to 4 days. The pasta will get drier and harder as it sits. The texture is perfect after 2 days in the refrigerator.

To clean the octopus, insert your fingers into the body and turn it inside out. Scrape away and discard the ink sac and other innards and then rinse the body well. Turn the body right side out. Remove and discard the eyes and black mouth, or beak, located at the center where the tentacles meet the body. Scrub the tentacles very well with rock salt, rinse, and repeat until you are sure the tentacles are clean.

Scrubbing with salt also breaks down the muscle fibers a bit to make the octopus more tender.

Place the octopus in a pot just big enough to accommodate it. Add the oil, sparkling water, and garlic, adding a little more sparkling water if necessary to cover the octopus. Bring the liquid to 180°F (82°C) over medium-high heat, then lower the heat to maintain the temperature at a steady 180°F (82°C). Braise the octopus uncovered at 180°F (82°C) until it is tender, about 1½ hours.

Remove the pan from the heat and let the octopus cool in the liquid. Once it is cool, transfer the octopus to a cutting board and chop it into bite-size pieces. Reserve the braising liquid. To prepare the octopus ahead of time, leave it whole in the braising liquid and refrigerate it for up to 1 day, then chop it when you are ready to serve the pasta.

Bring a large pot of salted water to a boil. Drop in the spaghetti and cover the pot to quickly return the water to a boil. Cook the pasta until it is tender but still a little chewy when bitten, 4 to 5 minutes. Drain the pasta and reserve the pasta water.

Transfer the drained pasta to a large, deep sauté pan along with ¾ cup (177 ml) of the octopus braising liquid and ¼ cup (60 ml) of the pasta water. Place the pan over medium heat and stir in the chopped octopus and 1 tablespoon (15 ml) of the lemon juice. Toss until the sauce reduces slightly, gets creamy, and coats the pasta, 1 to 2 minutes. Add a little more braising liquid and/or pasta water if necessary to create a creamy sauce. Keep the pasta moving until pasta and sauce become one thing in the pan. Taste it, adding salt, pepper, and up to 1 tablespoon (15 ml) additional lemon juice until it tastes good to you.

Dish out the pasta onto warmed plates.

# RED WINE SPAGHETTI WITH CRUNCHY VEGETABLES AND ROQUEFORT

MAKES 4 SERVINGS

This dish is a like a cheese plate in a different form. You get red wine, pungent cheese, and crunchy quick-pickled vegetables all at once. For the vegetables, you can switch the carrots to parsnips or fennel. Or use whatever vegetables you like.

PASTA SWAP Red Wine Semolina Dough is a key flavor in this dish. But you could extrude the dough into linguine, fusilli, or rigatoni, if you like.

8 ounces (227 g) Red Wine Semolina Dough (page 121)

Semolina, for dusting

½ cup (118 ml) water

2 tablespoons (30 ml) white wine vinegar

2 tablespoons (25 g) sugar

½ teaspoon (1.5 g) kosher salt

½ small clove garlic, smashed

1 black peppercorn

½ cup (36 g) small cauliflower florets

½ cup (50 g) finely chopped celery

¼ cup (35 g) peeled and finely chopped carrot

2 tablespoons (21 g) finely chopped cipollini onion

2 ounces (57 g) Roquefort or Gorgonzola cheese, crumbled (about ½ cup)

3 ounces (85 g) speck or prosciutto, finely chopped

Kosher salt and freshly ground black pepper

Fit your pasta extruder or stand-mixer attachment with the spaghetti plate. Set the extruder to medium speed; if using a stand-mixer attachment, feed the dough into the extruder in marble-size clumps, using a pushing tool to push the clumps through the extruder. The first few clumps may come out uneven; just throw them away. Continue gradually dropping marble-size clumps into the extruder and pushing them through, being careful not to overload it. As the pasta is extruded, cut it into 9-inch (23 cm) lengths and immediately dust it with semolina to prevent sticking.

Dry the pasta by placing it on wire racks that will fit in your refrigerator and refrigerate it uncovered for at least 8 hours or up to 4 days. The pasta will get drier and harder as it sits. The texture is perfect after 2 days in the refrigerator.

Combine the water, vinegar, sugar, salt, garlic, and peppercorn in a small saucepan and bring to a boil. Put the cut vegetables into a small heatproof container and pour the hot vinegar mixture over them. Let the mixture cool to room temperature, then cover and refrigerate the vegetables for

at least 1 hour or up to 2 days. Let the vegetables come back to room temperature before serving, 15 to 20 minutes.

Bring a large pot of salted water to a boil. Drop in the spaghetti and cover the pot to quickly return the water to a boil. Cook until the pasta is tender but still a little chewy when bitten, 4 to 5 minutes. The pasta will lose some of its red color.

Using a spider strainer or slotted spoon, drain the pasta by transferring it to a large, deep sauté pan. Reserve the pasta water. Stir in the Roquefort, speck, and 1 cup (237 ml) of the pasta water. Toss until the sauce reduces slightly, gets creamy, and coats the pasta, 1 to 2 minutes. Keep the pasta moving until pasta and sauce become one thing in the pan. Taste it, adding salt and pepper until it tastes good to you.

Dish out the pasta onto warmed plates. Using a slotted spoon, top each serving with some of the crunchy vegetables, leaving behind the garlic, peppercorn, and pickling liquid.

# 8
—
# HAND-FORMED PASTA

**WHEN I MAKE PASTA AT HOME, I RARELY USE ANYTHING OTHER THAN A ROLLING PIN, A KNIFE, AND MY HANDS.** It's therapeutic to mix flour and water and feel the dough take shape between my palms. I roll out the dough until, little by little, it flattens and stretches into a thin sheet. When I step back and look at the sheet of pasta, I see a blank slate. My mind clears. The possibilities seem endless. It relaxes me and puts a smile on my face.

Many restaurant chefs in Italy believe that pasta should always be made this way—the old-school way. I'm not such a stickler for rules. I do believe in innovation and progress. Believe me, if I get forty orders of eight different pastas at the restaurant on a busy night, you won't find anything but state-of-the-art machinery at my side. But there is value in the old-school method.

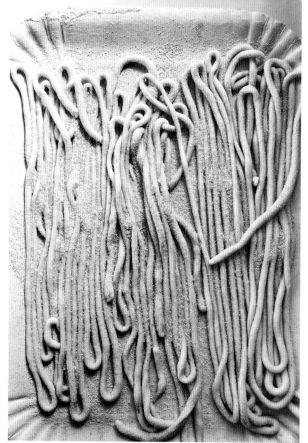

Making pasta by hand gives you a better feel for the dough. You learn what textures to look for and how to achieve them by adjusting the ingredients or kneading. Like everything else in cooking, you can always mechanize the process. But practicing preparations in their purest form is the best way to master technique. The cook who puts a rib-eye steak in a plastic bag and cooks it *sous vide* at a preset temperature has less knowledge and skill than one who works the grill, regulates the fire, manages hot spots, and rests the steak so that the meat appears as if it was cooked *sous vide* when you slice it. You may disagree, but there is culinary value in understanding what's behind the machines we use today and why they were manufactured in the first place.

At La Chiusa in Tuscany (see page 20), where I worked twenty years ago, the pasta chefs rolled *pici* by hand all day long. *Pici* resemble thick spaghetti, and when I visited recently, the pasta chef, Rosa, made it exactly the same way. She sifted flour into a bowl, mixed in a little oil and water,

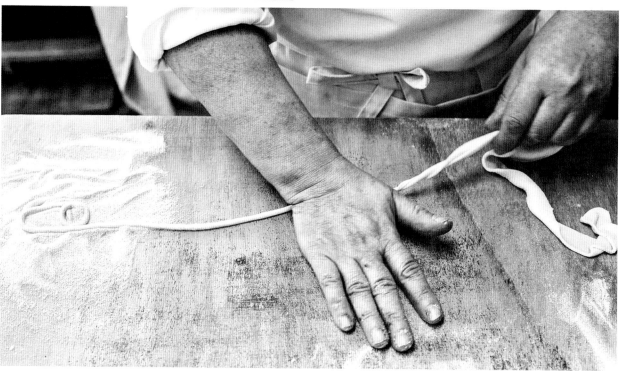

and stirred until the dough came together. She kneaded the raggy mass on a floured wooden board until it was smooth and supple like a baby's skin. Next, she rolled it into a circle with a metal pipe. "Why the metal?" I asked. "Sometimes I use wood," she said, "but the pipe is lighter." Then Rosa drizzled on some olive oil, spread it out with her hands, and cut the pasta dough into strips as wide as her thumb. She rolled the strips back and forth on the wood, constantly separating her palms and stretching the dough into thin ropes. Each rope got dusted in cornmeal, draped around her fingers, and laid to rest on a paper tray. When cooked, these noodles were so perfectly shaped yet looked so handmade on the plate. They were beautiful because of their imperfections—like a beautiful smile with a few crooked teeth. There is something special about that. Sure, the precision of high-quality spaghetti has its own appeal, but biting into the very handiwork of a skilled chef is a more profound experience.

As with *pici*, Italian cooks have left their fingerprints on all sorts of handmade pastas over the centuries. *Orecchiette* are a mixture of semolina and water that is pinched into pieces and shaped over a fingertip into "little ears." Sardinian *lorighittas* are strands of doubled-up fresh spaghetti twisted by hand into ring shapes known as *loriga*. And *strozzapreti*, "priest stranglers," are but little strips of dough rolled between palms to create a short rope-like shape—perhaps a wry reference to the gluttony of priests.

The stories behind these pasta shapes are half their charm. This chapter barely scratches the surface of the hundreds of Italian pastas you can make by hand. Some here are old-school, like *cavatelli* (see page 186) and *testaroli* (see page 197); others, such as dove pasta (see page 188), are original creations. None is very difficult to make. If you've read the other chapters in this book, you'll understand all the basics of making and handling these simple doughs. Even if you haven't, the recipes here include all of the necessary directions for turning out beautiful handmade pastas at home.

# PICI DOUGH

MAKES ABOUT 1 POUND (454 G)

This dough is similar to Egg Yolk and Bread Flour Dough (page 29) but without the egg. As Rosa at La Chiusa restaurant in Tuscany told me, "When no one had anything, the eggs were for the boss, not for the pasta." I turn this humble dough into equally humble Pici Aglio e Olio (page 181).

> 2¼ cups (310 g) bread flour (11.5 percent protein), plus more for dusting
>
> 1 tablespoon olive oil (15 ml)
>
> ¼ cup water (60 ml) or more if needed

Sift the flour into a bowl. Mix in the oil and water with a fork or spoon until the dough comes together. It will look raggy at first; continue adding water by the tablespoon (15 ml) until the dough can be gathered into a ball. You may need to add up to 4 tablespoons more water (¼ cup/60 ml), depending on the humidity in the room.

Turn out the dough onto a lightly floured work surface and knead it until it feels soft and smooth, about 3 minutes. Cover the dough and let it rest so it can relax, at least 5 minutes or up to 1 hour. Or wrap the dough in plastic wrap and refrigerate it for up to 3 days.

# ORECCHIETTE DOUGH

MAKES ABOUT 1 POUND (454 G)

For orecchiette, I use a semolina-and-water dough similar to Extruded Pasta Dough (page 120). Instead of extruding it, I add extra water to create a dough you can shape by hand. Try this shape in Orecchiette with Pig's Head Ragù and Black Walnuts (page 194).

2 cups (335 g) semolina
¾ cup (177 ml) water

Put the semolina in a bowl and slowly stir in the water. Knead the dough into a ball with your hands. It should be stiff but rollable. Shape the dough into a disk and set it aside, covered, for least 30 minutes, or wrap in plastic wrap and refrigerate for up to 3 days.

# CAVATELLI DOUGH

MAKES ABOUT 1¼ POUNDS (567 G)

A traditional pasta from Molise, *cavatelli* were also adopted by parts of Puglia, where they are called *capunti*. The dough sometimes includes ricotta cheese or potatoes, and it's formed into what looks like a little hot dog bun. You can form the shape by hand or with a small tabletop crank machine (see Sources, page 249). For *cavatelli* shaping directions, see Cavatelli alla Norma on page 186.

1 cup (227 g) ricotta impastata cheese (see page 241)
1¾ cups plus 2 tablespoons (284 g) tipo 00 flour, or 2¼ cups (284 g) all-purpose flour, plus more for dusting
2 eggs
⅛ teaspoon kosher salt

Stir together the ricotta, flour, eggs, and salt in a bowl. The mixture should come together as a mass of dough. Turn the dough out onto a lightly floured work surface and knead it until silky and smooth, about 5 minutes, kneading in a little flour if necessary to prevent sticking. Alternatively, you can combine the ingredients and knead the dough in a stand mixer fitted with the paddle attachment on medium speed for about 5 minutes. Depending on the humidity in the room, you may need to add more flour. The dough is ready if when you stretch it with your hands, it gently pulls back into place. Shape the dough into a disk, wrap it in plastic wrap, and refrigerate it for at least 30 minutes or up to 3 days.

## DOVE PASTA DOUGH

MAKES ABOUT 1 POUND (454 G)

Here is another semolina-and-water dough with a little salt for flavor. I like to cut this dough into shapes that resemble birds. Refer to the photographs of Dove Pasta with Quail Meatballs on page 188 to see what I mean.

2 cups plus 2 tablespoons (355 g) semolina
½ cup plus 2 tablespoons (148 ml) water
1 teaspoon (3 g) kosher salt

Combine the semolina, water, and salt in the bowl of a stand mixer fitted with the paddle attachment. Mix on medium speed for 7 minutes. Alternatively, combine the semolina, water, and salt in a bowl and stir with a wooden spoon for 8 minutes. The dough should resemble coarse streusel and feel fairly moist. On a work surface, gently knead the pieces of dough just until they can be gathered together into a smooth ball. Wrap the dough in plastic wrap and let it rest for 10 minutes or refrigerate it for up to 3 days.

## TESTAROLO BATTER

MAKES ABOUT 3½ CUPS (828 ML)

Some Italians consider *testarolo* to be the country's oldest pasta. It comes from the Lunigiana, an area partly in Tuscany and partly in Liguria, and is made from a loose batter seared in a hot pan, like a crepe. You cut the crepe into pieces, simmer the pieces, and serve them with a smooth sauce.

1 cup (125 g) durum flour
¾ cup (125 g) semolina
1 teaspoon (3 g) kosher salt
2⅔ cups (631 ml) water

Whisk together the durum flour, semolina, and salt in a bowl. Whisk in the water. The batter will be very thin, like crepe batter. Use the batter within 1 hour or refrigerate it in an airtight container for up to 2 days. Briefly whisk the batter again before using to recombine the ingredients.

# LORIGHITTAS WITH SEAFOOD

MAKES 4 SERVINGS

The island of Sardinia is home to dozens of unique handmade pastas with interesting shapes. This one comes from the town of Morgongiori and resembles a small rope shaped into a ring (*loriga* in Sardinian). It's usually served with simple tomato sauce or with a tomato and chicken *ragù*, but because the island is surrounded by such amazing seafood, I decided to serve it with scallops, squid, and *uni*. You can use whatever seafood is freshest (about 1½ pounds/680 grams total). You'll need a fine-mesh screen to dry the *lorighittas*. Any clean screen will do, or you can buy a pasta drying screen just for this purpose (see Sources, page 249).

PASTA SWAP Handmade farfalle would work, but this pasta is really about the shape of the *lorighittas*.

8 ounces (227 g) Lorighittas Semolina Dough (page 121)

8 baby squid (about 12 oz/340 g), cleaned and finely diced, or 1 pound (454 g) cuttlefish, cleaned and finely julienned

1 cup (237 ml) olive oil

¾ cup (126 g) finely diced yellow onion

4 sea scallops (about 4 oz/57 g), preferably unsoaked diver scallops, finely diced

16 pieces cleaned uni (about 10 oz/283 g or ¾ cup)

2½ tablespoons (37 ml) fresh lemon juice

2½ tablespoons (10 g) chopped fresh flat-leaf parsley

Kosher salt and freshly ground black pepper

To make the *lorighittas* completely by hand, divide the dough into a few pieces, roll the pieces on a long floured work surface into ropes about ¹⁄₁₆ inch (1.5 mm) in diameter, and then cut the ropes every 9 inches (23 cm) or so to make spaghetti. Or, to save time, fit your pasta extruder or stand-mixer attachment with the spaghetti plate. Set the extruder to medium speed; if using a stand-mixer attachment, feed the dough into the extruder in marble-size clumps, using a pushing tool to push the clumps through the extruder. The first few clumps may come out uneven; just throw them away. Continue gradually dropping marble-size clumps into the extruder and pushing them through, being careful not to overload it. As the pasta is extruded, cut it into 9-inch (23 cm) lengths and immediately dust it with flour to prevent sticking.

To form each *lorighitta* (see photos, page 180), flour your hands. Loosely wrap a piece of spaghetti twice around two fingers. The ends of the spaghetti should meet and there should be two rounds of spaghetti around your fingers. Now, remove your two fingers and pinch the two ends together. Gently roll the double rounds of spaghetti

together between your fingertips to create a rope shape reminiscent of laid, or twisted, rope; the finished pasta should look like the loop of a noose, with no extra rope. Lay the *lorighitta* on a fine-mesh drying screen and repeat with the remaining dough. Dust the *lorighittas* with flour and let them dry at room temperature (65°F to 75°F/18°C to 24°C) for at least 1 day or up to 2 days.

To clean each squid, pull away the head and tentacles from the hood (tube-like body), and then reach into the hood and pull out the entrails and the plastic-like quill, taking care not to puncture the pearly ink sac. Cut off the tentacles just above the eyes, and discard the head. Squeeze the base of the tentacles to force out the hard "beak," and rinse the tentacles and the hood under cold running water. Using the back of a paring knife or your fingers, pull and scrape off the gray membrane from the hood. Cut off and discard the 2 small wings on either side of the hoods. Chill the hoods and tentacles in ice water until ready to use. Then drain the squid, pat dry, and dice.

CONTINUED

If you don't have squid, you can use cuttlefish. The cleaning is similar. Grab the hard cuttlebone through the skin of the body and twist the bone to extract it through the skin. If the skin is tough, use a paring knife to make a small incision near the end of the body through which to extract the bone. Discard the bone. Work near a bowl of water so you can reserve the ink sacs. The ink sacs and entrails rest under the oval-shaped membrane you have just exposed. Work your fingers around the circumference of the oval-shaped membrane to separate the entire membrane (and the head and tentacles) from the rest of the body, taking care not to puncture the ink sacs inside. Squeeze the ink sacs into the bowl of water and reserve for another use (such as the risotto on page 234). Rinse the body under cold running water. Using the back of a paring knife or your fingers, pull and scrape off the dark membrane from the body. Finely julienne the body from top to bottom and set aside.

Bring a large pot of salted water to a boil. Drop in the *lorighittas* and cover the pot to quickly return the water to a boil. Cook the pasta until it is tender but still a little chewy when bitten, 10 to 12 minutes for 1-day-old pasta, 15 to 18 minutes for 2-day-old pasta.

Meanwhile, heat the oil in a large, deep sauté pan over medium heat. Add the onion and sweat it until it is soft but not browned, 3 to 4 minutes.

Using a spider strainer or slotted spoon, drain the pasta by transferring it to the pan. Reserve the pasta water. Add the squid, scallops, *uni*, lemon juice, and parsley to the pan. Toss until the liquid reduces slightly, gets somewhat creamy, and coats the pasta, 2 to 3 minutes, adding a little pasta water if necessary to create a creamy sauce. The seafood should be lightly cooked and no longer translucent. Keep the pasta moving until pasta and sauce become one thing in the pan. Taste it, adding salt and pepper until it tastes good to you.

Dish out the pasta onto warmed plates.

# PICI AGLIO E OLIO

**MAKES 4 SERVINGS**

*Pici* are like thick, hand-rolled spaghetti. The noodle is so thick, chewy, and delicious, you don't want to cover it up with much else. *Aglio e olio* (garlic and oil) is just right. I use garum—essentially Roman fish sauce, also known as *colatura di alici* or anchovy extract—to punch up the flavor. It has a complex umami character from the fermented fish. You can buy garum online from Buon Italia (see Sources, page 249), or substitute a good-quality Asian fish sauce like Three Crabs brand. As for a garnish, don't even consider it. This dish is about simplicity. Parmesan would be sacrilege!

**PASTA SWAP** You could roll the same dough into *strozzapreti*, but the method here is so unique, and the dough is really best for *pici*.

---

1 pound (454 g) Pici Dough (page 175)

1 cup plus 1 tablespoon (252 ml) extra-virgin olive oil

Semolina or cornmeal, for dusting

10 cloves garlic, cut into matchsticks

1 to 2 teaspoons (1.8 to 3.5 g) red pepper flakes

3 to 4 tablespoons (45 to 60 ml) garum or good-quality Asian fish sauce

1½ tablespoons (6 g) chopped mixed fresh herbs (parsley, oregano, and thyme are nice)

---

Roll out the dough on a lightly floured work surface about ⅛ inch (3 mm) thick and about 18 inches (46 cm) square. Rub the surface of the dough with about 1 tablespoon (15 ml) of the oil, coating it evenly. The oil enriches the dough and keeps it from drying out as you work.

Pour a pile of semolina or cornmeal near the corner of the work surface. Cut the dough square into strips ¾ to 1 inch (2 to 2.5 cm) wide. Starting at one end of a strip, use the heel of your palm to roll the strip gently back and forth on the work surface, stretching it lengthwise until it forms a rope about ¼ inch (6 mm) in diameter (see photo, page 174). If necessary, rub a little water on the work surface to help the rope stick and roll more easily. As you roll, set the shaped portion of the rope into the semolina or cornmeal pile to prevent it from sticking to itself. You should end up with a rope 5 to 6 feet (1.5 to 1.8 m) long in the pile of semolina or cornmeal. Pick up one end of the rope, drape it around a finger, and then continue to drape the entire rope around your fingers. Place the rope in parallel lines on a rimmed baking sheet dusted with semolina or cornmeal. Repeat with the remaining dough. Use the *pici* immediately or cover them and let them stand at room temperature for up to 2 hours. You can also freeze them in a single layer, transfer them to

a zipper-lock bag, and freeze them for up to 1 month. Take the pasta straight from the freezer to the boiling pasta water.

Bring a large pot of salted water to a boil. Drop in the *pici* and cover the pot to quickly return the water to a boil. Cook the pasta until it is tender but still a little chewy when bitten, 2 to 3 minutes.

Meanwhile, heat the remaining 1 cup (237 ml) oil in a large, deep sauté pan over medium heat. Add the garlic and cook it, stirring occasionally, until aromatic but not brown, 2 to 3 minutes. Remove the pan from the heat and stir in 1 teaspoon of the pepper flakes and 3 tablespoons of the garum.

Using tongs, drain the pasta by transferring it to the pan of sauce. Reserve the pasta water. Add 1¼ cups (296 ml) of the pasta water to the pan and stir vigorously over medium-high heat until the sauce reduces slightly, gets creamy, and coats the pasta, 2 to 3 minutes. Keep the pasta moving until pasta and sauce become one thing in the pan. Taste it, adding more pepper flakes and garum until it tastes good to you. Stir in the herbs.

Dish out the pasta onto warmed plates.

# PAGLIATA WITH SWEETBREADS

**MAKES 4 TO 6**
**SERVINGS**

If you find a very traditional trattoria in Rome, you might be lucky enough to try *pagliata*. It's a classic Roman preparation that calls for veal intestines that still have milk in them. You tie the ends closed, and then cook the intestines in tomato broth. They become very tender, and when you bite into them, the curdled milk squirts out. It is one of the greatest things that I have ever put into my mouth. You'll never find those innards in the United States, so I make the sauce with veal sweetbreads, milk, and tomato instead. I pair it with a pasta shape called *cappellacci dei briganti*, or "brigands' hats." This shape resembles the headgear of Italian outlaws who opposed the unification of Italy in the 1800s. It's a whimsical pairing of pasta and sauce. At the time that I developed the dish, we'd just gotten some new plates at the restaurant in the style of Victor Emmanuel, the first king of the newly united Italy. Only the finest of Roman pasta dishes could make the treaty between the brigands and the French-speaking king; hence, the *pagliata* with brigands' hats.

PASTA SWAP Rigatoni would actually be more traditional here.

---

12 ounces (340 g) Egg Yolk Dough (page 26), rolled into sheets about 1⁄16 inch (1.5 mm) thick

4 ounces (114 g) veal sweetbreads, preferably thymus

1 tablespoon (15 ml) olive oil

½ red onion, finely chopped

2 cloves garlic, smashed

¼ cup (60 g) whole canned San Marzano tomatoes

3 cups (710 ml) whole milk

Kosher salt and freshly ground black pepper

¼ cup (25 g) grated pecorino romano cheese

---

Lay a sheet of pasta on a lightly floured work surface. Using a round cutter 2 inches (5 cm) in diameter, cut the dough into rounds. To shape each piece of pasta (see photos, page 184), pick up a dough round and place it on your index finger so that your finger is about ½ inch (12 mm) from the top of the circle. Wrap the circle around your finger, overlapping one side of dough over the other, and pressing the fold gently against your finger so it stays put. Turn your finger so the seam is in the back. The pasta should look like a witch's hat with a slightly longer "brim" in the front. Fold that brim up onto the hat, gently pressing it against your finger so the front of the brim stays put against the tall part of the hat. Repeat the process with each dough round, placing the pieces on a floured rimmed baking sheet and dusting them with flour. Repeat with the remaining dough. You should have 60 to 70 pieces. Cover the pasta loosely and use it within 2 hours, or freeze it in a single layer, transfer it to an

airtight container, and freeze it for up to 1 month. Take the pasta straight from the freezer to the boiling pasta water.

Rinse the sweetbreads in cold water, then soak them in a bowl of ice water for 10 minutes. (Organs spoil easily, so it's important to keep the sweetbreads cold right up until you cook them.) Drain them, pat dry, and carefully remove the outer membrane and sinew. Slice the sweetbreads into strips 3 inches (7.5 cm) long.

Meanwhile, heat the oil in a large, deep sauté pan over medium heat. Add the onion and garlic and sweat them until they are soft but not browned, 4 to 5 minutes. Add the tomatoes, crushing them with your hand as you add them to the pan, and cook them, stirring occasionally, until they start to break down, about 5 minutes. Add the sweetbreads

CONTINUED

and milk and bring the mixture to just below a simmer. Turn the heat down to low and braise the mixture until the milk curdles and the sauce thickens, developing a consistency that resembles ricotta cheese, 30 to 40 minutes. Taste the sauce, adding salt and pepper until it tastes good to you.

Bring a large pot of salted water to a boil. Drop in the *cappellacci dei briganti* and cover the pot to quickly return the water to a boil. Cook the pasta until tender but still a little chewy when bitten, 2 to 3 minutes.

Using a spider strainer or slotted spoon, drain the pasta by transferring it to the sauce in the pan. Toss over medium heat until the sauce reduces slightly, reemulsifies and gets creamy, and coats the pasta, 1 to 2 minutes. Keep the pasta moving until pasta and sauce become one thing in the pan.

Dish out the pasta onto warmed plates and garnish with the pecorino.

# CAVATELLI ALLA NORMA

MAKES 6 SERVINGS

One of Sicily's most famous dishes, *pasta alla Norma* comes from Catania and includes some of the region's signature ingredients: eggplant, tomato, basil, and *ricotta salata*. Supposedly, a local playwright named Nino Martoglio loved the dish so much that he compared it to *Norma*, the famous opera by Vincenzo Bellini. The name stuck.

PASTA SWAP *Strozzapreti* (see page 199) would be a good substitute here.

1 pound (454 g) Cavatelli Dough (page 176)

1 cup (237 ml) extra-virgin olive oil

½ Spanish onion, finely chopped

4 pints (1.1 kg) grape tomatoes

Kosher salt and freshly ground black pepper

3 cups (710 ml) grapeseed or canola oil, for frying

1½ pounds (680 g) Japanese or other small eggplants (about 12 small eggplants), sliced into half-moons ¼ inch (6 mm) thick

2 red onions, halved and thinly sliced into half-moons

12 big, fresh basil leaves

2 tablespoons (8 g) chopped fresh flat-leaf parsley

¼ teaspoon (0.5 g) red pepper flakes

½ cup (50 g) grated Parmesan cheese

1 chunk ricotta salata cheese, for shaving

Cut the dough into 4 equal pieces and let them sit, covered, at room temperature for 5 to 10 minutes before rolling them out. Roll out according to the instructions for your *cavatelli* maker. For most tabletop models, you roll the dough into a rope to about ½-inch (13 cm) thickness, flatten it slightly, flour it well, and then feed it into the *cavatelli* maker. Secure the *cavatelli* maker to your work surface, then flour the dough and feed each sheet into it. Dust the *cavatelli* with flour and use immediately. You can also freeze them in an airtight container for up to 1 month. Take the *cavatelli* straight from the freezer to the boiling pasta water.

Heat the olive oil in a large, deep sauté pan over medium-low heat. Add the Spanish onion and sweat it, stirring occasionally, until it is soft but not browned, 8 to 10 minutes. Add the tomatoes and season them aggressively with salt. Cook the tomatoes slowly until they break down but remain chunky, about 1 hour, gently mashing them once they start to soften. Stir the sauce to emulsify the tomatoes and oil, and then taste the sauce, adding salt and pepper until it tastes good to you. Use the sauce within 3 hours, or transfer it to an airtight container and refrigerate it for up to 2 days or freeze it for up to 1 month.

Heat the grapeseed oil in a large saucepan or deep sauté pan over medium-high heat until it starts to smoke. Working in batches if necessary to prevent crowding, add the eggplant slices and fry, stirring to cook them evenly, until they are golden brown, 3 to 4 minutes. Using a slotted spoon, transfer the fried eggplant to paper towels to drain.

Turn down the heat to medium, add the red onions to the oil remaining in the pan and cook, stirring now and then, until nicely caramelized, 8 to 10 minutes. Drain off the excess oil (it can be cooled and reused for other frying), and then stir the eggplant back into the pan. Taste the mixture, adding salt and pepper until it tastes good to you. Use immediately or refrigerate the mixture in an airtight container for up to 8 hours.

Bring a large pot of salted water to a boil. Drop in the *cavatelli* and cover the pot to quickly return the water to a boil. Cook the pasta until it is tender but still a little chewy when bitten, 2 to 3 minutes.

Meanwhile, add the eggplant mixture to the pan of tomato sauce and warm the mixture over medium heat. Using a spider strainer or slotted spoon, drain the *cavatelli* by

transferring them to the sauce in the pan. Reserve the pasta water. Add 1½ cups (355 ml) of the pasta water, raise the heat to medium-high, and toss until the sauce reduces slightly, gets creamy, and coats the pasta, 1 to 2 minutes. Add a little more oil or pasta water if necessary to create a creamy sauce. Remove the pan from the heat and stir in the basil, parsley, and pepper flakes. Keep the pasta moving until pasta and sauce become one thing in the pan.

Dish out the pasta onto warmed plates and shave *ricotta salata* over each serving.

# DOVE PASTA WITH QUAIL MEATBALLS

**MAKES 6 SERVINGS**

This light first course combines meatballs and pasta in broth. If you don't want to make the quail stock, you can use a mix of chicken stock (page 242) and duck stock (page 242). And if you cannot find *bagoss* cheese, *Bitto* works well. You could even use Parmesan. You'll need a fine-mesh drying screen to make this pasta (see Sources, page 249).

4 ounces (112 g) Dove Pasta Dough (page 177), rolled into sheets between ⅛ inch and 1/16 inch (3 mm and 1.5 mm) thick

QUAIL MEATBALLS

1¼ pounds (567 g) whole semiboneless quail (about 4)

4½ ounces (128 g) pork fatback, cut into 1-inch (2.5 cm) pieces

2 cups (200 g) grated Parmesan cheese

1 cup (110 g) plain dried bread crumbs

3 eggs

1 teaspoon (3 g) kosher salt

½ teaspoon (1 g) freshly ground black pepper

2½ cups (591 ml) quail stock (page 242)

Tipo 00 or all-purpose flour, for dusting meatballs

1 ripe plum, halved, pitted, and cut into very thin half-moons (18 to 24 slices)

1 ripe apricot, halved, pitted, and cut into very thin half-moon slices (18 to 24 slices)

1 cup (114 g) grated bagoss, Bitto, or Parmesan cheese

8 fresh mint leaves, cut into chiffonade

Lay a pasta sheet on a lightly floured surface and trim the edges square. Cut the pasta into 2-inch (5 cm) squares with a crimp-cut cutter (the cuts should look square rather than like a zigzag). Stack about 5 squares at a time and use a sharp knife to cut the stack in half on the diagonal to make stacks of triangles. Use the tip of the knife to cut out a ½-inch (12 mm) triangular notch on each crimp-cut side about ½ inch (12 mm) away from the right angle of the triangle. The result should resemble a flat bird with wings on either side. To make the shape three-dimensional, pick up a piece and lightly spritz it with water. Then, pinch the longest side—the straight-cut side—of the triangle at the center to fold in the two sides, sort of like making a paper airplane, to bring the "wings" of the dove shape closer together. When doing this, pinch together only about ½ inch (12 mm) of the dough just at the longest side to make the body of the dove, leaving the rest of the triangle flat (the wings). Invert the dove pasta onto a flat pasta drying screen so that the pinched side is pointing up. Repeat with the remaining dough. You should have about 50 pieces of dove pasta. Dry the pasta on the screen at room temperature (about 70°F/21°C) for 2 days.

To make the meatballs, remove the bones from the quail and reserve them for making quail stock. You should have about 1 pound (454 g) quail meat and skin. Put the fatback and the quail in a single layer on a rimmed baking sheet and freeze until partially frozen, about 30 minutes. Put a stand-mixer bowl and paddle attachment and all the parts of a meat grinder in the freezer for 20 minutes.

Grind the cold quail (skin and meat) and fatback on the small die of the meat grinder into the cold bowl. If you don't have a meat grinder, you can grind them in a food processor, using short pulses until very finely chopped but not pureed. Fit the mixer with the cold paddle attachment, add the Parmesan, bread crumbs, eggs, salt, and pepper to the bowl, and mix on medium-low speed until blended.

Pinch off 1-inch (2.5 cm) pieces of the quail mixture and gently roll them between your palms into 1-inch (2.5 cm) balls. You should have about 35 meatballs. Use them within 1 hour or refrigerate them in an airtight container for up to 1 day.

Bring a large pot of salted water to boil. Drop in the pasta and cover the pot to return the water quickly to a boil. Uncover the pot partially and cook the pasta until tender yet firm, about 3 minutes.

Meanwhile, heat the stock in a saucepan over medium heat. Put the flour in a bowl and, working in small batches, roll the meatballs in the flour, patting off the excess. Add the meatballs to the stock and bring the liquid to a simmer. Simmer the meatballs until they reach an internal temperature of 160°F (71°C), 1 to 2 minutes.

Place 3 or 4 plum slices and 3 or 4 apricot slices in each of 6 warmed shallow bowls. Ladle 5 or 6 meatballs and between ⅓ and ½ cup (78 to 118 ml) of the stock into each bowl. Using a spider strainer or slotted spoon, drain the pasta by transferring it to the bowls, placing 7 or 8 pieces into each bowl. Garnish with the cheese and mint.

# CHITARRA WITH VEAL SHIN RAGÙ

**MAKES 6 SERVINGS**

This long, square strand pasta is named *chitarra* (Italian for "guitar") because it's cut on a pasta-cutting tool called a *chitarra* that has metal strings resembling guitar strings. At Vetri, we make this *ragù* with whole veal shins or shanks weighing 5 to 6 pounds (2.3 to 2.7 kg) each. But you can use shanks that have been cut every 2 to 3 inches (5 to 7.5 cm) across the bone, known as osso buco cut, which are much easier to find. If you like, add some other aromatics to the braise, such as bay leaf, garlic, or herbs like thyme or rosemary. Sometimes I soften up a long strip of lemon zest in hot water, then twist it over the top as a garnish.

**PASTA SWAP** *Pici, bucatini,* and spaghetti all work great here.

---

5 pounds (2.3 kg) veal shins or shanks, trimmed of excess fat and membrane

Kosher salt and freshly ground black pepper

Tipo 00 flour or all-purpose flour, for dusting veal shins

2 tablespoons (30 ml) grapeseed or canola oil

1 yellow onion, coarsely chopped

2 carrots, peeled and coarsely chopped

2 celery stalks, coarsely chopped

1 pound (454 g) Whole Egg and Semolina Dough (page 29), rolled into sheets about ⅛ inch (3 mm) thick

½ cup (114 g) unsalted butter

2 tablespoons (8 g) chopped fresh flat-leaf parsley

1 cup (112 g) grated pecorino al tartufo cheese (truffle pecorino)

1½ teaspoons (3 g) grated lemon zest

---

Heat the oven to 200°F (95°C). Season the shins all over with salt and pepper and then dust them with the flour, shaking off the excess. Heat the oil in a Dutch oven over medium-high heat. When the oil is hot, working in batches to prevent crowding, add the shins and cook them, turning them now and then, until they are deeply browned all over, 8 to 10 minutes. Transfer the shins to a plate.

Turn down the heat to medium and add the onion, carrots, and celery. Cook, stirring occasionally, until the vegetables are nicely browned and caramelized, 5 to 7 minutes. Return the shins to the pan, then add water to come about two-thirds of the way up the sides of the shins. Cover the pan and braise in the oven until the meat pulls easily off the bone, 12 to 14 hours.

Remove the pan from the oven and let the mixture cool in the pan. When cool enough to handle, remove the shins and pull off the meat from the bones, discarding the bones and any fat and gristle. Be vigilant. There will be tendons and pockets of chewy stuff that you want to discard. Shred the meat and set it aside. Pass the liquid and vegetables through a food mill fitted with the large die into a large, deep sauté pan, or pulse them briefly in a food processor just until the vegetables are finely chopped but not pureed, then transfer to a large, deep sauté pan. If the *ragù* mixture looks thin and watery, place the pan over high heat and boil it until it is the consistency of tomato sauce. Return the meat to the *ragù* and then taste the mixture, adding salt and pepper until it tastes good to you. You should have about 4 cups (946 ml) *ragù*. Use the *ragù* within a few hours or transfer it to an airtight container and refrigerate it for up to 3 days or freeze it for up to 2 months.

Lay a pasta sheet on a lightly floured work surface. Generously dust the sheet with flour, and then cut the sheet into pieces the length and width of your *chitarra*. Lay a piece lengthwise on the strings of the *chitarra* and roll a floured rolling pin back and forth over the pasta to press it into the strings (see photos, page 192). If the pasta doesn't cut all

CONTINUED

the way through, help it along by strumming your fingers across the strings like playing a guitar. Generously dust the noodles with flour and coil them into nests on a floured rimmed baking sheet. Cover and use within a few hours or refrigerate for up to 8 hours.

Bring a large pot of salted water to a boil. Drop in the pasta and cover the pot to quickly return the water to a boil. Cook the pasta until it is tender but still a little chewy when bitten, 1 to 2 minutes.

Meanwhile, heat 3 cups (710 ml) of the *ragù* in a large, deep sauté pan over medium heat. Reserve any remaining *ragù* for another use. Using tongs, drain the pasta by transferring it to the pan of *ragù*. Reserve the pasta water. Add the butter, parsley, and ½ cup (118 ml) of the pasta water and toss until the sauce reduces slightly, gets creamy, and coats the pasta, 1 to 2 minutes. Remove the pan from the heat and stir in ½ cup (56 g) of the pecorino and the lemon zest. Keep the pasta moving until pasta and sauce become one thing in the pan. Taste it, adding salt and pepper until it tastes good to you.

Dish out the pasta onto warmed plates and garnish with the remaining pecorino.

# TESTAROLO WITH PISTACHIO PESTO

MAKES 4 SERVINGS

Unlike other pastas, this one starts with a loose batter and is cooked like a crepe. The pancake gets deep brown and crisp on one side and is riddled with holes on the other. It is then cut into diamond shapes, put briefly into hot water, and then tossed with a smooth sauce. The dish originates in the Lunigiana, historical area that falls in both Tuscany and Liguria. The locals once cooked the crepes in glazed terra-cotta dishes (a *testo* in Italian) but now use giant cast-iron pans over a blazing-hot wood fire. I've tried it both ways and, whether you heat a cast-iron pan on the stove top or a terra-cotta dish in a hot oven, both work well.

PASTA SWAP Nothing compares with this pasta. It's irreplaceable.

3½ cups Testarolo Batter (page 177)

1 cup (150 g) shelled and peeled pistachios, preferably Sicilian

½ cup (118 ml) extra-virgin olive oil

Kosher salt and freshly ground black pepper

3 tablespoons (28 g) pine nuts

1 tablespoon (6 g) grated orange zest

½ cup (57 g) soft fresh goat cheese, crumbled

Heat a 10- or 12-inch (25 or 30 cm) round, heavy skillet (such as cast iron) over high heat. Let the skillet heat up until it is blisteringly hot, at least 15 minutes or up to 30 minutes.

When the pan is ready, measure about ¾ cup (177 ml) of the batter for a 10-inch (25 cm) pan or 1 cup (237 ml) of the batter for a 12-inch (30 cm) pan. Pour the batter into the hot pan, starting at the perimeter of the pan and moving gradually inward in a circular motion so the batter completely covers the pan bottom in an even layer. The batter should immediately blister and form bubble holes. Cook uncovered for 30 seconds. Then, turn down the heat to medium and cover the pan to partially steam the *testarolo*. Cook until the bottom is deeply browned and the *testarolo* starts to puff up and release itself from the pan, about 1½ minutes more. Scrape the *testarolo* out of the pan like a crepe and transfer it to a cooling rack.

Repeat with the remaining batter, letting the pan reheat over high heat for at least 5 minutes between each *testarolo*. You should have 4 *testaroli*, and you might have a little left over, depending on the size of your pan. When each *testarolo* is cool, cut it into 8 diamond shapes. The easy way to do this is to first cut the circle into eighths as if you are cutting a

CONTINUED

pizza. Then go around the outside of the circle and cut diamond shapes by notching out 8 triangles from the perimeter. Snack on those triangles or serve them separately. Alternatively, you can cut the circle into strips 2 inches (5 cm) wide, then cut the strips crosswise on an angle to create diamond shapes (lozenges). Use the pieces within 1 hour or freeze them in a single layer on a floured rimmed baking sheet, transfer them to a zipper-lock plastic bag, and freeze them for up to 1 month.

Grind the pistachios and oil in a food processor until the nuts are very finely chopped but not completely pureed, 1 to 2 minutes. Taste the mixture, adding salt and pepper until it tastes good to you. You should have about 1 cup (237 ml).

Bring a large pot of salted water to a boil. Drop in the *testarolo* pieces and cook them for 15 seconds, just to reheat and slightly hydrate them. Avoid overcooking them or they will turn to mush.

Meanwhile, toast the pine nuts in a large, deep sauté pan over medium heat, shaking the pan now and then, until they are lightly browned, 3 to 4 minutes. Transfer the pine nuts to a plate. Pour the pistachio pesto into the pan and gently heat it over medium heat. Using tongs, a spider strainer, or a slotted spoon, drain the *testarolo* pieces by transferring them to the pan of pesto. Toss them gently until well coated, 1 minute.

Dish out the *testarolo* pieces, browned side up, onto warmed plates and arrange them in a star or other attractive pattern. Drizzle on some of the pesto, and then garnish with the pine nuts, orange zest, and goat cheese.

# STROZZAPRETI WITH GREEN TOMATOES AND RAZOR CLAMS

MAKES 3 OR 4
SERVINGS

Always made by hand, *strozzapreti* (priest stranglers) are little strips of dough rolled between your palms. Each strip has a groove along its length that helps the pasta hold onto the sauce. Meaty green tomatoes bring the perfect texture and acidity to this recipe. If you use sweeter red tomatoes, add a little lemon juice to replicate that acid. And if you don't have razor clams, use another shellfish, like oysters, for a similar effect.

PASTA SWAP I've made this dish with *bucatini*, spaghetti, and *chitarra* and all three work great.

8 ounces (227 g) Pici Dough (page 175) or Culurgione Dough (page 29), rolled into sheets between ⅛ inch and ⅟₁₆ inch (3 mm and 1.5 mm) thick

4 large green tomatoes

6 tablespoons (90 ml) extra-virgin olive oil, plus some for drizzling

1 shallot, finely chopped

1 small clove garlic, smashed

5 razor clams

Kosher salt

¼ cup (16 g) chopped fresh flat-leaf parsley

Lay a pasta sheet on a floured work surface and cut it into strips ½ inch to ¾ inch (12 mm to 2 cm) wide. To form each *strozzapreto*, rest a strip in your palms and roll it between your palms to create a rough shape resembling a drill bit. Pinch off the spiraled portion in 2½- to 3-inch (6 to 7.5 cm) lengths and place them on a floured rimmed baking sheet. Repeat with the remaining dough. You should have about 75 pieces. Dust them with flour, cover loosely, and use within 4 hours or refrigerate for up to 8 hours. You can also freeze them in a single layer, transfer to a zipper-lock bag, and freeze for up to 1 month. Take the pasta straight from the freezer to the boiling pasta water.

Have ready a bowl of ice water. Bring a pot of water to a boil. Using a small, sharp knife, score an X on the bottom of each tomato, then drop the tomatoes into the boiling water and blanch them until the skins begin to split and curl back from the X, 30 to 60 seconds. Using a slotted spoon, transfer the tomatoes to the ice water and let cool a minute or two. Starting at the X, peel the skin from each tomato and discard it. Dice the tomatoes.

Heat ¼ cup (60 ml) of the oil in a large, deep sauté pan over medium heat. Add the shallot and garlic and sweat them until they are soft but not browned, 3 to 4 minutes. Remove

and discard the garlic. Add the diced tomatoes and cook them, stirring now and then to keep them from browning, until they are soft, 8 to 10 minutes. Turn down the heat to low and keep the sauce warm.

Meanwhile, shuck the razor clams and remove the meats from the shells. Rinse the clams and cut them into small pieces the size of coffee beans. Toss the clams in the remaining 2 tablespoons (30 ml) oil and season them with salt.

Bring a large pot of salted water to a boil. Drop in the *strozzapreti* and cover the pot to quickly return the water to a boil. Cook the pasta until it is tender but still a little chewy when bitten, 4 to 6 minutes.

Using a spider strainer or slotted spoon, drain the pasta by transferring it to the sauce. Reserve the pasta water. Add the clam mixture, parsley, and 1 cup (240 ml) of the pasta water and toss over medium-high heat until the sauce reduces slightly, gets creamy, and coats the pasta, 2 to 3 minutes. Keep the pasta moving until pasta and sauce become one thing in the pan. Taste it, adding salt until it tastes good to you.

Dish out the pasta onto warmed plates.

# 9

---

# GNOCCHI

---

*Ridi, ridi! Che la mamma ha fatto gli gnocchi!*
Smile, smile! Mom made gnocchi!
**— ITALIAN PROVERB**

**ANYTIME YOU COME ACROSS A PROVERB ABOUT FOOD, YOU KNOW THAT FOOD IS SOMETHING SPECIAL.** To Italians, gnocchi are special. Gnocchi could be as important to Italians as turkey is to Americans on Thanksgiving. Romans often eat gnocchi on Thursday, Ligurians enjoy it on Saturday, and in Campania, gnocchi are served on Sunday. In Campania, gnocchi are baked in the oven with sauce and mozzarella cheese (*gnocchi alla sorrentina*), while in Rome they are made with semolina and baked with butter and Parmesan (*gnocchi all romana*). Each region of Italy has its own gnocchi style and traditions. Those traditions are one of the things I love most about Italians. Their love of food isn't just about eating; it's imbued with history that breathes life into the very food itself. I know that if someone from Rome had Sunday dinner at someone's house in Campania and gnocchi were served, the Roman would tell everyone back home how crazy it was. Gnocchi on Sunday instead of Thursday. Unbelievable!

The history of gnocchi actually parallels the history of pasta. After all, gnocchi dough isn't all that different from pasta dough; it's just shaped into gnocchi (dumplings) instead. According to pasta historian Oretta Zanini De Vita, "The *gnocco* is the ancestor of almost all the Italian pastas." In her brilliant *Encyclopedia of Pasta*, she goes on to name dozens of its pasta descendants, including *cavatelli*, *orecchiette*, and *strozzapreti*. It makes sense. Just like pasta, the earliest gnocchi were made with only flour and water. Potatoes didn't come until much later. Sure, it may be the most popular vegetable for gnocchi now, but there's a whole world of gnocchi outside of the potato. You can make dumplings with all kinds of different flours and breads, pureed vegetables, and cheeses.

No matter what type of gnocchi you make, texture and flavor are still the two most important things to consider when making them. Not enough flour and you'll create soup when the dumplings go into the water. Too much flour—or too much kneading—and you'll make the ever popular "asshole stoppers," as they were lovingly called years ago in South Philly. But with the right amount of flour, maybe a little egg, and a gentle touch, gnocchi can taste like tender puffs of flavor that seem to float from the fork to your mouth.

Don't discount the importance of flavor. In a dish of pasta, a lot of the flavor comes from the sauce. But with gnocchi, flavor comes mostly from the dumplings themselves. The vegetable (or the cheese) should be the star of the show. If you add a sauce, think of it only as a final flourish that serves to bring out the flavors already in the gnocchi. To illustrate the point, take a bite of watermelon. Now, sprinkle a little coarse salt on the watermelon and taste it again. The salt serves only to heighten the flavor of the watermelon without covering it up. This is what sauce should do for gnocchi.

## WORKING WITH POTATOES

From waxy to starchy, I've tried every potato out there for gnocchi. Sometimes I use yellow potatoes, but I like russet (Idaho) potatoes best. They have the most starch and the least moisture. That's critical because excess moisture makes for gummy-textured gnocchi. If you have a lot of liquid in the dough, you have to add more flour to soak up the liquid, and when you mix the flour in, you develop gluten that makes the gnocchi gummy and heavy.

When I make gnocchi, I limit moisture in all steps of the process. I cook potatoes with the skins on to reduce the amount of water they absorb. It doesn't matter whether you boil, steam, or bake them. Leave the skins on. It also helps if you rice the potatoes while they're still hot. You don't have a potato ricer? Get one. They're cheap and it's the best tool for making potato puree. A food mill fitted with the fine die (plate) also works. Either way, rice the potatoes while they're still hot to allow excess steam to escape. If you let the cooked potatoes sit with the skins on, the moisture that would otherwise be released as steam will be reabsorbed into the potato starch, and then you're back to gummy gnocchi. It's best to rice the potatoes onto a wooden board and spread them out so even more moisture can evaporate. The drier the potato, the lighter the gnocchi.

Just don't let the potatoes sit there for too long. Warm potatoes mix more easily and quickly into the dough. If the potatoes are cold, you have to mix more rapidly, which then develops gluten in the flour and toughens the gnocchi. Here's how I like to do it: After the potatoes stop steaming but are still warm, I scatter the flour, Parmesan, beaten egg, and seasonings over the top. Then I scrape everything together with a bench scraper, cutting in the ingredients. The bench scraper minimizes stirring.

## WORKING WITH OTHER VEGETABLES

I love surprising people by making gnocchi out of anything but potatoes. Spinach, squash, cabbage—they all taste great. Just keep in mind that the preparation may be a little different. Like I said, russet potatoes are relatively high in starch and low in water (about 20 percent starch and 75 percent water). Other vegetables may be the opposite. Winter squash has about 8 percent starch and 88 percent water, and spinach has only 4 percent starch but 91 percent water. Just as with potatoes, you want to get rid of that excess moisture to ensure light-tasting gnocchi. To do that, I cook the vegetable first, then puree it and either drain away or cook out the excess liquid.

## CHOOSING FLOUR

You'll come across gnocchi recipes made with all kinds of flour, but I always use double-zero flour. It is very finely milled, which means it distributes evenly throughout the dough, creating a smooth-textured dumpling. You can use all-purpose flour, but the gnocchi won't be quite as silky because all-purpose flour is more coarsely ground. Look for finely milled flour with about 9 percent protein.

Always mix in the flour gently. The flour is only there to hold together the vegetable puree. If you overwork the gluten, it will make your gnocchi taste tough instead of tender. Get your hands in there and feel the dough as you mix or knead. If the dough feels stiff when you're mixing it, the gnocchi will taste stiff when cooked. Stop mixing or kneading the moment the dough holds together and still feels somewhat tender.

## SHAPING GNOCCHI

You can shape gnocchi several different ways. Sometimes I roll the dough into ropes and cut the ropes into little pillows. Other times I pipe balls of dough into a bowl of flour, and still other times I make football shapes (quenelles) using two spoons. It all depends on the firmness of the dough and the shape I want to make. Potato gnocchi tend to be firm enough to roll into ropes. That's the method I use for Potato Gnocchi with Corn Crema and Corn Salad (page 206) and for Baccalà Gnocchi with Squid Salad (page 213). To make a dimple in that shape of gnocchi, you just put a finger into each one, or you roll them on a grooved wooden gnocchi board or along the tines on the back of a fork. Some people say the dimple helps the gnocchi cook evenly. I say it acts like a spoon and helps the dumpling pick up some extra sauce!

Of course, round and oval gnocchi have no dimples or grooves, but that's fine. If you want a round shape and the dough is firm enough, you can just roll it into balls between your palms like cookie dough. If the dough is loose and delicate, spoon it or pipe it into dollops into a bowl of flour, and then roll the dollops into balls in the flour. That's how I shape my spinach gnocchi and the squash gnocchi on page 211.

## BOILING AND SAUCING

Boiling gnocchi is similar to boiling pasta. You can use the same amount of water and salt—about 5 quarts (5 L) water and 2 tablespoons (18 g) kosher salt per 1 pound (454 g) of dough. But gnocchi are more delicate than noodles, so go for a low boil rather than a rolling boil. Sometimes they'll float, sometimes they won't. The cooking time depends on the type of gnocchi you're making. They're all a little different, so I usually boil a single dumpling first and time the boiling, then I set a timer and cook the rest of the gnocchi for that amount of time. It could take anywhere from 2 to 5 minutes, depending on the gnocchi and even the humidity and temperature of the room you're working in. You're looking for a somewhat springy texture in the cooked gnocchi. As the starch in the dumpling absorbs water, it swells and softens, or gelatinizes, and has a springy, almost jelly-like texture. To see if the starch is gelatinized, squeeze a dumpling between your fingers. It should have some bounce-back. If it just flattens out, boil the gnocchi a little longer.

With most pasta, you put the drained noodles in a pan of sauce and stir them together to marry pasta and sauce. But gnocchi often go straight from the water to the plate. Then you spoon some sauce over the top. If you are going to sauté or bake the gnocchi after boiling them, it's best to shock them in ice water as soon as they come out of the boiling water to stop the cooking. If the gnocchi are made correctly, they will be tender, so use a spider strainer or slotted spoon to drain them.

If you're new to gnocchi, try making the potato gnocchi on page 206 first. You can serve these basic dumplings with nothing more than butter and cheese. They are a great place to start. But be adventurous, too. Dumplings are simple, so there's no reason not to explore. Try broiled Cabbage Gnocchi with Sausage and Toasted Bread Crumbs (page 216) or creamy Goat Cheese Gnocchi with Prosciutto Crisps (page 218). Either way, smile, because you've made gnocchi!

# CHESTNUT GNOCCHI WITH PORCINI RAGÙ

MAKES 6 TO 8
SERVINGS

There's no egg in these dumplings, so they're very delicate. That means you have to be extra careful when you cook them. Keep them at a gentle simmer instead of a vigorous or even low boil, so they don't fall apart. You'll be rewarded with a superlight texture and just a hint of sweet chestnut. Of course, you could use an egg instead of the oil, but I prefer the taste without the egg. And if you can't find fresh porcini, use whole chanterelle mushrooms.

1 pound (454 g) yellow or gold potatoes, such as Yellow Finn or Yukon Gold potatoes

1 cup (106 g) chestnut flour, sifted

½ cup (76 g) tipo 00 flour, or ½ cup plus 2 tablespoons (76 g) all-purpose flour, plus some for dusting

3 tablespoons (45 ml) olive oil

⅛ teaspoon (0.3 g) freshly grated nutmeg

Kosher salt and freshly ground black pepper

½ red onion, minced

1 clove garlic, smashed

4 thyme sprigs

1½ pounds (680 g) porcini mushrooms, sliced if large

2 tablespoons (30 ml) dry white wine

2 cups (473 ml) chicken stock (page 242)

¼ cup (25 g) grated Parmesan cheese

Combine the potatoes (unpeeled) and salted water to cover by 1 inch (2.5 cm) in a saucepan. Cover, bring the water to a boil over high heat, and boil until a knife slides easily in and out of the potatoes, 20 to 25 minutes.

Remove the pan from the heat and transfer the potatoes to a cutting board. Immediately peel off and discard the skins. Wear gloves if the potatoes feel too hot to handle. Coarsely chop the potatoes, and then pass them through a potato ricer or a food mill fitted with the fine die onto a large, lightly floured cutting board or smooth work surface, covering the board or surface with the potatoes. (Spreading out the potatoes helps to evaporate excess moisture.) Sprinkle both flours, 1 tablespoon (15 ml) of the oil, and the nutmeg evenly over the potatoes. Season with about ½ teaspoon (1.5 g) salt and ¼ teaspoon (0.5 g) pepper. Using a bench scraper, cut the layered ingredients into the potatoes, repeatedly scraping, cutting, and mixing until the dough comes together.

Gently knead the dough just until it has a uniform consistency, 1 to 2 minutes. Be careful not to overwork the dough or it will develop excess gluten, which will make the gnocchi tough. Flour the bench scraper or a knife and cut the dough in half. Roll each half on the floured surface

into a long rope about ½ inch (12 mm) in diameter. Use the floured bench scraper or knife to cut the rope crosswise into ½-inch (12 mm) pieces. Gently roll a cut side of each piece on a lightly floured grooved gnocchi board (or on a clean comb or the tines of a fork) to notch the exterior and create an oval shape. As the gnocchi are formed, transfer them to a generously floured rimmed baking sheet and shake the sheet pan to dust the gnocchi with the flour. You should have about 175 gnocchi.

Use the gnocchi within 1 hour or cover them loosely and refrigerate them for up to 8 hours. You can also freeze the gnocchi in a single layer, transfer them to a zipper-lock bag, and freeze them for up to 2 weeks. Take the gnocchi straight from the freezer to the boiling water, adding 30 seconds or so to the cooking time.

Have ready a bowl of ice water. Bring a large pot of salted water to a boil. Drop the gnocchi into the boiling water and cover the pot to quickly return the water to a low boil. Adjust the heat so that the water simmers, stirring gently. Cook the gnocchi until springy to the touch and tender

CONTINUED

throughout, 3 to 5 minutes. Squeeze a dumpling between your fingers. It should have some bounce-back. If it just flattens, the gnocchi are not done yet. Using a spider strainer or slotted spoon, immediately transfer the gnocchi to the ice water and let them sit in the water for 30 seconds to stop the cooking. Transfer the gnocchi to dry kitchen towels and pat them dry.

Meanwhile, heat the remaining 2 tablespoons (30 ml) oil in a large deep, sauté pan over medium heat. Add the onion, garlic, and thyme and sweat the onion until it is soft but not browned, 4 to 5 minutes. Add the mushrooms and cook until they release some of their liquid and shrink a little, about 5 minutes. Pour in the wine and cook until the wine evaporates, 1 to 2 minutes. Pour in the stock and bring the mixture to a simmer. Adjust the heat so that the mixture simmers gently, and then simmer to blend the flavors, 15 to 20 minutes. Taste the *ragù*, adding salt and pepper until it tastes good to you.

Add the gnocchi to the *ragù*, shaking the pan until the gnocchi are well coated and heated through, 1 to 2 minutes. Discard the thyme and garlic, and then dish out the gnocchi onto warmed plates. Garnish with the Parmesan.

# SQUASH GNOCCHI WITH BROWN BUTTER AND CRISPY SAGE

MAKES 4 TO 6
SERVINGS

Italian Tonda Padana squash is about the size of a basketball and weighs close to 8 pounds (3.6 kg). It's pretty high in starch and low in water, so it's great for gnocchi. If you can't find Tonda Padana squash, use kabocha squash instead.

½ Tonda Padana squash (about 4 lb/1.8 kg)

½ cup plus 1 tablespoon (128 g) unsalted butter

2 whole eggs

2 egg yolks

½ cup (50 g) grated Parmesan cheese

½ cup (47 g) almond flour, plus some for dusting

¼ cup (30 g) finely crushed amaretti cookies or almond macaroons

½ teaspoon (1.5 g) kosher salt

⅛ teaspoon (0.3 g) freshly grated nutmeg

8 to 12 fresh sage leaves

¾ cup grated bagoss (85 g), Bitto (80 g), or Parmesan (75 g) cheese

To make the squash easier to peel, jab the squash all over with a knife (to allow steam to escape), and then microwave it on high power until the skin softens, about 2 minutes. Peel the squash with a vegetable peeler or paring knife. Scoop out and discard the seeds and strings, then cut the flesh into 1- to 2-inch (2.5 to 5 cm) chunks.

Put the squash chunks in a heavy pot and add water to a depth of ¼ inch (6 mm). Add 1 tablespoon (15 g) of the butter, cover the pot, and bring the liquid to a simmer over high heat. Turn down the heat to medium-low and simmer, covered, until the squash is tender, 15 to 20 minutes. Mash the squash in the pan (or puree it with a handheld blender or in a food processor), and then continue cooking the squash, stirring often to prevent burning, until much of its water evaporates and the puree reduces in volume, about 1 hour. When it's done, the squash should be the consistency of a loose dough and thick enough to cling to an upended spoon.

Measure out 1½ cups of the puree and reserve the rest for another use. Transfer the puree to a bowl, let cool slightly, then add the whole eggs, egg yolks, Parmesan, almond flour, cookie crumbs, salt, and nutmeg, and mix with a spoon until the dough comes together (it will be loose). Spoon the dough into a zipper-lock bag, seal closed, and refrigerate it until it is somewhat firm, at least 3 hours or up to 24 hours.

Snip a corner from the bag and pipe 1-inch (2.5 cm) dollops of the dough into a bowl of almond flour or all-purpose flour. Scoop up a dollop with floured hands, roll into a ball, and then place it on a floured rimmed baking sheet. Repeat with the remaining dough. You should have 50 to 60 gnocchi.

Use the gnocchi immediately or cover them loosely and refrigerate them for a few hours. You can also freeze them in a single layer, transfer them to a zipper-lock bag, and freeze them for up to 2 weeks. Take the gnocchi straight from the freezer to the boiling water, adding about 30 seconds to the cooking time.

Bring a large pot of salted water to a boil. Drop in the gnocchi and cover the pot to quickly return the water to a low boil. Cook the gnocchi until springy to the touch and tender throughout, 3 to 5 minutes. Squeeze a dumpling between your fingers. It should have some bounce-back. If it just flattens, the gnocchi are not done yet.

Meanwhile, melt the remaining ½ cup (114 g) butter and sage together over medium heat in a small sauté pan until the butter turns golden brown and the sage is crisp, about 7 minutes.

Using a spider strainer, transfer the gnocchi to warmed plates, allowing 10 to 12 gnocchi per serving. Spoon the brown butter over the gnocchi and sprinkle with the cheese. Garnish with the crispy sage.

# BACCALÀ GNOCCHI WITH SQUID

MAKES 6 TO 8
SERVINGS

To give potato gnocchi a kick in the pants, I like to add *baccalà*, or salt cod. It gives the dumplings a light, flaky texture and a shot of briny flavor. If you can't find squid, you can use sea scallops instead. Cut the scallops into coins about ⅛ inch (3 mm) thick, and then cut the coins into strips.

4 ounces (114 g) baccalà (salt cod) fillet

1½ pounds (680 g) russet potatoes (about 2)

¼ cup (25 g) grated Parmesan cheese

1 lemon

½ cup (76 g) tipo 00 flour, or ½ cup plus 2 tablespoons (76 g) all-purpose flour, plus some for dusting

Kosher salt and freshly ground black pepper

1 egg, beaten

2 pounds (907 g) baby squid, cleaned

¼ cup (60 ml) olive oil

1 tablespoon (3 g) finely chopped fresh chives

To remove the excess salt from the *baccalà*, soak the fillet in water to cover in the refrigerator for 2 to 3 days, changing the soaking water two or three times each day. Drain the *baccalà*, remove any skin, and then finely chop it. Set aside.

Combine the potatoes (unpeeled) and salted water to cover by 1 inch (2.5 cm) in a saucepan. Cover, bring the water to a boil over high heat, and boil until a knife slides easily in and out of the potatoes, 25 to 30 minutes.

Remove the pan from the heat and transfer the potatoes to a cutting board. Immediately peel off and discard the skins. Wear gloves if the potatoes feel too hot to handle. Coarsely chop the potatoes, and then pass them through a potato ricer or a food mill fitted with the fine die onto a large, lightly floured cutting board or smooth work surface, covering the board or surface with the potatoes. (Spreading out the potatoes helps to evaporate excess moisture.) Let the potatoes stand for 5 minutes, and then sprinkle the Parmesan evenly over the potatoes. Weigh out 2 ounces (57 g/about ⅓ cup) of the *baccalà* and sprinkle it evenly over the top. Using a Microplane or other fine-rasp grater, grate the zest from the lemon over the *baccalà*. (Reserve the lemon for use later.) Scatter the flour evenly over the top and season with about ½ teaspoon (1.5 g) salt and ¼ teaspoon (0.5 g) pepper. Finally, pour the egg evenly over the top. Using a bench scraper, cut the layered ingredients into the potatoes, repeatedly scraping, cutting, and mixing until the dough comes together.

Gently knead the dough just until it has a uniform consistency, about 1 minute. Be careful not to overwork the dough or it will develop excess gluten, which will make the gnocchi tough. Shape the dough into a rectangular block, then flour the bench scraper or a knife and cut slabs 1 inch (2.5 cm) wide from the block. Roll each slab on the floured surface into a rope about ½ inch (12 mm) in diameter. Using the floured bench scraper or knife, cut the rope crosswise into ½-inch (12 mm) pieces. Gently roll a cut side of each piece on a lightly floured grooved gnocchi board (or on a clean comb or the tines of a fork) to notch the exterior and create an oval shape. As the gnocchi are formed, transfer them to a generously floured rimmed baking sheet and shake the baking sheet to dust the gnocchi with the flour. You should have about 200 gnocchi.

Use the gnocchi within 1 hour or cover them loosely and refrigerate them for up to 8 hours. You can also freeze them in a single layer, transfer them to a zipper-lock bag, and freeze them for up to 2 weeks. Take the gnocchi straight from the freezer to the boiling water, adding 30 seconds or so to the cooking time.

To clean each squid, pull away the head and tentacles from the hood (tube-like body), and then reach into the hood and pull out the entrails and the plastic-like quill, taking care

CONTINUED

not to puncture the pearly ink sac. Cut off the tentacles just above the eyes, and discard the head. Squeeze the base of the tentacles to force out the hard "beak," and rinse the tentacles and the hood under cold running water. Using the back of a paring knife or your fingers, pull and scrape off the gray membrane from the hood. Cut off and discard the 2 small wings on either side of the hoods. Chill the hoods and tentacles in ice water until ready to use. Then drain the squid, pat dry, and dice.

Have ready a bowl of ice water. Bring a large pot of salted water to a boil. Drop the gnocchi into the boiling water and cover the pot to quickly return the water to a low boil. Adjust the heat so that the water simmers, stirring gently. Cook the gnocchi until springy to the touch and tender throughout, 3 to 5 minutes. Squeeze a dumpling between your fingers. It should have some bounce-back. If it just flattens, the gnocchi are not done yet. Using a spider strainer, immediately transfer the gnocchi to the ice water and let them sit in the water for 30 seconds to stop the cooking. Transfer the gnocchi to dry kitchen towels and pat them dry. Reserve the gnocchi water.

Cut the squid hoods crosswise into slices ¼ inch (6 mm) wide, and cut the tentacles in half. Pour gnocchi water to a depth of ⅛ to ¼ inch (3 to 6 mm) into a large, deep sauté pan and place over medium heat. Add the remaining 2 ounces (57 g/about ⅓ cup) chopped *baccalà* and the squid tentacles and cook until the tentacles are half-cooked, about 1 minute. Cut the reserved lemon in half and squeeze the juice (without seeds) into the pan. Add the squid hoods, gnocchi, oil, and chives. Shake the pan until the sauce thickens slightly and the squid tubes just begin to turn opaque, about 30 seconds.

Dish out the gnocchi and squid onto warmed plates.

# SWISS CHARD GNOCCHI WITH BROWN BUTTER AND PARMESAN

**MAKES 4 TO 6 SERVINGS**

I see gnocchi made with spinach and potato quite a bit. It's a great combination. But spinach isn't the only green leafy vegetable out there. Swiss chard adds a little more flavor.

1 russet potato (12 oz/340 g)

4 ounces (112 g) Swiss chard

½ cup (50 g) grated Parmesan cheese

½ cup (76 grams) tipo 00 flour, or ½ cup plus 2 tablespoons (76 g) all-purpose flour, plus some for dusting

⅛ teaspoon grated nutmeg

Kosher salt and freshly ground black pepper

1 egg, beaten

½ cup (114 g) unsalted butter

Combine the potato (unpeeled) and salted water to cover by 1 inch (2.5 cm) in a saucepan. Cover, bring the water to a boil over high heat, and boil until a knife slides easily in and out of the potato, 25 to 30 minutes.

Remove the pan from the heat and transfer the potato to a cutting board. Reserve the potato water in the pan. Peel off and discard the potato skin (wear gloves if necessary). Coarsely chop the potato, and then pass it through a potato ricer or a food mill fitted with the fine die onto a large, lightly floured cutting board or smooth work surface, covering the board or surface with the potato. (Spreading out the potato helps to evaporate moisture.) Let stand for 5 minutes.

Meanwhile, return the potato water to a boil and set up a bowl of ice water. Remove and discard the tough stems and ribs from the Swiss chard, then blanch the leaves in the boiling water for 3 minutes. Immediately transfer the chard leaves to the ice water to stop the cooking. Transfer the chard to a colander and press out most of the water. Transfer the chard to a food processor and pulse until finely chopped.

Spread the chard evenly over the surface of potato. Scatter 1 tablespoon (6 g) of the Parmesan, the flour, and the nutmeg evenly over the top. Season the mixture with salt and pepper, and then use a bench scraper to cut all of the seasonings into the potatoes, repeatedly scraping and mixing the ingredients until they are blended. Taste the mixture, adding more salt and pepper until it tastes good to you. Use the bench scraper to stir in the egg just until the dough comes together.

Knead the dough on a lightly floured work surface for 3 to 4 minutes. It will be soft. Flour the bench scraper or a knife and cut the dough into 4 pieces. Roll each piece on the floured surface into a long rope about ½ inch (12 mm) in diameter. Using the floured bench scraper or knife, cut the ropes crosswise into ½-inch (12 mm) pieces. As the gnocchi are formed, transfer them to a generously floured rimmed baking sheet and shake the baking sheet to dust the gnocchi with the flour. You should have about 100 gnocchi.

Use the gnocchi immediately or cover them loosely and refrigerate them for a few hours. You can also freeze them in a single layer, transfer them to a zipper-lock bag, and freeze them for up to 2 weeks. Take the gnocchi straight from the freezer to the boiling water, adding 30 seconds or so to the cooking time.

Melt the butter in a sauté pan over medium heat and cook until the liquid looks golden and the milk solids brown on the bottom of the pan, 6 to 8 minutes. Keep warm over low heat.

Bring a large pot of salted water to a boil. Drop in the gnocchi, in batches if necessary to prevent crowding, and cover the pot to quickly return the water to a low boil. Gently cook the gnocchi until springy to the touch and tender throughout, 3 to 5 minutes. Squeeze a dumpling between your fingers. It should have some bounce-back. If it just flattens, the gnocchi are not done yet.

Using a spider strainer or slotted spoon, drain the gnocchi, letting them drip-dry for a moment, then dish them out onto warmed plates. Spoon the brown butter over the top. Garnish with the remaining Parmesan.

# CABBAGE GNOCCHI WITH SAUSAGE AND TOASTED BREAD CRUMBS

**MAKES 6 TO 8 SERVINGS**

People taste these gnocchi and ask me, "What's in this dish?" And I say, "Cabbage, no potato." "But it's gnocchi, isn't it?" they ask. Of course it is! You see, gnocchi just means dumplings. You can make gnocchi with almost anything. For a crispier texture, blast the crumb-topped gnocchi in a hot oven until browned on top. A little brown butter here doesn't hurt either.

¼ head green cabbage (about 7 oz/200 g)

12 slices white sandwich bread

2 cups (473 ml) whole milk

1 link fresh Italian sausage (about 4 oz/114 g)

1 small clove garlic, smashed

¾ cup (113 grams) tipo 00 flour, or ¾ cup plus 2½ tablespoons (113 g) all-purpose flour, plus some for dusting

Kosher salt and freshly ground black pepper

2 eggs, beaten

4 tablespoons (57 g) unsalted butter

⅔ cup (72 g) plain dried bread crumbs

¾ cup (75 g) grated Parmesan cheese

Bring a large pot of salted water to a boil. Add the cabbage and boil until the leaves are tender, 4 to 5 minutes. Remove the pot from the heat and transfer the cabbage to a cutting board. When cool enough to handle, trim out the tough, woody core and stems and discard. Finely chop the tender leaves. You should have about 1½ cups chopped (150 g).

Soak the bread in the milk in a bowl for 5 minutes. Squeeze out the bread like a sponge to remove as much milk as possible, wringing it in cheesecloth if necessary to remove and discard all the milk. Set the bread aside.

In a sauté pan over medium heat, cook the sausage and garlic clove until the sausage is cooked through. Transfer to a cutting board and finely chop it. Discard the garlic.

Combine the bread, cabbage, sausage, and flour in a bowl and stir with a wooden spoon until fully mixed. If the bread doesn't fall apart, mash it with the spoon until it does. Taste the dough, adding salt and pepper until it tastes good to you. Stir in the eggs. Cover and refrigerate the dough for at least 2 hours or up to 24 hours.

Melt the butter in a sauté pan over medium heat. Add the bread crumbs and cook, stirring now and then, until they are toasted and golden brown, 4 to 5 minutes. Remove from the heat and set aside.

Spoon 1-inch (2.5 cm) dollops of dough into a bowl of flour. Gently scoop up a dollop with floured hands (the dough will be loose), roll the dollop into a ball, and then place it on a floured rimmed baking sheet. You should have 50 to 60 gnocchi.

Use the gnocchi immediately or cover them loosely and refrigerate them for a few hours. You can also freeze them in a single layer, transfer them to a zipper-lock bag, and freeze them for up to 2 weeks. Take the gnocchi straight from the freezer to the boiling water, adding 30 seconds or so to the cooking time.

Bring a large pot of salted water to a boil. Working in batches to prevent crowding, drop in the gnocchi and cover the pot to quickly return the water to a low boil. Gently cook the gnocchi until springy to the touch and tender throughout, 3 to 5 minutes. Squeeze a dumpling between your fingers. It should have some bounce-back. If it just flattens, the gnocchi are not done yet.

Using a spider strainer or slotted spoon, drain the gnocchi, letting them drip-dry for a moment, then dish them out onto warmed plates. Top each serving with a spoonful of the bread crumbs and some Parmesan.

# 10

—

# RISOTTO

**IF YOU ARE FLYING INTO MILAN'S LINATE AIRPORT, YOU MIGHT THINK YOU'RE SOMEWHERE IN CHINA.** Through the plane window, rice paddies stretch as far as the eye can see. Northern Italy has the perfect climate for growing short-grain and medium-grain rice, ingredients that are the heart and soul of risotto. The Po River brings water to these fields from the Italian Alps up north. In the spring, the fields get flooded, and each grain of rice germinates and grows into a new plant over the summer. Each new plant grows thousands of new grains. Rice is pretty amazing when you think about it like that. But so is the fertility of the Po Valley in northern Italy. This region has been producing high-quality rice since the late 1400s. And now Italy is the largest rice producer in all of Europe.

## TYPES OF RICE

On the world stage, Italian rice is known as short-grain or medium-grain rice. But Italians get even more specific. They have four categories: *comune* rice, slightly longer *semifino*, medium-long *fino*, and longer, slender *superfino* rice. Short, fat *comune* rice is best for soups. *Fino* varieties like Maratelli are great for rice balls and *sartù*, Neapolitan rice timbales. For risotto, you can use some varieties of *semifino* like Vialone Nano, but *superfino* varieties are best. Arborio, Carnaroli, Volano, Elba, and other *superfino* types create the creamiest risotto while still retaining a little bite.

Generally, the longer the rice grain, the more al dente the finished risotto. That's because long-grain rice is high in amylose, a type of starch that gives rice its firmness. Amylose is what causes long-grain rice like basmati to cook up light and separate. Short-grain rice is higher in a sticky type of starch called amylopectin. That starch creates the "gluey" texture of Japan's sticky rice. We can also thank amylopectin for the smooth, buttery texture of Italian risotto.

Most Italians like a firm chew in their risotto. That's why Carnaroli is king. It's got enough amylopectin to make risotto rich and creamy but also enough amylose to keep the rice al dente when fully cooked. As with pasta, a silky yet firm texture is very important to Italians.

### Acquerello Carnaroli

It is texture that makes Carnaroli rice so special. Born in 1945, this rice is a cross between Vialone and Lencino varieties. The plants grow nearly twice as tall as other *superfino* types and tend to fall over from their own weight. That's why Carnaroli rice almost became extinct in the 1980s. Fortunately, it was saved by a farmer from the Lombardian territory of Lomellina. However, not all Carnaroli rice on the market is created equal. As with dried pasta and other food products, some producers grow and process their rice using artisanal methods; others cut corners.

There isn't much else to a dish of risotto, so I use the highest-quality rice I can. Just as Carnaroli is the king of rice, Acquerello is, in my opinion, the king of Carnaroli. Italians excel at craftsmanship, and Acquerello takes rice craftsmanship to a whole new level. The craftsmen at

Acquerello combine time-honored methods with cutting-edge technology. The Carnaroli rice goes through at least twenty steps before it is vacuum-packed. First and foremost, the rice is aged. Right after harvest, rice is fairly wet from the flooded fields, and the starch inside is soft. If you cooked it right away, the rice would fall apart. Aging firms up the starch. The longer rice ages, the more compact and stable the starch becomes. You can fully cook well-aged rice, but each grain still remains intact. The craftsmen at Acquerello experimented with aging times from a few months to more than seven years. The sweet spot was found to be about eighteen months. If you like fine aged wine, try some of Acquerello's longer-aged rice. It has a deep, yet flexible structure that cooks up into exceptionally creamy risotto with rice grains that do not lose their shape.

The other important factor is how Acquerello mills the rice. Most rice is milled with electric roller mills—just like wheat. Roller mills are fast but rough on the grains. They smash the rice grains together until the bran falls off, and in this process, they scratch or crack the white endosperm inside. With *superfino* varieties, the goal is to keep the starchy white endosperm intact so the rice releases the maximum amount of starch into risotto without losing its shape.

Acquerello uses an older-style helix mill that keeps the rice moving in a circular pattern so the grains do not get damaged. Helix mills slowly and gently thin out the bran until it becomes a fine powder. At that point, the germ is like a little crushed pebble, which means the bran can be sieved out and the germ can be retained. Just like wheat germ, rice germ is full of valuable nutrients such as B vitamins, vitamin E, and various minerals. Most white rice does not include any part of the germ. But here's the revolutionary thing about Acquerello: its Carnaroli rice includes the germ. In 2012, Acquerello received a US patent for its unique method of enriching rice. The rice and crushed germ is put back into the helix mill for about fifteen minutes and the friction generates just enough heat—about 105°F (40°C)—for the germ to be reabsorbed into the rice. The result is nutritious white rice that still makes perfect risotto. Brilliant!

If you're ever in the province of Vercelli, stop by the Colombara Estate where Acquerello Carnaroli is grown,

harvested, milled, and packaged. It's worth the trip. Rice has been cultivated there since the late 1400s, and the Rondolino family, who now runs the business, has preserved the old stone workshops, the school, and even the dormitory where the *mondine* (rice weeders) lived while they worked the fields. You will be transported back in time. And the stories you will hear will give you a deeper appreciation for everything that goes into that chewy-tender risotto on your plate!

## A GOOD START TO RISOTTO

I'll say it for wheat pasta, and I'll say it for rice: starting with great rice will always give you a leg up on creating a superior dish of risotto. After that, the success of the dish depends mostly on technique.

I like to begin with *soffritto*, the flavor base of countless Italian sauces and *ragù*. It's Italy's version of French mirepoix. Sometimes I use only onion; sometimes a little carrot, leek, garlic, or maybe some chopped pancetta. Use whatever aromatics you like to begin building flavor in the pan. I mince the vegetables pretty small so they don't eclipse the beautiful grains of rice in the finished dish. You can cook the aromatics in olive oil, butter, or both—just don't overcook them. You don't want to brown the vegetables because that will darken the risotto.

You do, however, want to toast the rice. When the vegetables are translucent, add the rice and cook it until it gets a little brown around the edges. That step adds a layer of toasted, nutty flavor—and it doesn't darken the risotto. Toasted rice creates one of those subtle differences between good risotto and remarkable risotto. Always toast the rice.

## ADDING LIQUIDS

I usually add wine for another layer of flavor. Not every risotto needs it, but I like at least a little for some acidity. Plus, the alcohol brings out flavors in the other ingredients. About ⅓ cup (78 ml) wine per 1 cup (195 g) of rice is a good amount. I add the wine to the toasted rice, then let it completely evaporate in the pan so that the risotto doesn't taste too winey.

After that, I usually add stock about ½ cup (118 ml) at a time. The needed amount of liquid will vary according to the hardness of the rice. Sometimes I use water for the liquid, but stock builds flavor. If it's Shellfish Risotto (page 231), I use shellfish stock (page 243), and for Duck Risotto with Orange Sauce (page 236), duck stock (page 242). You are going for a subtle taste, so avoid highly reduced stocks. An intense veal stock boiled down to a demi-glace would overpower the rice—plus the texture would be too thick. Everything you add to a pan of risotto should serve to enhance the rice rather than overshadow it.

## TO STIR OR NOT TO STIR

This is a touchy subject. I'm sure some Italians would put a knife in my back after reading this, but you don't *always* have to stir. It's true that stirring the rice the entire 20 to 30 minutes that it cooks will rough up the surface of the kernels and release starch, which thickens the liquid and creates a nice, creamy risotto. Without a doubt, you will achieve the best results with this method. But in a restaurant kitchen, when you're in the weeds during dinner service, the last thing you want to do is stir risotto for a half hour. We came up with a method for making risotto in which we add only about one-third of the stock, stirring all the while. Then we stop the stirring and put the pan of risotto in the oven for 6 to 7 minutes. When we take it out, it sits with a lid on it for anywhere from 15 minutes to 2 hours. Just before serving, we put the pan back over a burner, gradually add the remaining stock and stir the risotto like mad. The key to this method is at the end when you *mantecare*, or emulsify, all the elements. You basically want to blend together the stock, the starch from the rice, and any added fats to create a smooth sauce. Precooking the rice still brings a fair amount of its starch to the surface. Then we just stir the starch into the mix at the end of cooking instead of the entire time. Even discerning palates can't distinguish risotto cooked by this oven method. Taste it for yourself in Duck Risotto with Orange Sauce (page 236).

## DONENESS

Once you have made risotto a few times, you'll be able to just look in the pan to see if it's done. It should look like rice soup that is missing some broth. You want it smooth but not too thick, and the rice grains should be plump and soft with a little bite left in them. Pop a grain of rice into your mouth to test it. It should feel soft but need at least a little chewing before it dissolves. If the rice is really chewy, cook it a bit longer. Start testing the rice early. You can always cook it more, but if it's overcooked, you can't get back to al dente. That term has many definitions. In Italy, it means the rice is still pretty chewy, what I would call "extra crispy." In America, people go the other way—they like it a little too soft for my taste. I prefer it with just enough bite so that you have to chew, but when you do, the rice gradually melts into the rest of the sauce in your mouth, creating a luxurious, velvety experience.

When the risotto gets to that point, take the pan off the stove. There should still be a fair amount of liquid in it. Don't worry, as the rice will absorb more liquid off the heat. It's ready when you put the risotto on a plate and it slowly flattens out but still holds together as rice and sauce. It shouldn't get lumpy and pasty on the plate. Keep in mind that the risotto may sit on the plate for several minutes before it is eaten. I like to make it extra soupy. That way the rice has some time to breathe, and the texture is perfect when you finally take a bite.

And you thought risotto was just a dish of rice! As with everything else in cooking, beautiful products and careful technique are what create great plates of food. I know I said it earlier, but I'll say it again: one without the other will only ever achieve a certain level of cuisine. To reach higher, you need both.

# TOMATO RISOTTO

MAKES 4 SERVINGS

In the south of Italy, spaghetti with tomato is the quintessential pasta dish. Everyone loves it. So I thought, "What would be the northern representation of that dish?" Risotto with tomato!

2 large, ripe beefsteak tomatoes (about 1½ lb/680 g each)

¼ cup plus 1 tablespoon (75 ml) extra virgin olive oil

¼ cup (42 g) finely chopped yellow onion

¾ cup (145 g) Carnaroli rice

4 cups (946 ml) boiling water

Kosher salt and freshly ground black pepper

Best-quality balsamic vinegar, for drizzling

Cut 4 thin cross-sectional slices from the center of 1 tomato and set the slices aside. Chop the remaining portion of that tomato and all of the second tomato into small cubes. Heat 1 tablespoon (15 ml) of the oil in a saucepan over medium heat. Add the onion and sweat it until it is soft but not browned, 4 to 6 minutes. Add the rice and sauté the rice until it is translucent around the edges and starts to brown a little, 2 to 3 minutes. This is an important step to develop the right flavor and texture in the rice; make sure the rice absorbs some of the oil. Add the chopped tomatoes and cook them until they start to break down and the rice has absorbed most of the tomato liquid, 5 to 6 minutes.

Gradually add the boiling water about ½ cup (118 ml) at a time, stirring almost constantly over medium-high heat until the rice absorbs the water after each addition. When the rice is done, it should be tender but still a little chewy when bitten and should have released most of its starch, creating a creamy sauce in the pan. This process will take 25 to 30 minutes. Near the end of cooking, add a little more boiling water if necessary and stir the rice like crazy to release as much starch as possible and create the sauce. Drag your spoon through the rice to the bottom of the pan; the sauce should slowly fill in the line you made.

Remove the pan from the heat and gradually add the remaining ¼ cup (60 ml) oil, stirring until the risotto is creamy. Taste the risotto, adding salt and pepper until it tastes good to you.

Dish out the risotto onto warmed plates and garnish with the reserved tomato slices and a drizzle of balsamic vinegar.

# RISOTTO ALLA MILANESE

MAKES 4 SERVINGS

This dish is forever linked to the centuries-old Duomo cathedral in Milan. Apparently, in 1574, a master glassmaker who was in charge of making stained glass for the cathedral enlisted an able disciple who was given the nickname Zafferano because he used saffron to color the glass. The yellow of the saffron never failed to make a beautiful golden color, achieving stunning effects in the windows. The master glazier said to his disciple, "I see it now. You'll end up putting saffron in your risotto, too!" The daughter of the glassmaker was engaged to marry a wealthy merchant. At some point during the wedding, the party moved toward the table holding four steaming pots of risotto, traditional at Italian weddings. Everyone was amazed to see that the risotto was golden yellow, as if it were made of gold. It was the wedding gift of all wedding gifts from the disciple. The surprise was greeted with warm enthusiasm. News of the extraordinary dish traveled fast: the next day, all of Milan was eating golden risotto.

6 cups (1.4 L) beef stock or chicken stock (page 242), heated to a boil

1 tablespoon (2 g) saffron threads

3 tablespoons (42 g) unsalted butter

½ cup (84 g) finely chopped yellow onion

1¾ cups (340 g) Carnaroli rice

¾ cup (75 g) grated Parmesan cheese, plus some for garnish

3 tablespoons (45 ml) extra-virgin olive oil

2 ounces (57 g) bone marrow (about 2 tablespoons), finely chopped

Kosher salt and freshly ground black pepper

Combine 1 cup (237 ml) of the boiling stock and the saffron threads in a heatproof cup and set aside.

Heat 2 tablespoons (28 g) of the butter in a saucepan over medium heat. Add the onion and sweat it until it is soft but not browned, 4 to 6 minutes. Add the rice and sauté the rice until it is translucent around the edges and starts to brown a little, 2 to 3 minutes. This is an important step to develop the right flavor and texture in the rice; make sure the rice absorbs some of the oil.

Gradually add 5½ cups (1.3 L) of the boiling stock about ½ cup (118 ml) at a time, stirring almost constantly over medium-high heat until the rice absorbs the stock after each addition. Add the stock with the saffron as the last addition. (It's best to add the saffron near the end of the cooking so that it retains maximum flavor and aroma.) When the rice is done, it should be tender but still a little chewy when bitten and should have released most of its starch, creating a creamy sauce in the pan. This process will take 25 to 30 minutes. Near the end of cooking, add a little more boiling stock if necessary and stir the rice like crazy to release as much starch as possible and create the sauce. Drag your spoon through the rice to the bottom of the pan; the sauce should slowly fill in the line you made. The risotto should be a beautiful golden yellow.

Remove the pan from the heat and add the Parmesan, oil, bone marrow, and the remaining 1 tablespoon (15 g) butter, stirring until the risotto is creamy. Taste it, adding salt and pepper until it tastes good to you.

Dish out the risotto onto warmed plates and garnish with a little Parmesan.

# SQUID INK RISOTTO WITH SEPPIA SALAD AND RICOTTA

**MAKES 4 TO 6 SERVINGS**

I learned this dish at Taverna Colleoni dell'Angelo in Bergamo's old city. It was one of the restaurant's old-school specialties. The texture of the ricotta pairs perfectly with the cuttlefish, or *seppia* in Italian, and a touch of red pepper flakes heats things up while the ricotta cools them down. If you can't find cuttlefish, use squid and julienne both the bodies and tentacles.

2 pounds (907 g) cuttlefish, (about 1½ pounds/680 g cleaned; see page 180)

4 tablespoons (60 ml) olive oil

⅓ cup (56 g) chopped yellow onion

¼ cup (60 ml) dry white wine

2 teaspoons (10 ml) fresh lemon juice

1 tablespoon (4 g) chopped fresh flat-leaf parsley

Kosher salt and freshly ground black pepper

1 cup (227 g) ricotta impastata cheese (see page 241)

Pinch of red pepper flakes, plus some for garnish

1 cup (195 g) Carnaroli rice

1 teaspoon (5 ml) squid ink

6 to 7 cups (1.4 to 1.7 L) boiling water

Reserve the ink sacs from the cuttlefish. Finely julienne the cuttlefish bodies.

Heat 1 tablespoon (15 ml) of the oil in a sauté pan over medium heat. Add the onion and sweat it until it is soft but not browned, 4 to 6 minutes. Add the cuttlefish and sweat for 2 minutes. Add the wine and cook for 5 minutes. The cuttlefish will start to give up its liquid. If necessary, add just enough water to almost cover the cuttlefish, and then cover and braise it over low heat for 22 minutes. Drain off any excess liquid, and then stir in 1 tablespoon (15 ml) of the oil, the lemon juice, and the parsley. Taste the salad, adding salt, pepper, and additional lemon juice and oil until it tastes good to you.

Puree the ricotta in a blender or food processor until super-smooth, 2 to 3 minutes, scraping down the sides a few times. Add the pepper flakes and season the mixture with salt and pepper. Puree the ricotta again, and then taste it, adding salt and pepper until it tastes good to you.

Heat the remaining 1 tablespoon (15 ml) oil in a saucepan over medium heat. Add the rice and sauté the rice until it is translucent around the edges and starts to brown a little,

2 to 3 minutes. This is an important step to develop the right flavor and texture in the rice; make sure the rice absorbs some of the oil.

Add the squid ink to the boiling water and squeeze the cuttlefish ink sacs into the water, extracting their ink. Gradually add 6½ cups (1.5 L) of the inky water about ½ cup (118 ml) at a time, stirring almost constantly over medium-high heat until the rice absorbs the water after each addition. When the rice is done, it should be tender but still a little chewy when bitten and have released most of its starch, creating a creamy sauce in the pan. This process will take 25 to 30 minutes. Near the end of cooking, add a little more water if necessary and stir the rice like crazy to release as much starch as possible and create the sauce. Drag your spoon through the rice to the bottom of the pan; the sauce should slowly fill in the line you made. Taste the risotto, adding salt and pepper until it tastes good to you.

Dish out the risotto onto warmed plates and spoon the pureed ricotta over the risotto. Spoon the cuttlefish salad on top and garnish with red pepper flakes.

# DUCK RISOTTO WITH ORANGE SAUCE

MAKES 6 SERVINGS

Here's a play on the classic French duck à l'orange. The flavors work perfectly, so why not make risotto with them? More importantly, this recipe shows you how to make risotto a few hours ahead of time. You parcook the rice in the oven, then finish it later on the stove top. The duck *ragù* and orange sauce can also be made hours or even a day or two ahead, so when it comes time to serve, the whole dish comes together quickly.

1 duck (4 to 5 lb/1.8 to 2.3 kg)

Kosher salt and freshly ground black pepper

4 tablespoons (60 ml) grapeseed or canola oil

1 cup (168 g) finely chopped yellow onion

½ cup (61 g) peeled and chopped carrot

½ cup (51 g) chopped celery

½ cup (21 g) dried porcini mushrooms

1⅓ cups (315 ml) dry white wine

7 cups (1.7 L) duck stock (page 242), plus more if needed

1 cup (237 ml) fresh orange juice

1 cup (195 g) Carnaroli rice

6 fresh basil leaves

To make the duck *ragù*, heat the oven to 350°F (175°C). Remove the giblets from the duck and reserve them for another use. Trim away any excess fat from the duck. Cut the leg-thigh portions from the body by pulling each leg away from the body, bending the leg to find the hip joint, and then driving your knife straight through the joint. Remove the breasts by cutting slits on either side of the breastbone, and then working the knife carefully around the rib cage, keeping the knife against bone at all times and pulling the breast away from the carcass. Reserve the carcass to make duck stock. Separate the legs from the thighs by driving a cleaver straight through the joint.

Season the duck pieces all over with salt and pepper. Heat 2 tablespoons (30 ml) of the oil in a Dutch oven over medium-high heat. When the oil is hot, add the duck pieces, skin side down in a single layer, and sear them, turning them only once, until most of the fat is rendered out and the skin is deeply browned all over, 6 to 8 minutes per side. Transfer the pieces to a plate.

Drain off all but 2 tablespoons (30 ml) of the fat from the pan (strain and reserve the rendered fat for another purpose; it will keep frozen for 8 to 10 months—duck fat is great for frying potatoes) and return the pan to medium heat. Add ¾ cup (126 g) of the onion, the carrot, and the celery to the

pan and sweat the vegetables until they are soft but not browned, 4 to 5 minutes. Add the porcini, and then deglaze the pan with 1 cup (237 ml) of the wine, scraping up any browned bits from the pan bottom. Return the duck and any accumulated juices to the pan, and then add water to come about three-fourths of the way up the sides of the duck pieces. Cover and braise the duck in the oven until the meat is very tender, 2 to 3 hours.

Remove the pan from the oven and let the duck cool in the pan. When it is cool enough to handle, pick and shred the meat from the bones, discarding the fat and skin; reserve the bones to make duck stock. Skim any excess fat from the surface of the braising liquid, then pass the braising liquid and vegetables through a food mill fitted with the large die, or pulse them briefly in a food processor just until the vegetables are finely chopped but not completely pureed. If the *ragù* is watery, return it to the pan and boil it over medium heat until slightly thickened, then mix the shredded meat into the *ragù*. Taste the *ragù*, adding salt and pepper until it tastes good to you. You should have about 3½ cups (828 ml) meaty *ragù*. Use it within 2 hours or refrigerate it in an airtight container for up to 3 days.

To make the orange sauce, pour 2 cups (473 ml) of the stock into a saucepan, bring to a boil over high heat, and boil until reduced by about half, 10 to 15 minutes. Add the orange juice and boil again until the liquid is reduced by about half (to about 1 cup/237 ml), 10 to 15 minutes. Taste the sauce, adding salt and pepper until it tastes good to you. Use the sauce within 2 hours or refrigerate it in an airtight container for up to 3 days.

Heat the oven to 400°F (200°C). Heat the remaining 2 table-spoons (30 ml) oil in an ovenproof saucepan over medium heat. Add the remaining ¼ cup (42 g) onion and sweat it until it is soft but not browned, 4 to 6 minutes. Add the rice and sauté the rice until it is translucent around the edges and starts to brown a little, 2 to 3 minutes. This is an important step to develop the right flavor and texture in the rice; make sure the rice absorbs some of the oil. Pour in the remaining ⅓ cup (78 ml) wine and simmer it until the pan goes dry, 2 to 3 minutes.

Stir in 2 cups (473 ml) of the stock, bring it to a boil over high heat, and then cover the pan and set it in the oven for 6 minutes. Remove the pan from the oven and let it stand, covered, for up to 2 hours, stirring every 15 minutes or so to release some steam.

When you are ready to serve the dish, bring the remaining 3 cups (710 ml) stock to a boil in a small saucepan. Put the risotto pan over medium-high heat. Add the boiling stock to the risotto 1 cup (237 ml) at a time, stirring constantly until the rice absorbs the stock after each addition. Stir vigorously to release the starch in the rice. When the rice is done, it should be tender but still a little chewy when bitten and have released most of its starch, creating a creamy sauce in the pan. This process will take 10 to 15 minutes (about half the time of risotto cooked completely on the stove top). Near the end of cooking, add a little more boiling stock if necessary and stir the rice like crazy to release as much starch as possible and create the sauce. Drag your spoon through the rice to the bottom of the pan; the sauce should slowly fill in the line you made. Stir in 2 cups (473 ml) of the duck *ragù*; reserve any remaining *ragù* for another use. Taste the risotto, adding salt and pepper until it tastes good to you.

If the orange sauce has been refrigerated, reheat it in a saucepan over medium heat. Stack the basil leaves, roll them up lengthwise, and then cut crosswise into thin slices (chiffonade).

Dish out the risotto onto warmed plates and spoon some of the warm orange sauce over each serving. Garnish with the basil.

# STOCKS, SAUCES, AND OTHER BASICS

THE WORD *BASIC* MAY IMPLY THAT THE RECIPES IN THIS SECTION ARE IN SOME WAY OPTIONAL. The real meaning is exactly the opposite. Stocks and sauces are the very cornerstones of good cooking.

As I mentioned in Playing with Flavor (page 137), layers are the key to an amazing dish of food. Chefs are always looking to build layers, and step one is to make stock. If you cheap out and use premade stock, don't expect your cooking to soar. It will be built on a shaky foundation.

I've worked in restaurants where a single stock was used to flavor dozens of different dishes, with no changes to it whatsoever. I never understood that. If I'm making a mushroom dish, maybe I'll make chicken stock, but I'll add mushrooms stems to the stock. If I'm making a duck dish, I'll use duck stock, not chicken stock. Fish dishes gets fish stock.

Think of these basic recipes as a starting point. Add whatever layers of flavor that make the most sense for the dishes you are cooking. Béchamel (page 245) is a great example. White sauce can go in any number of different directions. I offer just three: béchamel with onion, truffle béchamel, and Taleggio béchamel. But you could make porcini béchamel by adding dried porcini and their soaking liquid in place of some of the milk. Or Castelmagno béchamel by stirring in some grated Castelmagno at the end. Dozens of different cheeses could flavor béchamel. Pick your favorite and build flavor from the bottom up.

Although these recipes may seem like an afterthought here at the end, they form the very backbone of many of the other recipes in the book. Start here and work your way backward through the chapters. Fortunately, most of these preparations can be made ahead and be refrigerated or frozen, so you'll have them on hand whenever you need them.

## NOTES ON BASIC INGREDIENTS

To clear up any confusion, here is what I mean when I refer to various ingredients throughout this book.

### Butter

I always use unsalted butter, but in most recipes, you could use salted butter. Just add a little less salt when seasoning the dish, and make sure to taste it. Either way, buy the freshest butter that you can.

### Eggs

I use large eggs from chickens pastured on a local farm. I recommend you do the same. Fresh, pastured eggs taste better than factory-farmed eggs and have a rich color, which then paints the pasta or whatever you're cooking with that gorgeous hue. Sometimes I call for ½ an egg, beaten, so that the recipe won't make too much volume of dough for a home cook. In those cases, beat a large egg in a spouted measuring cup and pour out half the egg to use in the recipe.

## Flours

Specific flours are called for throughout the book. Whenever possible, weigh them instead of using volume measurements. Volumes change depending on whether you dip a measuring cup into the flour or spoon the flour into the cup and level it off with a knife. We used the spooning and leveling method for the volume-to-weight conversions here. But weights are always constant—especially if one flour is ground more finely than another. For example, Italian tipo 00 flour is ground superfine and American all-purpose flour is ground more coarsely. The volumes are different: 1 cup tipo 00 flour equals 1 cup plus 3 tablespoons all-purpose flour, even though both amounts weigh 150 grams. Be very careful when switching flours for pasta. For best results, go by weights!

## Oils

Olive oil is my choice for general cooking and sautéing. I use extra-virgin oil when the oil won't see any heat, as in dressings and purees, or when it sees only a little heat, like when I'm sweating vegetables or stirring the oil into cooked sauces. The delicate flavor of very fine extra-virgin oil dissipates with heat, so reserve your best olive oil for drizzling onto food just before serving. Use your least expensive olive oil for sautéing. For high-heat searing and grilling, I prefer grapeseed oil because it has a high smoke point and a clean, neutral flavor. You could use canola oil instead of grapeseed. Sometimes I blend oils, such as extra-virgin olive oil with a mild-flavored oil like grapeseed. I use blends mostly for vinaigrettes but also sometimes for panfrying. Just mix extra-virgin olive oil and grapeseed or canola oil in a ratio of one to one.

## Weight and Volume Measures

The recipes in this book were tested using metric weights of the ingredients, as well as US volume measures. The latter have been included because most American cooks are comfortable using volume measures, but the metric weights are much more accurate. That's because US volume measures fail to capture the precision of metric weights. For example, the difference between ¾ cup all-purpose flour and the next largest volume measure, which is 1 cup, is ¼ cup flour, or 31 grams. That ¼-cup/31-gram difference can have a noticeable effect on a pasta dough, possibly causing it to fail. In some cases, the accurate volume measure falls somewhere between ¾ cup and 1 cup, such as

14 tablespoons/109 grams flour. In this particular case, the volume is expressed as ¾ cup plus 2 tablespoons to make the measure as accurate and as user-friendly as possible. This is the sort of fudging that necessarily occurs when converting metric weights (grams and milligrams) to American volume measures (cups, tablespoons, and teaspoons). If you plan to double or triple a recipe, the primacy and accuracy of the weights become even more critical. For the most successful results, I recommend that you purchase an inexpensive digital gram scale and use the metric weights in the recipes.

### Onions

Yellow onions are workhorses in my kitchens. Sometimes I use Spanish onions; they are a bit larger and sweeter but basically the same. For a little less pungency, I use white onions here and there. Red onions taste milder and work well in raw preparations. But if you are out of yellow onions, you can use red onions or white onions without drastically affecting the recipe.

### Parmesan Cheese

When I call for Parmesan cheese, I am referring to Parmigiano-Reggiano. Everything else is a knockoff. Use the real thing.

### Ricotta Cheese

I use *ricotta impastata*, a creamy type of ricotta that is low in water. I often use Grande brand, which is labeled *ricotta del pastaio*. If you can't find *ricotta impastata*, drain your ricotta in a sieve overnight to remove excess water, and then whip it in a food processor.

### Salt

Most of the recipes call for kosher salt. Diamond Crystal is my go-to brand. Different grinds and brands of salt measure differently, so be careful if you're swapping out salt. For instance, 1 teaspoon Diamond Crystal kosher salt equals ½ teaspoon fine table salt or fine sea salt and ¾ teaspoon Morton's kosher salt, and all of those spoon measures weigh 3 g.

# VEAL STOCK

MAKES ABOUT 4 CUPS (1 L)

Stocks are vital to good cooking, and good technique is vital to good stock. I'm not a big fan of dark, syrupy stocks. I like to make them like tea, gently flavoring the water so it has a clear taste that's not too overpowering. I do roast the bones to develop flavor, but if you like a lighter stock, roast the bones for about half the time given here.

    5 pounds (2.3 kg) veal bones
    5 cups (1.2 L) water
    2 tablespoons (30 ml) olive oil
    1 yellow onion, chopped (1½ cups/252 g)
    2 large carrots, chopped (1½ cups/185 g)
    3 celery stalks, chopped (1½ cups/152 g)
    2 sprigs rosemary, 5 sprigs flat-leaf parsley,
    10 peppercorns, 1 clove garlic, and 1 bay leaf, tied in
    a cheesecloth sachet with kitchen string

Heat the oven to 400°F (200°C). Lay the bones in a single layer in a roasting pan and roast them until they are deeply browned, 1½ to 2 hours. Transfer the browned bones to a stockpot and place the roasting pan over medium heat. Add about 1 cup (237 ml) of the water to deglaze the pan, scraping up any browned bits on the pan bottom. Scrape the pan contents into the stockpot and add the remaining 4 cups (946 ml) water.

Place the stockpot over medium heat and bring the liquid to just under a simmer. Do not let it boil. If it boils, your stock will be cloudy. Adjust the heat so that a few bubbles occasionally and lazily come to the surface. Cook the stock for 1 hour, skimming any impurities from the surface now and then.

Meanwhile, heat the oil in a large sauté pan over medium heat. Add the onion, carrots, and celery and sauté the vegetables until they are deeply browned, 8 to 10 minutes. After the stock has cooked for 1 hour, add the sautéed vegetables. Cook the stock gently for another 6 hours, skimming the surface now and then. Add the sachet and cook for another

2 hours, skimming the surface as before. The total cooking time should be about 8 hours.

Remove the pot from the heat. Using tongs, remove the bones, any large vegetable pieces, and the sachet and discard them. Let the stock cool until warm. Line a medium-mesh sieve with cheesecloth and strain the stock through the cheesecloth into a large container. Label, date, and refrigerate the stock for up to 1 week or freeze it for up to 3 months. Remove the fat from the surface before using.

BEEF STOCK Use beef bones in place of the veal bones and proceed as directed for veal stock.

CHICKEN STOCK Use chicken bones in place of the veal bones and roast them for only 1 hour. Proceed as directed for veal stock.

DUCK STOCK Use duck bones in place of the veal bones and roast them for only 1 hour. Proceed as directed for veal stock.

GOOSE STOCK Use goose bones in place of the veal bones and roast them for only 1 hour. Proceed as directed for veal stock.

MARROWBONE STOCK Use veal marrowbones in place of the veal bones. Halve them lengthwise (ask your butcher to cut them for you) to reveal the marrow and make it easier to slide it out. You can also use cross-cut marrow bones. Place the bones in a roasting pan and warm them to about 90°F (32°C) in a very low oven, just until the marrow begins to soften, then slide the marrow out of the bones. Refrigerate and reserve the marrow for the Saffron Gnocchi Sardi with Bone Marrow (page 113) or Risotto alla Milanese (page 228) or another use. Roast the bones and proceed as directed for veal stock.

QUAIL STOCK Use quail bones in place of the veal bones and roast them for only 45 minutes. Proceed as directed for veal stock.

# FISH STOCK

MAKES ABOUT 2 QUARTS (2 L)

The bones of scorpion fish work amazingly well in this stock. Halibut bones are good, too. But you can use the bones of whatever type of white fish you are cooking. This stock takes less than an hour to make.

8 cups (1.9 L) water

5 pounds (2.3 kg) white-fish bones

1 yellow onion, finely chopped (1½ cups/252 g)

4 celery stalks, finely chopped (1¼ cups/126 g)

2 lemons

10 flat-leaf parsley stems, 10 black peppercorns, 1 clove garlic, and 1 bay leaf, tied in a cheesecloth sachet with kitchen string

Combine the water and fish bones in a stockpot over medium heat and bring the liquid to just under a simmer. Do not let it boil. If it boils, your stock will be cloudy. Adjust the heat so that a few bubbles occasionally and lazily come to the surface. Skim any impurities from the surface, and then add the onion and celery. Cook for 30 minutes, skimming off impurities now and then. Cut the lemons in half, squeeze the juice into the pot, and then add the spent rinds. Drop in the sachet and cook the stock for another 15 minutes.

Remove the pot from the heat. Using tongs, remove and discard as many of the fish bones as possible, along with any big vegetable pieces. Line a medium-mesh sieve with cheesecloth. Let the stock cool until it is warm and then strain it through the cheesecloth into a large container. Label, date, and refrigerate the stock for up to 1 week or freeze it for up to 3 months.

SHELLFISH STOCK Use lobster, crab, or shrimp shells in place of the fish bones and proceed as directed for fish stock. Note that this recipe produces a colorless shellfish stock, while the crab stock at right includes tomatoes.

# CRAB STOCK

MAKES ABOUT 4 CUPS (1 L)

After this stock simmers, I like to smash up the shells to extract as much flavor as possible. Just whirl the whole mixture in a blender, and then strain it. We're not going for a subtle flavor here. You should get a strong taste of crab.

1 tablespoon (15 ml) grapeseed or canola oil

4 large blue crab shells

½ cup (84 g) chopped yellow onion

½ cup (61 g) chopped carrot

½ cup (51 g) chopped celery

1 cup (240 g) canned whole San Marzano tomatoes

Heat the oil in a stockpot over medium heat. Add the crab shells and sauté them, cracking the shells a little with a wooden spoon, until they are golden brown, 10 to 15 minutes. Add the onion, carrot, and celery and sauté the vegetables until they are tender and lightly browned, 10 to 12 minutes. Add the tomatoes, crushing them with your hand as you drop them into the pot, and scrape up any browned bits on the pan bottom. Raise the heat to medium-high and simmer the mixture until the liquid has reduced by about half, 5 to 10 minutes. Add enough water to cover the ingredients by about 1 inch (2.5 cm) and bring the liquid to a simmer. Turn down the heat to low and simmer the stock gently for 1 hour.

Remove the pot from the heat and let the stock cool until it is warm. Line a medium-mesh sieve with cheesecloth. Working in batches, transfer the contents of the pot to a blender and blend until almost smooth. As each batch is blended, pass it through the prepared sieve, pressing on the solids to extract as much liquids as possible. Transfer the stock to a large container, and then label, date, and refrigerate it for up to 1 week or freeze it for up to 3 months.

# TOMATO SAUCE

MAKES ABOUT 4 CUPS (1 L)

This sauce develops layers of tomato flavor by combining two separate sautés: one with canned San Marzanos and one with fresh plum tomatoes. It's important to use the highest-quality ingredients you can. Underripe or subpar tomatoes will not make good tomato sauce.

½ cup (120 ml) olive oil

1 yellow onion

2 cloves garlic

1 can (28 oz/794 g) whole canned San Marzano tomatoes (about 3½ cups)

1 pound (454 g) fresh plum tomatoes (about 8)

Kosher salt and freshly ground black pepper

Heat 6 tablespoons (90 ml) of the oil in a saucepan over medium heat. Coarsely chop half of the onion and add it to the pan. Smash 1 garlic clove and add it to the pan as well. Sweat the onion and garlic until they are soft but not browned, 4 to 6 minutes. Add the canned tomatoes, crushing them with your hand as you add them to the pan, and simmer the tomatoes until they start to break down, 15 to 20 minutes.

Remove the pan from the heat and remove and discard the garlic. Let the mixture cool slightly, then transfer to a blender and puree until smooth. Set aside.

Have ready a bowl of ice water. Bring a pot of water to a boil. Using a small, sharp knife, score an X in the skin on the bottom of each tomato. Blanch the tomatoes in the boiling water until the skin on each tomato begins to split and curl back a little from the X, 30 to 60 seconds. Using a slotted spoon, immediately transfer the tomatoes to the ice water and let them stand until cooled, a minute or two. Starting at the X, peel the skin from each tomato and discard it. Cut each tomato in half lengthwise and dig out and discard the seeds, gel, and the base of the stem from each half. Finely chop the tomato flesh. This preparation is called tomato *concassé*.

Heat the remaining 2 tablespoons (30 ml) oil in a large saucepan over medium heat. Mince the remaining onion half and garlic clove and add them to the pan. Sweat the onion and garlic until they are soft but not browned, 4 to 5 minutes. Add the tomato *concassé* and simmer the mixture until the tomatoes start to break down, 5 to 7 minutes. Add the reserved pureed tomato sauce and simmer the mixture for 15 to 20 minutes to blend the flavors and thicken the sauce. Taste the sauce, adding salt and pepper until it tastes good to you.

Use the sauce within a couple hours, or transfer it to an airtight container and label, date, and refrigerate it for up to 1 week or freeze it for up to 3 months.

# BÉCHAMEL

MAKES ABOUT 4 CUPS (1 L)

I like béchamel to taste like a thick milk sauce with a hint of nutmeg. If you want it thinner or thicker, add more or less or less milk. I also use white pepper to keep the béchamel white. If you substitute black pepper, use half as much because it is twice as strong.

5 tablespoons (76 g) unsalted butter

½ cup (75 g) tipo 00 flour, or ½ cup plus 2 tablespoons (75 g) all-purpose flour

4 cups (946 ml) whole milk

1 teaspoon (3 g) kosher salt

1 teaspoon (2 g) freshly ground white pepper

Pinch of freshly grated nutmeg

Melt the butter in a saucepan over medium heat. Whisk in the flour to make a roux (it will look like lumpy batter). Whisk and cook the flour until it smells a little nutty and turns a light tan, 2 to 3 minutes. This is called a blond roux. (If you continue cooking the flour until it is deep brown, it is called a brown roux and has a deeper, toasted flavor but less thickening power.)

Meanwhile, bring the milk to a simmer in a saucepan over medium-high heat. When the roux is ready, remove the milk from the heat and slowly whisk it into the roux until it is fully incorporated and the mixture is free of lumps. Simmer the mixture gently over low heat, stirring now and then, until it thickens, 15 to 20 minutes.

Remove from the heat. For a silky texture, strain the béchamel through a fine-mesh sieve. Add the salt, pepper, and nutmeg, and then taste the sauce, adding more salt, pepper, and/or nutmeg until it tastes good to you. The nutmeg should be subtle.

Use the béchamel within 20 or 30 minutes. Or let it cool completely, cover it with plastic wrap pressed directly onto the surface to prevent a skin from forming, and refrigerate it for up to 2 days. Reheat the béchamel in a saucepan over low heat before using.

**BÉCHAMEL WITH ONION** Add ¼ cup (42 g) minced yellow onion to the melted butter and sweat the onion until it is soft but not browned, 5 to 6 minutes. Stir in the flour and proceed as directed for béchamel. Strain the sauce through a fine-mesh sieve to remove the onion.

**TRUFFLE BÉCHAMEL** Stir in 1 tablespoon (15 ml) white truffle paste along with the salt, pepper, and nutmeg and proceed as directed for béchamel.

**TALEGGIO BÉCHAMEL** After simmering the béchamel until thickened, remove it from the heat and whisk in 1½ pounds (680 g) Taleggio cheese, chopped, until the cheese melts and the sauce is smooth, then proceed as directed for béchamel. Makes about 6 cups (1.4 L).

# VINCOTTO

MAKES ABOUT 2 CUPS (473 ML)

Literally "cooked wine," this thick, sweet sauce is similar to balsamic syrup. It's easy to make and keeps well, but if you want to buy it, it's pretty widely available. Try it on vanilla ice cream!

4 cups (946 ml) dry red wine

3 cups (600 g) sugar

10 black peppercorns

1 cinnamon stick, about 3 inches (7.5 cm) long

Combine all of ingredients in a saucepan, place over high heat, and bring to a boil, stirring to dissolve the sugar. Turn down the heat to medium-high and vigorously simmer the mixture until it has reduced by about half and has thickened to the consistency of thin syrup, 35 to 40 minutes.

Strain the mixture through a fine-mesh sieve and use it within 1 hour, or transfer it to an airtight container and store in a cool cupboard for up to 1 month.

# SOURCES

You can find just about everything you need in your local stores or online to make a dish of pasta. Here's where you can find the oddball items like a *chitarra* and canned snails.

## Equipment

**ARCOBALENO**
160 Greenfield Road
Lancaster, PA 17601
717-394-1402
www.arcobalenollc.com
Pasta extruders, pasta sheeters, and other pasta machines.

**ARTISANAL PASTA TOOLS**
Sonoma, California
707-939-6474
www.artisanalpastatools.com
*Corzetti* stamps, *garganelli* boards, rolling pins, and other pasta tools.

**FANTE'S**
1006 South Ninth Street
Philadelphia, PA 19147
800-443-2683
www.fantes.com
Pasta machines, pasta rollers, pasta cutters, *chitarre*, *corzetti* stamps, gnocchi boards, drying screens, drying racks, and other pasta-making supplies.

**FRANCO CASONI**
Via Bighetti 73
16043 Chiavari
Province of Genoa, Italy
+ 39 0185301448
www.francocasoni.it
*Corzetti* stamps custom-made in Italy.

**KING ARTHUR FLOUR**
135 US Route 5 South
Norwich, VT 05055
800-827-6836
www.kingarthurflour.com
Digital scales, bench scrapers, boards, and other pasta-making supplies.

**KITCHENAID**
Customer Experience Center
PO Box 218
St. Joseph, MI 49085
800-541-6390
www.kitchenaid.com
Stand mixers, extruded-pasta presses, pasta rollers, pasta cutters, meat grinders, and other mixer attachments.

**WEBSTAURANT STORE**
717-392-7472
www.webstaurantstore.com
Baking sheets, terrine molds, and other kitchen equipment.

## Flour, Dried Pasta, Rice, and Other Dry Products

**ALLEN CREEK FARM**
PO Box 841
Ridgefield, WA 98642
360-887-3669
www.chestnutsonline.com
Chestnut flour.

**BUON ITALIA**
75 Ninth Avenue
New York, NY 10011
212-633-9090
www.buonitalia.com
Setaro pasta (including porcini pasta, *funghi ai funghi*), tipo 00 flour, semolina, garum (*colatura di alici*), *vincotto*, white truffles, truffle paste, truffle oil, and other dry products.

**EATALY**
200 Fifth Avenue
New York, NY 10010
212-229-2560

43 East Ohio Street
Chicago, IL 60611
312-521-8700

www.eataly.com
Setaro pasta, Afeltra pasta, and other dry products.

**GUSTIAMO**
1715 West Farms Road
Bronx, NY 10460
718-860-2949
www.gustiamo.com
Martelli pasta, Acquerello rice, San Marzano and Mount Vesuvius tomatoes, Sicilian pistachios, garum (*colatura di alici*), and other dry products.

**HAYDEN FLOUR MILLS**
4404 North Central Ave.
Phoenix, AZ 85012
480-557-0031
www.haydenflourmills.com
Durum flour, *farro*, *farro* flour, semolina, and polenta.

**IL MERCATO ITALIANO**
PO Box 9751
Green Bay, WI 54308
920-884-6010
www.ilmercatoitaliano.net
Amaretti cookies, *farro* flour,
San Marzano tomatoes, polenta,
semolina, and other dry products.

**KING ARTHUR FLOUR**
135 US Route 5 South
Norwich, VT 05055
800-827-6836
www.kingarthurflour.com
All-purpose flour, durum flour, semolina,
almond flour, and other flours.

**SEVERINO PASTA COMPANY**
110 Haddon Avenue
Westmont, NJ 08108
856-854-7666
www.severinopasta.com
A small American company making
high-quality artisan pasta.

## Vegetables

**GREEN MEADOW FARM**
130 South Mount Vernon Road
Gap, PA 17527
717-442-5222
www.glennbrendle.com
High-quality vegetables, fruit, and other
foods grown by Amish farmers.

**MAXIMUS INTERNATIONAL FOODS**
15 Bicknell Road
Weymouth, MA 02191
617-331-7959
www.maximusfood.com
Wild and cultivated mushrooms.

## Cheese

**BUON ITALIA**
75 Ninth Avenue
New York, NY 10011
212-633-9090
www.buonitalia.com
*Gorgonzola dolce*, *ricotta salta*, *robiola*,
and other Italian cheeses.

**DI BRUNO BROTHERS**
930 South Ninth Street
Philadelphia, PA 19147
888-322-4337
www.dibruno.com
Parmigiano-Reggiano, *Gorgonzola
dolce*, *mozzarella di bufala*, *ricotta
salata*, sheep's milk ricotta, *ricotta
impastata*, and other Italian cheeses.

**EURO GOURMET**
10312 Southard Drive
Beltsville, MD 20705
301-937-2888
www.eurogourmet.biz
*Burrata* and other Italian cheeses.

## Meat and Fish

**BORDER SPRINGS FARM**
743 VFW Drive
Patrick Springs, VA 24133
276-952-5485
www.borderspringsfarm.com
High-quality grass-fed lamb never
treated with hormones or antibiotics.

**BUON ITALIA**
75 Ninth Avenue
New York, NY 10011
212-633-9090
www.buonitalia.com
*Baccalà* (salt cod), *lardo*, salted anchovies,
squid ink, and other cured meats and fish.

**CHEFSHOP.COM**
PO Box 3488
Seattle, WA 98114
800-596-0885
www.chefshop.com
Canned snails.

**CREEKSTONE FARMS**
604 Goff Industrial Park Road
Arkansas City, KS 67005
620-741-3366
www.creekstonefarms.com
High-quality grass-fed, grain-finished
Black Angus beef certified by the USDA.

**D'ARTAGNAN**
280 Wilson Avenue
Newark, NJ 07105
800-327-8246
www.dartagnan.com
Duck, goose, rabbit, lamb, foie gras,
and other meats.

**DI BRUNO BROTHERS**
930 South Ninth Street
Philadelphia, PA 19147
888-322-4337
www.dibruno.com
Pancetta, prosciutto, and other
cured meats.

**GEORGE L. WELLS MEAT COMPANY**
982 North Delaware Avenue
Philadelphia, PA 19123
800-523-1730
www.wellsmeats.com
Duck, rabbit, lamb, and other meats.

**LA TIENDA**
1325 Jamestown Road
Williamsburg, VA 23185
888-331-4362
www.tienda.com
*Baccalà* (salt cod) and squid ink.

**SAMUELS & SON SEAFOOD**
3400 South Lawrence Street
Philadelphia, PA 19148
800-580-5810
www.samuelsandsonseafood.com
Halibut, squid, cuttlefish, and other
seafood.

# ACKNOWLEDGMENTS

## From Marc Vetri

What started out as a simple book about pasta has taken a great many twists and turns. This is the first book I wanted to write, and it's the subject I know the most about. But a decade ago, I wasn't able to get anyone interested in a single-subject pasta book. When Ten Speed Press finally gave me the go-ahead a few years back to write this book, I started gathering pasta dishes from all of the Vetri family restaurants. I revisited every plate of pasta that we ever made or even experimented with over the years. They were all great, but I realized that pasta dishes alone were not enough. Don't get me wrong; eating a delicious dish of pasta can be an amazing experience. But for pasta to be truly inspiring, there must be a story behind it.

So I talked to as many people as possible, from chefs, farmers, and seed growers to dried-pasta artisans and little old ladies with hands the size of baseball mitts from kneading and rolling dough their entire lives. I spent hours online scouring scholarly articles in English and Italian to find out the science behind the perfect plate of pasta. Every corner I turned revealed a potential new chapter. *Mastering Pasta*, which began as a straightforward collection of Vetri family recipes, grew into a rigorous study of one of the most interesting and versatile dishes in the history of cuisine. I have many people to thank for this journey.

The discussion started with a question, "Hey, you feel like doing a pasta book?" David Joachim, the man who wrote my previous two books with me, replied, "I'm down!" He is like my business partner in writing. He is the yin to my yang. I write stories, and he makes them sound like I know how to write stories. Without him there is no book—just random words on a page.

Many late nights after service was finished at Vetri, chef Adam Leonti and I sat and talked about what this book would look like and what it would include. At every corner, we both got excited about what the other had found. He was the ultimate sounding board, and this book is just as much a part of him as it is a part of me.

Then came selling the book. I've heard so many horror stories about publishers and editors from my colleagues. "It was a nightmare!" "Can you believe they want me to do this?!" I've heard so much screaming and ranting that I was reluctant to reveal that I never really had any problems with my publisher. We just kind of talk and work it out. Ten Speed Press is simply the best publishing house for chefs. Throughout all three books I have published, Aaron Wehner and his team have been the greatest people to work with. As long as they remain interested in publishing my books, I am happy to continue working with them.

My family of business partners stands behind me at all times, and I am fortunate to have an extremely deep bench. Jeff Benjamin has been an invaluable partner for more than fifteen years. But as a human being and friend he is unquantifiable. As with every project that we do, Jeff has been there with support and guidance throughout. On a day-to-day and even hour-to-hour basis, the two people on whom I rely the most are Jeffrey Michaud and Brad Spence. These two dedicated chefs are the heart and soul of the Vetri family of restaurants.

During the search for the right photographer for this book, I received many portfolios to peruse. One photographer stood out: Ed Anderson. While we researched and wrote the book, Ed's photos never failed to capture our amazing travels through Italy and beyond.

As I mentioned, this journey took many turns. At least one fork in the road was placed by Dan Barber. In October 2013, Dan invited me to a seed conference at the home of his restaurant, Stone Barns Center for Food & Agriculture in Pocantico Hills, New York. The conference took place about a week before I was supposed to leave for Italy on the first leg of our research trip. The timing was so close that I declined the invitation. Dan sent me an email, saying, "Too bad. It's really shaping up to be a good event. Great speakers and terrific chefs, etc. If you somehow free up the time, let us know and we'll save a seat." I felt like he had just told me that I couldn't eat chocolate anymore. I reworked my schedule, attended the conference, and it turned out to be one of the most inspiring events of my career. I never imagined that a seed conference would be so informative and interesting. No speaker was more captivating than Dr. Stephen Jones, whose presentation completely changed the course of this book. Without that experience, as well as the numerous trips out to the Bread Lab at Washington State University for research and collaboration with his amazing team, this book, as it stands now, would not have been possible.

In Italy, many people helped me and my team navigate the worlds of pasta and rice. Alicia Walter gave us countless introductions. Oretta Zanini De Vita showed us the pasta of Rome. Vincenzo Setaro from Pastificio Fratelli Setaro and Paolo from Premiato Pastificio Afeltra took us on amazing tours of their factories and recounted the complicated history of Italian dried pasta. Dania and Umberto Luccherini from La Chiusa, where I made fresh pasta twenty years ago, were as courteous and friendly as ever. Acquerello's Maria Nava Rondolino taught us about high-quality rice. Marco Rossi and Stefano Arrigoni were always a phone call away with great advice. And Mark Issa was the best of companions. He rides shotgun like no one else!

After returning from that first research trip to Italy, a gentleman named Steve Koenigsberg walked into Vetri for dinner alone. We started talking and I learned that, at one time, Steve was immersed in the study of pasta flours in Rome. We talked forever that night, and our discussion led to further emails and late-night telephone calls about the science of pasta, semolina, and wheat flour. Steve was instrumental in helping me come to many of the conclusions in this book. He led me down the right roads in order to find the documented research. It was serendipitous for him to walk into the restaurant at that precise moment.

As if on cue, in the midst of this continuing research, my great friend Chris Bianco from Pizzeria Bianco in Phoenix came to Philadelphia to cook with me. We started talking wheat and milling, and he introduced me to J. D. McLelland, a film producer and director who was in the middle of shooting a documentary called *The Grain Divide*. A couple of phone calls later, we were back on a plane to Seattle to harvest wheat and deepen my understanding by talking with pioneers in the grain industry such as Glenn Roberts from Anson Mills. Like everything that occurred in the process of writing this book, it was as if these chance meetings were supposed to happen. These guys helped shape not only this book but also an amazing start to another chapter of learning in my life.

Nearly a year of deep research eventually informed my theory that some dried pastas have a more pleasant chewiness than others. But I needed solid proof. So I phoned Nathan Myhrvold, the genius behind *Modernist Cuisine*, the landmark book of science-based cooking. What I got in return was so much more than I expected. I laid out my theory in a lengthy email, and Nathan replied, "This pasta question you ask is very important and your theory seems plausible." He then described how he would do the research. His food scientist, Larissa Zhou, would review the relevant academic papers, and then test and analyze several dried pastas both raw and cooked to determine the differences in their pasting properties or, as I call it, their creaminess. We held weekly conference calls for months. Their work not only helped shape our research but also gave us an amazing look into the inner workings of Myhrvold's Cooking Lab. I can't thank Nathan and his team enough for their generosity and dedication to the culinary world.

Maja and Antonio Adiletta from Arcobaleno have been two great partners in our quest to make the perfect extruded pasta. Their machines continue to evolve as our love for using them grows. We are lucky to have them in our backyard.

When it came time for photography, Paola Andrea basically moved into my house for a week with every beautiful plate, wooden board, and piece of silverware she could find. The photo shoot was perfectly executed with her expertise and great eye.

Throughout this entire book-writing process, my assistant, Carolyn Pagnotta, has been a beacon of light. From making sure recipes were done and ingredients were ordered to booking flights and cars, you name it, she handled it with grace.

A far-reaching team brought this book together, and a big part of that team consists of the cooks in our restaurants. They all inspire me to push forward every day. I feel like a composer in a great musical. I have all of these amazing musicians, and we make beautiful music together. Special thanks to the cooks at Vetri, who listen to my daily rants and humor me.

"To the world you may be just someone, but to someone you may be the whole world." Whoever wrote those words was expressing the way I feel about my wife, Megan. I can't possibly write in an acknowledgment how much I appreciate this amazing woman. I can only say I love you . . . more.

## From David Joachim

Marc, I can't thank you enough for your generosity and big, open, curious heart. This time you took me to the core of Italy and once again shared your boundless passion for that country's cuisine. You also taught me the absolute best way to prepare octopus: braised in olive oil with sparkling water. Whole wheat spaghetti never tasted so good.

Adam Leonti was the key grip throughout this project, working deftly behind the scenes and showing me the finer points of how to fold *culurgiones* and blister a *testarolo*. Thanks Adam. You inspired me to grow out my beard again.

Some of these recipes come from deep within the Vetri family archives. When all I had were bare-bones notes, Jeffrey Michaud and Brad Spence filled in the details. You guys are the best.

Testing a recipe is not as simple as cooking a dish and throwing a dinner party. It's more like putting your meal under a microscope: you first measure, prepare, and observe the dish, and then modify the recipe instructions based on the test results. It's detailed work, and I'm glad Carrie Havranek and her inquisitive mind joined me in the kitchen lab to help make these recipes as accurate, readable, and "cookable" as possible.

Of course, the tasting is more fun, especially with food as laser focused on flavor as Marc's. Many mouths tasted and gave opinions and suggestions. Thanks especially to Dave Pryor, Selene Yeager, Matt Morrison, Jaime Livingood, Mark Taylor, Trisha Mae, Heather Jones, Chad Shafer, the Peoples family, Christine Bucher, and Maddox and August Joachim.

I ate pasta all over Italy and the United States while researching and writing this book. For showing me new spins and dialed-in standbys, thanks to the pasta chefs at Torre del Saracino, Da Enzo, La Toretta, Ristorante Cocchi, La Chiusa, Osteria della Brughiera, Osteria Le Cantine D, Molinari's, Del Posto, The Spotted Pig, flour + water, Osteria Mozza, Quince, and Hearth.

Marc and I did a ton of research into the science behind a great dish of pasta. Big thanks to Dr. Stephen Jones and Jonathan McDowell for welcoming us into the Bread Lab at Washington State University and allowing us to turn it into the Pasta Lab. Our pasta tests with various wheat flour varietals, conversations about wheat gluten, and subsequent email discussions on all things wheat were vital to the understanding of pasta texture and flavor described in this book.

At the *Modernist Cuisine* Cooking Lab in Seattle, Nathan Myhrvold and Larissa Zhou went above and beyond to document the various textures of dried pastas. Thank you Larissa for your in-depth lab work and beautiful microscope images of starch and protein. Thanks also to cereal scientist R. Carl Hoseney for vetting our explanation of protein coagulation and starch gelatinization in dried pasta.

I'd also like to acknowledge Carolyn Pagnotta for keeping the lines of communication open at Vetri family central. Getting a hold of chefs and recipes isn't always easy. You made it easier.

To Mark Issa, thanks for being Mr. Fix-It in Italy and providing video documentation of all the pastas we made, ate, and researched there.

To Andy Schloss, thank you as always for your stimulating conversation, general advice, and big-picture perspective on the book.

And to my wife, Christine, you lucked out with this project. You've been vegetarian for twenty-five years and don't always get to sample the hundreds of recipes I develop and test each year. I'm glad you got to enjoy most of the delicious plates of food this time around. I could watch you eat forever.

# SELECTED BIBLIOGRAPHY

## Books

Artusi, Pellegrino. *Science in the Kitchen and the Art of Eating Well*. New York: Marsilio Publishers, 1997.

Bastianich, Lidia. *Lidia's Commonsense Italian Cooking*. New York: Knopf, 2013.

Bertolli, Paul. *Cooking by Hand*. New York: Clarkson Potter, 2003.

Boswell, Christopher with Elena Goldblatt. *Pasta: Recipes from the Kitchen of the American Academy in Rome*. New York: Little Bookroom, 2013.

Bruno, Pasquale, Jr. *Pasta Tecnica*. Chicago: Contemporary Books, 1985.

Bugialli, Giuliano. *Bugialli on Pasta*. New York: Simon and Schuster, 1988.

*Cook's Illustrated* magazine, eds. *The Complete Book of Pasta and Noodles*. New York: Clarkson Potter, 2002.

Delcour, Jan A., and R. Carl Hoseney. *Principles of Cereal Science and Technology*. Saint Paul, MN: American Association of Cereal Chemists, 2010.

Ghedini, Francesco. *Northern Italian Cooking*. New York: Hawthorn Books, 1973.

Gosetti della Salda, Anna. *Le Ricette Regionali Italiane*. Milan: Solares, 2005.

Gray, Rose, and Ruth Rogers. *The River Cafe Cookbook*. London: Ebury Press, 1995.

Green, Aliza. *Making Artisan Pasta: How to Make a World of Handmade Noodles, Stuffed Pasta, Dumplings, and More*. Beverly, MA: Quarry Books, 2012.

Hazan, Marcella. *Essentials of Classic Italian Cooking*. New York: Knopf, 1992.

Hildebrand, Caz, and Jacob Kenedy. *The Geometry of Pasta*. Philadelphia: Quirk Books, 2010.

Italian Academy of Cuisine. *La Cucina: The Regional Cooking of Italy*. New York: Rizzoli, 2009.

Joachim, David, and Andrew Schloss. *The Science of Good Food: The Ultimate Reference on How Cooking Works*. Toronto: Robert Rose, 2008.

Kill, R. C., and K. Turnbull, eds. *Pasta and Semolina Technology*. Oxford: Blackwell Science, 2001.

Kruger, James E., Robert B. Matsuo, and Joel W. Dick. *Pasta and Noodle Technology*. Saint Paul, MN: American Association of Cereal Chemists, 1996.

Legendre, George L. *Pasta by Design*. London: Thames & Hudson, 2011.

Marchetti, Domenica. *The Glorious Pasta of Italy*. San Francisco: Chronicle Books, 2011.

May, Tony. *Italian Cuisine: Basic Cooking Techniques*. New York: Rizzoli, 1992.

McGee, Harold. *On Food and Cooking: The Science and Lore of the Kitchen*. New York: Scribner, 2004.

McNaughton, Thomas. *Flour + Water: Pasta*. Berkeley, CA: Ten Speed Press, 2014.

Myhrvold, Nathan, Chris Young, and Maxime Bilet. *Modernist Cuisine: The Art and Science of Cooking*. 5 vols. Bellevue, WA: The Cooking Lab, 2011.

Phaidon Press, eds. *The Silver Spoon*, new ed. London: Phaidon Press, 2011.

Pomeranz, Y., ed. *Wheat: Chemistry and Technology*. 2 vols. Saint Paul, MN: American Association of Cereal Chemists, 1988.

Serventi, Silvano, and Françoise Sabban. *Pasta: The Story of a Universal Food*. New York: Columbia University Press, 2003.

Skinner, Robert P. *Manufacture of Semolina and Macaroni*. Washington: Government Printing Office, 1902.

Vetri, Marc. *Il Viaggio di Vetri: A Culinary Journey*. Berkeley, CA: Ten Speed Press, 2008.

———. *Rustic Italian Food*. Berkeley, CA: Ten Speed Press, 2011.

Zanini De Vita, Oretta. *Encyclopedia of Pasta*. Berkeley, CA: University of California Press, 2009.

———. *Popes, Peasants, and Shepherds: Recipes and Lore from Rome and Lazio*. Berkeley, CA: University of California Press, 2013.

———, and Maureen B. Fant. *Sauces & Shapes: Pasta the Italian Way*. New York: W. W. Norton, 2013.

## Articles

Adler, Jerry. "Artisanal Wheat On the Rise." *Smithsonian Magazine*, December 2011.

Brouns, Fred J. P. H., Vincent J. van Buul, and Peter R. Shewry. "Does Wheat Make Us Fat and Sick?" *Journal of Cereal Science* 58, no. 2 (September 2013).

Cafieri, S., S. Chillo, M. Mastromatteo, N. Suriano, and M. A. Del Nobile. "A Mathematical Model to Predict the Effect of Shape on Pasta Hydration Kinetic during Cooking and Overcooking." *Journal of Cereal Science* 48, no. 3 (November 2008).

Cafieri, S., M. Mastromatteo, S. Chillo, and M. A. Del Nobile. "Modeling the Mechanical Properties of Pasta Cooked at Different Times." *Journal of Food Engineering* 100, no. 2 (September 2010).

Czap, Nick. "Pasta With a Perfectionist's Touch." *New York Times*. April 1, 2013.

Delcour, J. A., J. Vansteelandt, M.-C. Hythier, and J. Abécassis. "Fractionaltion and Reconstitution Experiments Provide Insight into the Role of Starch Gelatinization and Pasting Properties in Pasta Quality." *Journal of Agricultural and Food Chemistry* 48, no. 9 (August 2000).

Del Nobile, M. A., A. Baiano, A. Conte, and G. Mocci. "Influence of Protein Content on Spaghetti Cooking Quality." *Journal of Cereal Science* 41, no. 3 (May 2005).

Dexter, James E., and Robert R. Matsuo. "Relationship Between Durum Wheat Protein Properties and Pasta Dough Rheology and Spaghetti Cooking Quality." *Journal of Agricultural and Food Chemistry* 28, no. 5 (May 1980).

Fardet, A., P. M. Baldwin , D. Bertrand , B. Bouchet , D. J. Gallant , and J.-L. Barry. "Textural Images Analysis of Pasta Protein Networks to Determine Influence of Technological Processes." *Cereal Chemistry* 75, no. 5 (September/October 1998).

Jones, Stephen. "Kicking the Commodity Habit: On Being Grown Out of Place." *Gastronomica: The Journal of Food and Culture* 12, no. 3 (Fall 2012).

Kratzer, Andreas Markus. "Hydration, Dough Formation and Structure Development in Durum Wheat Pasta Processing." PhD diss., Swiss Federal Institute of Technology, Zurich, 2007.

Novaro, P., M. G. D'Egidio, B. M. Mariani, and S. Nardi. "Combined Effect of Protein Content and High-Temperature Drying Systems on Pasta Cooking Quality." *Cereal Chemistry* 70, no. 6 (August 5, 1993).

Philpott, Tom. "In Which Top Chefs Have Their Minds Blown by Scientists." *Mother Jones*. October 4, 2013.

Robbins, Jim. "A Perennial Search for Perfect Wheat." *New York Times*. June 5, 2007.

Sissons, Mike. "Role of Durum Wheat Composition on the Quality of Pasta and Bread." *Global Science Books* 2, no. 2 (June, 2008).

Strom, Stephanie. "A Big Bet on Gluten-Free." *New York Times*. February 17, 2014.

Vansteelandt, Jan. "The Role of Durum Wheat Starch and Its Interactions in Pasta Quality." *Publications of the Laboratory of Food Chemistry and Biochemistry, KU Leuven* (January 2000).

———, and J. A. Delcour. "Physical Behavior of Durum Wheat Starch (*Triticum durum*) during Industrial Pasta Processing." *Journal of Agricultural and Food Chemistry* 46, no. 7 (June 25, 1998).

Xing, Huajing, Pawan Singh Takhar, Greg Helms, and Brian He. "NMR Imaging of Continuous and Intermittent Drying of Pasta." *Journal of Food Engineering* 78 (2007).

Zhang, Lifen, Takahisa Nishizu, Shiho Hayakawa, and Kiyokazu Goto. "Effects of Different Drying Conditions on Pasta Quality." Paper presented at International Congress on Engineering and Food, Athens, Greece, May 2011.

Zhou, Z., K. Robards, S. Helliwell, and C. Blanchard. "Ageing of Stored Rice: Changes in Chemical and Physical Attributes." *Journal of Cereal Science* 33 (2001).

Zweifel, C., S. Handschin, F. Escher, and B. Conde-Petit. "Influence of High-Temperature Drying on Structural and Textural Properties of Durum Wheat Pasta." *Cereal Chemistry* 80, no. 2 (March/April 2003).

# INDEX

Copyright © 2015 by Marc Vetri
Photographs copyright © 2015 by Ed Anderson

All rights reserved.
Published in the United States by Ten Speed Press, an imprint of
the Crown Publishing Group, a division of Random House LLC,
New York, a Penguin Random House Company.
www.crownpublishing.com
www.tenspeed.com

Ten Speed Press and the Ten Speed Press colophon are
registered trademarks of Random House LLC.

All photographs are by Ed Anderson with the exception
of those noted here: page 13 by Stephen Jones and
Kim Binczewski (Washington State University) and page 116
by Modernist Cuisine, LLC.

Library of Congress Cataloging-in-Publication Data

Vetri, Marc.
  Mastering pasta / Marc Vetri with David Joachim ;
photography by Ed Anderson.
      pages cm
  Includes bibliographical references and index.
  1.  Cooking (Pasta)  I. Joachim, David. II. Title.
  TX809.M17.V46 2014
  641.82'2—dc23
                                    2014020868


Hardcover ISBN: 978-1-60774-607-2
eBook ISBN: 978-1-60774-608-9

Printed in China

Design by Betsy Stromberg
Illustration on page 10 by GRei/Shutterstock.com
Vetri author photograph by Ed Anderson
Joachim author photograph by Olaf Starorypinksi

10 9 8 7 6 5 4 3 2

First Edition